TAX, DRUGS AND ROCK 'N' ROLL

TAX, DRUGS AND ROCK 'N' ROLL

DAMIAN CORLESS

mB
MIRROR BOOKS

MIRROR BOOKS

1

First published in hardback in Great Britain and Ireland
in 2024 by Mirror Books, a Reach PLC business.

www.mirrorbooks.co.uk
@TheMirrorBooks

ISBN: 9781915306593
eBook ISBN: 9781915306609

Photographic acknowledgements:
MirrorPix

Every effort has been made to trace copyright,
Any oversights will be rectified in future editions.

Editor: Christine Costello
Cover design: Adam Ward

Printed and bound by CPI Group (UK) Ltd,
Croydon, CR0 4YY.

This book was printed using
FSC approved materials.

For Martin and Kay and the young people of Ireland, the Irish Netherlands and Irish America. Sophie, Ollie, Max, Caitlin, Darragh, Darcy and the newest New Yorker, Maeve.

CONTENTS

CONTENTS

PROLOGUE

HAPPY ACCIDENTS & THE BEST LAID PLANS

WHEN HAROLD Macmillan became British Prime Minister he was asked what would steer the course of his government. "Events, dear boy, events," he answered, never foreseeing that he himself would be unseated by the unthinkable sex and spying scandal that was the Profumo Affair.

When I was a schoolboy I had a very set picture of my life at 40, which was that I'd be a schoolteacher married with children and living in a three-bedroom semi-D in the Dublin suburbs. But then events intervened and that future never came to pass, apart from the semi-D.

In the space of 18 months, two seeming disasters deflected my life off course in what turned out to be happy accidents. The first was when Bono crashed his car into a telegraph pole outside our house, setting off a freakish chain of events that left both my parents in hospital. The second involved a bizarre unplanned outburst at an interview for a job for life at Dublin Airport.

The Bono incident happened on the bleak evening of 4 February 1981, three days after U2 finished touring their debut album *Boy* across Ireland, Britain, Europe and the USA. I'd seen them pack out Dublin's TV Club on their hometown leg a couple of days before Christmas and they were tighter and hotter than ever, like The Beatles returned from Hamburg.

When I arrived home at teatime that day, my glasses steamed

up the moment I entered the kitchen where my mother was making the perfect meal for a dank, freezing February – egg and chips. The table was being cleared when there was a frenetic ringing of the doorbell.

It was young Mick Campbell from across the road and he was in a right tizzy, telling us to get out and see! Right outside our front door a car had swerved suddenly across the oncoming lane and ploughed into a telegraph pole.

Dad Martin and Mam Kay joined the growing scrum of concerned neighbours at the scene while I stayed inside to finish my tea. In the confusion, nobody paid much attention to the phone cables trailing from the felled pole that lay on the grass verge in front of the now-abandoned crashed car. Nobody except my Dad.

He instantly recognised the danger posed by the steel cables strewn across the width of the road, forming a tripwire. He was a senior engineer with the Department of Posts & Telegraphs and had cut his teeth climbing up and down poles just like the one now lying beside him on the grass verge. He began shooing the neighbours away from the pole and tripwires.

He and my mother were in the act of herding away the crowd and trying to stop the traffic when one driver, ignoring their calls to halt, carried on regardless and sprang the trap. At the same moment, our Jack Russell terrier, Snert, ran to my Dad and my mother followed to catch him, so all three were bunched together in the wrong place when disaster struck.

Blanking my Dad's frantic signals to stop, the rubbernecking motorist just kept going, snagging the fallen wires. The car lurched onwards like a harpooned whale. High on a nearby gable wall, the wires strained at their bracket. The bracket formed the third point of a joined-up triangle completed by the moving car and the fallen pole. (Yes, a diagram here would be helpful.) As the cable jerked rigid, it shot the pole into the air. It flew upwards and one of the steel footholds struck the back of my mother's head. The projectile reached its maximum altitude and the cable snapped. The mast fell back to earth, slamming my luckless father violently to the ground.

My egg and chips finished, I ventured out to see what all the excitement was about. An ambulance was pulling away. I couldn't see my parents. My sister Mary told me they were the occupants of the ambulance. My other siblings Ivan and Anne Marie had gone with them. Those moments that followed remain a bit of a blur, but the kids milling around were gibbering excitedly that the driver of the crashed Fiat, who'd vamoosed early in the episode, was none other than local celebrity Bono from U2.

When he came to give his account of the incident in the 2006 book *U2 By U2*, Bono's memory did not serve him too well. In his 2023 autobiography, *Surrender* it hadn't improved – he said he'd "wrapped his car around a lamppost" and got the road wrong.

In his earlier account, he said he'd bought his second-hand Fiat Uno 127 "while we were recording *War*", placing the accident more than 18 months after it actually happened. Aside from that, he confirmed and amplified what the kids on the road who'd witnessed the crash had said. Approaching my parents' house with his sweetheart Alison in the passenger seat, he'd realised he wasn't wearing his seatbelt so he "started struggling to put it on".

He continued, "When I looked up I was heading at speed towards a telegraph pole, so I tried to slam on the brakes, but my heels were wet and my foot slipped and I hit the accelerator instead." He smashed into the pole at speed just as he got his belt on.

The young couple had been setting out for a party to celebrate the end of U2's exhausting world tour, so there was a bottle of wine on the back seat. When they hit the pole, the bottle shot forward and smashed on the back of his seat, dousing him with alcohol. Thinking to himself, "I'd better get my arse out of there to a police station and get breathalysed," he ran around the corner to his friend Reggie Manuel's house and asked his pal to whisk him to a Garda station.

Bono concluded his account saying that the heedless driver who'd snagged the wires "ended up resurrecting the pole and slamming it down on poor old Mr and Mrs Corless. I wasn't there but that didn't stop them suing me, because they knew what I didn't, that you should never leave the scene of an accident. You will be happy to hear, they survived."

My parents did indeed survive to tell the tale, although my mother was left with a long scar and my Dad with limited mobility in his left arm and shoulder for the rest of his life. My parents didn't sue because Bono had left the scene of the crash. They sued because they were both badly injured. There were no hard feelings, though.

Ever the gentleman, Bono arrived at our house later that evening to inquire after the wellbeing of my parents. They were still receiving treatment in the Mater Hospital, but my sister Mary who was holding the fort said she'd pass on his good wishes. I can still picture my mother, four short years later, cheering at the telly as Bono waltzed across the world stage with a girl he'd plucked from the Live Aid audience at Wembley. She was waltzing along with them in our living room, filled with a heartfelt delight for the local boy made so, so good.

While the Bono crash was far from a happy accident for my parents, it set me thinking – not for the first time – that surely there ought to be more to life than a teaching job and a suburban semi-D when a bunch of northside Dubs not so different from me were in pursuit of the American Dream and were actually starting to achieve it.

That summer I got my qualifications as a secondary school teacher knowing I never wanted to see the inside of a classroom again. A word of advice to anyone considering going into teaching – *never* go back to your old school and *never* teach in the local school. They know where you live. The pupils that is. They are everywhere, they know your every move, and they delight in broadcasting what you've been up to, to you and the rest of the school, in the corridor outside their classroom at 8.58 on a Monday morning.

I'd been gigging in bands for three years, playing bass on an Irish Top 30 single and appearing on the *Non Stop Pop* TV show hosted by Gerry Ryan. But as the certainty of becoming a pop star dipped under 100%, an alternative to teaching as a fallback was now required.

I fetched up one morning to Dublin Airport for an interview to join the Dublin Airport Authority (DAA) as a clerical officer. On offer was a job for life with ample opportunities for promotion.

After 20 minutes the smiles on the faces of the interview panel told me I'd breezed through – and then it happened. As they closed the paperwork, one remarked: "I see you play in a rock band. That must be fun."

Except I didn't play in a rock band, having been sacked just days before for being a rubbish bassist. It wasn't so much that I was rubbish, but the slap-bass technique of Level 42 and Paul Young was now all the rage and I just couldn't get my thumb to obey. So I was out and an admittedly gifted string slapper was in. I didn't fully realise how upset I was at being fired until the very end of that fateful interview.

Instead of bringing proceedings to an agreeable conclusion I let it all out. I still don't know where it came from but it erupted. I informed the panel angrily that being in a band *is* great fun until you're stabbed in the back by the bastards you'd thought were your friends. I can't recall the exact language, but it was textbook Tourette. This was too much information for a clerical officer post and I left the shocked panel to pick their jaws off the long table, knowing for sure that 40 years in a blue blazer at the national airline's HQ had flown out the window. In the grand scheme of things, my public meltdown turned out to be one of those life-enhancing happy accidents when I landed what seemed the best job in the world as a rock writer at the precise time when music was about to assume an unprecedented role in Irish life at home and abroad.

I have been privileged to have had a front row seat for a social and cultural revolution that not only astonished the watching world but amazed the Irish themselves. And I got that position not by any grand plan but mostly because that's how events unravelled. The meet-the-parents random accident involving Bono wasn't the first U2 event that changed the course of my life.

If I hadn't witnessed the beginnings of U2 by the sheer chance of where I lived, I wouldn't have joined a band where I got to see far-flung parts of Ireland from the back of a van and lend my guitar strap to one of the Bay City Rollers when he snapped his. If I hadn't joined a band, I wouldn't have fallen into music writing as a failed musician, and I wouldn't have got to spend quality time with pop stars like Cher, Carole King, Iggy Pop, The Pixies, Guns N' Roses, R.E.M, Michael Hutchence, Bob Geldof and Phil Collins, writers including John Irving, John Mortimer and Nick Hornby, plus lots of top actors including a charmingly flatulent Michael Caine who displayed an admirable knowledge of Irish history. And I wouldn't be the only person in the world who possesses a copy of Duran Duran's *A View To A Kill* autographed by George Michael, who groaned then grinned.

If I hadn't fallen into that writing job, I wouldn't have been the only one in the office that lunchtime MTV rang and so would never have nabbed the gig as MTV Europe's first news correspondent. And if I hadn't fit the profile that college elders thought might appeal to young students, I'd never have landed the lecturing slot which led me to introduce Arthur Mathews to Graham Linehan, the pair who gifted us *Father Ted.*

This book seeks to explore, acknowledge and give thanks for the vital contribution of British musicians, producers, directors, creatives and footballers to Ireland's spectacular reversal of fortune that launched a reformed society, the Celtic Tiger carnival and the excesses that followed.

By far the greatest homegrown force for change in this period were U2 and half of Dublin's Fab Four are English by birth. U2's role in the making and shaping of modern Ireland extends far beyond the realm of music, and the four Dubliners were instrumental in resurrecting their hometown from a sorry backwater to a vibrant capital city worthy of that title.

I write from lived experience, of the band, and of a uniquely adventurous time, when Ireland would boldly go where no-one had ever imagined, and pop stars from the telly would come to live amongst us.

From the first time I saw U2 as a teenager, the band had a profound impact on my life. Myself and my friend Bart Cronin caught them just down the road in a Finglas school hall in May 1978, around a month after they changed their name from The Hype. We were only there because there was nothing else to do and because a friend of ours, Sean D'Angello was a member of the Lypton Village collective which comprised U2 and The

Virgin Prunes, chipping in as a sometime roadie for both bands. That night in Finglas, U2 played mostly covers, but they still wiped the floor with the other bands on the bill. Myself and Bart were smitten.

Over the summer and autumn of 1978, we scheduled our lives around U2 gigs, watching them gradually shed the Tom Robinson and Wire covers in favour of original numbers like 'Out Of Control', 'Concentration Cramp' and 'Stories For Boys'. As good as some of the self-penned songs were, the ever reliable roof-raising closer was a hopped-up rampage through Ramones' 'Glad To See You Go', a joyously manic send-off from a killer to his victim. By the end of the year it wasn't unknown for the band to play their entire canon of six or seven originals, and then start the whole set over again.

By the close of 1979, the group had moved on from doing lunchtime canteen gigs and midweek pub residencies to touring Britain and not long after they set about winning over America. Having devoted maybe a year of our young lives exclusively to following U2, there was a void to be filled and myself and Bart filled the gap by forming our own band.

With the prospects of pop stardom fading, and having sabotaged my job for life at Dublin Airport, I landed a job as staff writer with the music magazine *Hot Press*. My job interview for *Hot Press* presented the odd scenario of me, the candidate, wearing a sober brown suit and tie, while my three interrogators were dressed like The Jimi Hendrix Experience. I got the job.

My job as a music hack fitted the bill known as High Prestige, Low Income. I'd regularly fly to London first class to stay at the five-star Kensington Hilton – we knew it as Ken Hill – where I couldn't afford to eat in the restaurant or even look in the mini-bar. So I'd sit on the luxury double bed, turn on the telly and open my briefcase to take out the corned beef sandwiches I'd made early that morning.

When you're young, free and single, the high prestige usually more than makes up for the low income and in my early days in the job the regular shots of self-esteem were boosted when – it transpired – I was in at the start of something big, and the end of something great.

The start of something big came first in the gloomy summer of 1985.

One Saturday I was in the gym when I was tracked down with a phone call from one of my bosses. They'd set up an interview with a young musician who'd just released a movie soundtrack album and had completely forgotten about the appointment.

Since I had a key to the office, they asked if I would hop on my bike and meet her there. And hurry, because the interview was arranged for five minutes ago and she was a prodigy destined for great things.

So I hopped on my bike and rode like the wind and when I arrived I found a young woman called Enya huddled in the doorway sheltering from the rain with her lyricist and manager Roma Ryan.

I interviewed the soft-spoken prodigy, not knowing the first thing about her. She could have been a novice nun practising for her vow of silence and I had no questions prepared. When I played back the tape it was decided that the interview would appear as a longer-than-usual five-line photo caption.

Some years later when Enya was a global star with her own fairytale castle in Dublin's exclusive Killiney, I interviewed her again at length only this time I was fully prepped. Once again, when I listened back to what she'd said of substance, a five-line photo caption would have done grand.

A few months later, in December 1985, I conducted what

would turn out to be Phil Lynott's last print interview. It was a measure of how far his stock had slumped that the assignment had been passed down the line to me, the office junior. Five or six years earlier a Phil Lynott interview would have been fought over by the mag's writers as sure-fire cover material. I was told to keep the piece short.

In the event, short was all it deserved. Some of it was unusable. There were wild mood swings between euphoria and rage. A couple of innocent questions triggered terrifying outbursts. A jokey remark about his wealth brought an angry barked threat to terminate the session.

Three weeks later on Christmas Day, Phil collapsed at his home in Kew. After a brief rally, he died on 4 January 1986 of pneumonia and heart failure due to septicaemia, which had in turn been brought on by years of hard living. Ireland's much-loved Black Pearl was only 36.

In denial about his own creative decline, in that final interview he insisted his banishment to the wilderness was down to the fact that, "Fashion changed. All of a sudden you got all these people wearing dresses and lipstick." And he did leave this world out of favour, but the passage of time has proven Coco Chanel's adage that while fashion passes, style remains. For the record, Dublin's most beloved minstrel son was born in West Bromwich.

It's said that if you live long enough you'll see everything. While this is patently untrue, in recent times I've been put right on a couple of pop facts concerning myself that I'd never have believed if it hadn't been for some incidental words that had nothing to do with the matters in hand. Again, random events.

In the early 1980s, I was still living in the family home on Willow Park Road which had recently received an extension. My bandmate Emmett O'Reilly moved into one of the new houses a couple of hundred metres up the road and immediately began waffling on that Francis Rossi of Status Quo was living in the semi-D opposite him.

"Yes, Emmett. The millionaire rockstar. You have a greasy-haired, denim-clad hippy living across the road. Now will you just give it a rest!"

Fast-forward four decades and I'm just finishing up a lengthy interview with Rossi for this book when I mention that I'm back living close to where I grew up, and I bring up how Emmett kept prattling on all those years ago.

"Oh yeah, that was me," he replied.

But the bolt from the blue that really floored me came a quarter century after the event and from a most unexpected source.

I'd been on nodding terms with Sinéad O'Connor since the early 1980s when our bands both frequented Temple Lane rehearsal studios in Temple Bar. When I first encountered her as a journalist she took an instant dislike to me. My earliest attempt to interview her was in 1990. I was newly installed as editor of *In Dublin* and it was an ordeal. She kept me waiting for the best part of the day before granting me a hostile 10 minutes, telling me my line of questioning was ignorant.

Five years later she marched into the *In Dublin* offices and presented a three-page typed rebuttal to a piece I'd written, taking grave exception to my use of the word 'truculent' to describe her often truculent behaviour. I'd left the editor's seat a year earlier, so she demanded that the new editor print her rejoinder in full. The editor was delighted. For one thing it meant she had Sinéad O'Connor writing for her and for another it meant she got to fill three editorial pages for free.

So there was no love lost between me and Sinéad from the outset and I did nothing to mend fences with a humorous jibe I penned in 1993 when Sinéad paid the then enormous sum of

£11,000 to buy a full page of ad space in *The Irish Times* for a long and rambling poem she'd written.

I was still editing *In Dublin* and in the next issue ran a limerick of my own composition, along with fake critiques from Prince, *Hot Press* and others.

Intentionally scanning woefully, it went…

There was a young girl called Sinéad
To whom not enough attention was paid
She was basically good
But misunderstood
Fuck off! Fuck off! Fuck off! Everyone fuck off!

A couple of days after the mag came out, a young woman screamed into reception through the letterbox that we were all a shower of bastards.

Our receptionist Jenny swore that when she ran to the door, the figure running away down the laneway was Sinéad herself, although Jenny had only caught her from the back. Trouble was, poor Jenny (who's sadly no longer with us) was not the most reliable witness in the world.

Then, 25 years later, I was sitting in the kitchen of Aslan frontman Christy Dignam whose life story I was writing. Christy and Sinéad had recorded together and would pass away within weeks of each other in 2023.

Over the course of many months working together with Christy on his book, I'd never mentioned any of my various run-ins with Sinéad. This lunchtime however, in the course of giving his thoughts on the singer, from the dim depths of his mind Christy came out with…

"I remember one day I was walking through this laneway in town and there was this girl shouting in the letterbox of the *In Dublin* office. She was screaming: 'Yiz fuckin bastards!' And I said to myself, that's Sinéad O'Connor and she's screaming in the letterbox 'Yiz are a shower of fuckin bastards!'"

Sorry for ever doubting you gentle Jenny...

Damian Corless, 2024

Introduction

THEY CAME FOR THE TAX BREAKS, BUT STAYED FOR THE CRAIC

"It's extraordinary how potent cheap music is."

– Noël Coward

"WHAT I have always liked about the Irish Republic is that it is, of all the societies that I know, the least 'sexy'." So said English poet Donald Davie of a land frozen in time midway through the 20th Century. At the start of the 1980s Ireland looked very much like that same icebound place, but there was a thaw underfoot. The thaw very soon became a great disruption and, by the mid-1990s, grotty Dublin had jumped the queue to the front of the planet's sexiest hotspots. This was not just astounding, but transformative. I was very privileged to see it, and even be a small part of it.

I've written *Tax, Drugs and Rock 'n' Roll* to tell the story of how an influx of British pop stars in the early 1980s was a small but significant catalyst in the miraculous transformation of Ireland from poor, downtrodden and insular to rich, confident and outward looking. It's a personal story because

INTRODUCTION

I was fortunate to be up close and personal with Dublin's *Top Of The Pops* tax exiles, clubbing with them, playing football with them, interviewing them for my day job. In the space of a decade or so, the country was turned upside down, seeing itself in a whole dazzling new light and viewed anew by a bedazzled and somewhat bewildered watching world.

This is also a story of how my hometown of Dublin reclaimed its place as a capital city after decades of neglect, decay and a lot of wanton destruction. This was Ireland's Cinderella story come true. As the story opens, a joyless mantra was wailed every morning to the nation by its father confessor, broadcaster Gay Byrne. "The country is banjaxed," he'd groan, without fear of contradiction. In the '80s, Ireland was the sick man of Europe.

The thousands fleeing joblessness each week left by cattle boat because air travel was strictly for the rich, adding to the island's stifling isolation. The capital city, Dublin, was a crumbling wreck, its "killer smog" sensationalised in *the New York Times*. The decayed Georgian waterfront lining the River Liffey resembled rows of rotten sooty teeth.

Physical isolation and the Troubles spilling from Northern Ireland had choked tourism to a trickle. When the summer of '85 did bring a sudden influx of visitors, they were foreign reporters who came to gleefully report on moving statues in church grottos, egging on one British MP to mock "a country peopled by peasants, priests and pixies". The current affairs magazine *Magill* assembled a panel of experts to predict the state of Ireland by the close of the millennium. Those soothsayers concluded that Ireland would enter the 21st Century with "a smaller, older population", "continuing high unemployment", a "steady loss of young people through emigration" and "no end to violence in the North".

Instead, precisely the opposite happened. By the mid-1990s

the population had begun to swell with migrants, most of them young, many of them of a different skin colour to the white-bread host society. An end to the Troubles had come within touching distance as huge crowds in Dublin and Belfast cheered US President Bill Clinton as he called terrorists "yesterday's men". In 1994 a top economist presented investment bank Morgan Stanley with a fresh forecast of Ireland's prospects. The report's eye-catching title bore the words 'Celtic Tiger', a term that would serve as shorthand for the economic miracle to come.

Millions of words have been written about the Celtic Tiger years and the catastrophic economic crash that followed. This book is about the time just before all that, a time that set the scene for those two well-thumbed chapters in recent Irish history. It examines a pivotal period when a new generation with great expectations remade their self-image and the image Ireland presented to the world. This was a generation who were not suffering an identity crisis – they knew who they were, and they wanted more from life than the hard toil of digging roads or nursing night-shifts far from where they grew up

Irish music was a key vehicle for this take-off and British pop stars helped create the mood music overture for an astonishing reversal of fortunes. The huge success in America of a host of young, MTV-friendly British bands at the start of the 1980s was dubbed the Second British Invasion of the States in reference to the original invasion led by The Beatles in the 1960s. Status Quo's Francis Rossi set the ball rolling on the Second British Invasion of Ireland, closely followed by Sting and Andy Summers of The Police. But it was the arrival of a cluster of younger, freshly-minted MTV superstars that got Ireland its new English colony. Far from attracting hostility from the natives, these settlers were warmly embraced (well, mostly).

INTRODUCTION

Frankie Goes To Hollywood, Spandau Ballet and Def Leppard were among those who landed into a crumbling wreck of a capital city. They'd come for the tax breaks introduced by the Irish government in 1969 which allowed artists, writers and musicians to keep a large chunk of their earnings, and to double their money by taking advantage of a loophole in UK tax law which allowed them big savings if they stayed out of Britain for a year.

Many of these young millionaires arrived to endure a humdrum year of enforced exile beyond the grasp of the UK taxman. What they found confounded their low expectations. Ireland was very much a home from home. Holly Johnson spoke fondly of the time Frankie Goes To Hollywood ran a village pottery shop for a day as a favour to its elderly owner Alice. The store enjoyed its best sales ever (although mostly of egg cups). Spandau Ballet judged local talent contests in tough suburban pubs. Francis Rossi and Def Leppard frontman Joe Elliott provided me with similar reasons as to why overcast, downcast Ireland made for a much better tax haven than far-flung islands in the sun.

Finding themselves thrown together in Dublin, the Frankies, Spandaus and Leppards became good buddies, making Dublin's Pink Elephant an unlikely rival to Studio 54 as the world's nightclub with the most celebrities per square metre, or so the *New York Times* raved anyway. When the three bands combined their football talents to take on Dermot Morgan's Showbiz XI in the summer of 1986 a profound change was already blowing in the Irish wind and they were part of it, not least in spreading the word to the rest of Planet Pop that Ireland was open for business, while at the same time opening Irish eyes to the boundless new horizons beyond their lonely shores.

By the time Rolling Stone Ronnie Wood threw his stellar

housewarming party in County Kildare less than a decade later, Ireland's culture, society, economy and image were changed beyond recognition, with music as the beating heart of that change.

By the mid-1990s the 'sceptic isle' of 'police and priests' mocked by Bob Geldof in 'Banana Republic' had, to a remarkable extent, been bundled into the dustbin of history.

Of course, virtually all the heavy lifting in uprooting and overthrowing the old order had been done by natives on the warpath like U2, Sinéad O'Connor and the mutinous young people of Ireland.

Suddenly, everything went *Whoosh*!

Chapter 1

JOHN LENNON C/O BEATLE ISLAND, MAYO

"I hope we're a nice old couple living off the coast of Ireland, looking at our scrapbook of madness."

– John Lennon when asked in his final interview for his vision of when I'm 64

IN THE 1960s, the way Ireland's youth listened to music was revolutionised by two relatively affordable new arrivals. The dinky Dansette record player allowed teens to play their music of choice in their bedroom, away from the bulky and static music source controlled by their parents. Then the portable transistor radio (tranny) freed kids to bring their music outside onto the streets, the beach, anywhere. The undisputed kingpins of pop were The Beatles, who were especially beloved in Ireland because, as John Lennon put it in an early interview, "We're Irish!"

By 1966 The Beatles were getting crucified by the British tax man. The Fab Four were liable to pay a 95% supertax imposed by Harold Wilson's Labour government. An indignant John Lennon helped George Harrison with the lyrics to the protest song 'Taxman' which grumbled "There's one for you, nineteen for me". The band's manager Brian Epstein found himself hopelessly out of his depth making the giant leap from running a record store to guiding the finances of a global machine, which left The Beatles constantly reacting to money demands rather than planning for them.

Epstein had explored a rudimentary tax haven in the Bahamas but had managed to lose money on the venture. He had also set up offshore Swiss bank accounts for the four Beatles but such was the torrent of cash coming in that in late 1966 their accountant, Harry Pinsker, told them to spend, spend, spend or face a ruinous tax bill. Pinsker later revealed, "I suggested to the boys that they bought freehold property and went into retail trading."

By now cosseted from the outside world by their incredible fame, the band dispatched their Mister Fixit Alistair Taylor in the late spring of 1967 in search of a place where they could all live, Yellow Submarine fashion, in perfect harmony. Taylor returned with photos of the Greek island of Leslo, which had the added attraction of four satellite islands, one for each Beatle. Their Greek Odyssey was eventually foiled by the newly installed junta of the generals, who had ousted the democratic government in a coup and installed a brutal regime of torture and repression. The new tyrants immediately banned long hair, rock music and all dissenting views.

Around the same time as the Fab Four handed Taylor his mission to find a communal hideaway, Lennon sent him on a solo run to spend some of his tax avoidance cash on a windswept island off the west of Ireland which he'd spotted for sale in a Sunday newspaper. Taylor's mission was to bid anonymously, in the knowledge that if it became known that a Beatle was in the market the price would jump tenfold.

The auctioneer who penned the ad was R.G. Browne. His son, Michael, told me, "He (R.G) wrote catchy ads for the quality English Sunday papers. The ads had to be good because in those days you couldn't give away the islands in Clew Bay."

In the way of close communities, Michael ended up acting for Taylor and they secured Dornish for £1,550. The uninhabited island (actually two islands, linked by a rock causeway) was known to have the best grazing in Clew Bay and in beating off several local farmer bidders Lennon put assorted noses out of joint. Taylor, who paid in cash, later recalled, "Everybody was offering me money to allow their animals to graze."

John's original intention was to build a getaway for himself, his wife Cynthia and infant son Julian. Shortly after buying Dornish the Beatle arrived to inspect his pet project.

Michael told me, "I arranged to bring him out on a charter boat supplied by boat builder Paddy Quinn. It was a strict condition that there was to be no disclosure of the owner."

He needn't have worried. Paddy Quinn later revealed, "It was only afterwards I discovered it was John Lennon. Beatlemania and the Swinging Sixties hadn't quite reached the west of Ireland." Electricity had only reached the area a few years earlier at the start of the '60s.

Indeed, according to Browne, "It was only when the psychedelic caravan arrived some time later that people began to suspect the new owner was out of the ordinary."

The caravan in question, painted in multicoloured swirls, was floated over from the mainland on a jerry-built raft having drawn incredulous stares on its road trip through the west of Ireland.

On that first scouting trip in 1967 John did his best to be Mr Ordinary.

Browne said, "He was very pleasant and very practical. He was very interested in costings and he was determined to build a house that fit in with the local architecture. All of his entourage were business types in suits except for one hippy in a kaftan called Magic Alex. But even he was there on business.

"I asked what Alex was there for and John explained that he was working on a mechanism to stop people copying Beatles records. John was very businesslike. There was nothing airy-fairy about him. He wanted somewhere to provide him with isolation, but that would also be close to his work bases in Liverpool and London."

By chance, while Lennon was kicking the soil on his tax efficient real estate purchase, another superstar of the Beatles-led British Invasion of America, Peter Noone, was also in the west of Ireland looking at the old Noone family homestead with similar views on Britain's punitive taxes. Noone was the frontman of Herman's Hermits who had reportedly outsold the Beatles in the States in 1965. The group's second US No 1, 'I'm Henry The Eighth, I Am', had been drummed into Peter as a youngster by his Roscommon-born grandfather Thomas. In 1967, with 'There's A Kind Of Hush' riding high in the charts on both sides of the Atlantic, Noone trekked cross country from his Galway base to Four Mile House in County Roscommon, vacated by Thomas 50 years earlier.

Noone said, "Thomas was a fabulous musician and inspired all the Noones to sing and play. His brother James was killed in the war and Thomas was silent. He was only really relaxed when he was playing music. I was too young to figure out a way to get him to open up."

The singer continued, "Me and my friends rented horses and went on the most arduous pub crawl imaginable from Galway to Four Mile House. Most of it is but a hazy memory as me and my friends tried to drink like men. I was young and naive enough to survive with nothing more than a sore arse and probably a sore liver too, but a 17-year-old old Mancunian can recover by lunchtime.

"After the ride we ended up in the best hotel in Dublin which was more to my taste and we ate lamb chops with a decent vintage Bordeaux."

One year later John Lennon would have precisely the same adverse reaction to roughing it in rural Ireland.

John's five-year marriage to Cynthia began to crumble and his plans to build a family holiday home on Dornish were long-fingered. In May 1968 Cynthia arrived back early from a holiday to find John with Yoko Ono in the family home. Precisely 31 days later John and Yoko were in Clew Bay, on public view for the first time as an official item. They landed by helicopter on Dornish where John walked her around his fantasy island and the visitors settled briefly into the caravan for a smoke.

After a couple of hours they thought the better of roughing it and flew the couple of miles to the nearest five-star hotel on the mainland, the Great Southern in the village of Mulranny. Although one reporter seemed disappointed that "Mr Lennon's meal only consisted of soup and rice", the same report said the entourage included Ronan O'Rahilly and three others.

O'Rahilly was the Irish founder of Britain's flagship pirate pop station, Radio Caroline, and the manager of George Lazenby who had just signed up to replace Sean Connery as the second James Bond in *On Her Majesty's Secret Service*. During the shooting of the film, O'Rahilly persuaded Lazenby to commit career suicide by ditching the role because Bond "was all over". Paying warm tribute to his former agent at the time of O'Rahilly's death in 2020, Lazenby mused, "Who knows what would have happened had Ronan not got a hold of my brain?" Another report named another Bond icon, Robert Shaw, as one of the "three others" accompanying John and Yoko. Shaw had skyrocketed to fame in sync with The Beatles, playing the terrifying SPECTRE psychopath Donald Grant, out to crush Sean Connery's Bond in *From Russia With Love*.

In sharp contrast to Lennon's brief flirtation, Shaw would turn his Mayo tax arrangement into a permanent love affair. In the meantime however, the colourful story of Beatle Island – as it was now known – was only beginning.

The Beatles press officer Derek Taylor once said, "John had an MTV-level concentration span. He got bored very quickly and pushed things aside, whether it was a song or a business deal." And so it was that Dornish became an afterthought until John got wind of a serial squatter called Sid Rawle on the lookout for somewhere to plant a new age commune. Born to a Gypsy mother and a farmer father who was thrown off his farm, Rawle wanted all land to be confiscated from its owners and redistributed equally amongst the people. He was a fanatical campaigner for equality, but saw himself as first amongst equals, styling himself King Of The Hippies. To emphasise the point, he dressed in the flowing robes of a high priest.

Lennon and Rawle had a mutual friend in Swami Vishnu Devananda. The Swami had introduced The Beatles to the little known practice of yoga in 1965 when the band were filming *Help!* in the Bahamas where the holy man was holding mindful retreats for the tax averse on the sun-kissed haven.

Four years later, in the autumn of 1969, Devananda and Rawle made world headlines by leading a hippie invasion of the north Dublin fishing village of Skerries. 'Hippies Take Option On Island' blared the *Daytona Beach Morning Journal*. The Florida paper reported breathlessly that a band of hairy drop-outs had fetched up in Skerries just days after London police evicted them from their Piccadilly squats. Rawle told the press that they'd put down a $4,800 deposit on the uninhabited St Patrick's Island off the Dublin coast. Their plan was to establish a commune which, according to the Daytona paper, would "start with 500 British drop-outs".

The Montreal Gazette wrote that Rawle and his sponsors, including the Beat poet Allen Ginsberg, would have "no difficulty" raising the full $48,000 asking price. Even more disturbingly, one hippie boasted, "We will offer facilities for the IRA if they want them." Local man, Sean Rooney, told the Canadian paper, "I don't like the idea. Imagine having that big bunch of unwashed wastrels out there."

The more the hippies clarified their plans for St Patrick's, the more the people of Skerries vented their outrage. The would-be settlers saw St Patrick's as the first of many alternative island communities around the British Isles, housing some 20,000 drop-outs (except they objected to the term 'drop-outs', preferring 'heads'). They would build their own schools which would not "process" young minds. Thugs would be barred, but not drugs.

Striking while the iron was hot, the hippies hired a boatman for a trip to the island two miles offshore. Another Florida newspaper, *The Sarasota Journal*, opened its report, "Swami Vishnu Devananda stood on his head with joy. His two hippie companions cried: 'This is wild! This is beautiful!' Irish tempers boiled." Local councillor, future government minister and the man who would leave Celine Dion speechless, Ray Burke, fumed, "They will be stopped."

Residents were split. Some people had decided they had no objections to what they saw as an opportunity to make money selling goods and services to the hippies. Others felt that civilisation itself was under threat.

One of the Swami's companions, Frank Harris, told the crowd, "We are not bringing in thousands of screaming, long-haired, drug-ridden, sex-starved hippies. We want to use the island as a living laboratory, to find a way of life. If there is no water on the island, then our project falls through."

There was no fresh water on the island, although that seemed a minor matter when the would-be settlers discovered that the island was overrun by vicious giant rats. On further investigation, the giant rats proved even more fearsome than the hippies had originally thought, when they discovered that a couple of years earlier the authorities had released almost 40 large Manx cats expecting them to make short work of the rats. When the officials came back some months later, the rats had killed and eaten all the cats. The political establishment was already scouring the planning and property laws to make sure the hippies never cemented one brick on top of another on St Patrick's.

But no sooner had one door shut then another opened and when word reached The Beatles' Apple HQ – built as part of the retail trading end of their tax avoidance schemes – of the hippies' defeat in Skerries, Lennon summoned Sid Rawle and offered him Beatle Island as his promised land. Rawle assembled some 30 English drop-outs and they made their home in two large army surplus tents.

"It was heaven and it was hell," Rawle later recalled. It was mostly hell. The island was lashed by storms which blew the tents inside out. Crops failed. Their trips to the mainland to buy supplies with their meagre finances met with suspicion by some and outright hostility by a small few who organised into an anti-commune committee.

In March 1971, *The Connacht Telegraph* carried a story headlined 'Hippie Republic Under Siege'. It claimed, "After a year of seething anger, Westport has finally declared war on The Republic Of Dornish."

Photographer Liam Lyons, who covered that story, told me, "That headline was exaggerated. There was little hostility, though people were worried about drugs. But mostly the Diggers, as they were known, were a tourist attraction. You'd have visitors getting into canoes and paddling out to see them. They were mostly wealthy kids dropping out."

The commune became so well known that post began arriving from around the world addressed simply to Beatle Island or Hippie Island, Ireland.

"Some press guys would come down trying to stir it," Browne, the solicitor, said, "but the hippies were a harmless bunch. The biggest fear locals had about them wasn't drugs, but that they'd drown. They'd come in and out on the tide on little home-made boats. The sea has to be respected, and there was a fear they didn't respect it enough."

The hippies sensed far more hostility than concern from the locals. One told reporters, "We have now got a lunatic fringe in Westport who are whipping up hate against us. They keep on imagining us as Charlie Mansons who will come in the middle of the night and slice their heads off for bread." Claiming that their van parked on the mainland had been pummelled to pieces, he added, "There is also a campaign of terror directed against pub owners in the town as well as shop owners who supply us with goods. The two boatmen told us that they could no longer taxi us in from the island as their children had been threatened and told that their boats would be smashed if they carried us."

The island dwellers called themselves The Tribe Of The Sun which proved to be a horrible misnomer. Beatle Island was a barren, storm-swept, godforsaken rock, shunned even by rabbits and, having led his people to their island paradise, the self-styled King Of The Hippies Sid Rawle couldn't hack it. While his disciples struggled to make potatoes and turnips grow in the poor soil, he spent as much time away from his sodden camp followers as he could find excuses for, claiming he had to go on far away fundraising trips for weeks at a time. These absences included a stint painting houses in Dublin and making a counter-cultural mark selling vegetarian fast food as one of the founders of the Glastonbury Festival, with the first event headlined by Tyrannosaurus Rex. After weeks away he'd arrive back for a few days and vanish again, eventually never to return.

Demoralised by the incessant wind and rain and the blockade of supplies and services from the mainland, the hippies finally abandoned Beatle Island. The reason presented to the watching world was that an oil-filled lantern had toppled during one of the frequent violent storms, starting a blaze that destroyed their communal tent and all of their food stores. Some questioned whether the all-consuming fire offered a convenient way out for a community that had come to the very end of its tether.

Lennon's murder in 1980 crushed the couple's whimsical dream of reviving their plans to live on Dornish. In 2006, Yoko reflected, "It was a place where we thought we could escape the pressures and spend some undisturbed time together. We often discussed the idea of building a cottage there. It was so beautiful, so tranquil, yet so isolated, it seemed a perfect place to get away from it all." In 1984, she sold Beatle Island to a local farmer, giving the £30,000 raised to an Irish orphanage.

Lennon might have become Ireland's most admired and famous rock exile, but his restless nature eventually drew him to New York, the city that doesn't sleep. It's doubtful if he'd have chosen the isolation of Ireland even if an attractive new tax scheme had been in place when he visited in 1967 and 1968. Others would deem the new dispensation an offer they couldn't refuse though, led by Lennon's comic hero and friend Peter Sellers.

In 1969 Ireland's Finance Minister Charles Haughey introduced a far-sighted tax exemption aimed at enticing high-profile writers, artists and musicians to take up residence free of income tax on their creations. Invited to explain his scheme at Harvard University, Haughey stated that when it came to music, he had in mind the composers of "operas, ballets and symphonies". And that interpretation of the tax law took hold in Ireland, with virtually no Irish musicians availing of it for more than a decade until U2's canny management team twigged that it could have wider applications.

In his 2022 autobiography, musician Paul Brady wrote, "I asked was it (the Artists' Tax Exemption) not just for foreign writers. The prevailing assumption amongst us Irish artists at the time was that this was just a legal ploy by Haughey to show himself off as a patron of the arts and that it was only on offer to famous artists from outside the country. Ozzie Kilkenny, (the accountant he shared with U2) said that wasn't the case and he duly applied." And in one fell swoop the fortunes of Irish acts were utterly transformed, discovering a way to enjoy financial parity of esteem living cheek by jowl with rock exile pioneers like Status Quo and The Police.

Leslie Charteris, creator of *The Saint*, also availed of Ireland's generous new tax dispensation although he openly despised and resented his enforced stay in Dublin which seemed insufferably drab and dull after years writing scripts in Hollywood. Charteris bluntly declared, "Everything I write is designed to be milked to the last drop of revenue."

According to the broadcaster Emer O'Kelly, who endured an uncomfortable dinner party with Charteris as the prickly host, "He bought a small apartment in Ballsbridge and spent the requisite number of nights in it annually 'and not one more' as he said to me when I had the doubtful pleasure of meeting him."

He put it to his Irish guests, "Why on earth would anyone who didn't have to, live in Ireland?"

Wolf Mankowitz on the other hand took to Irish living so well that he moved to West Cork in 1969 and remained until his death three decades later. Mankowitz, a Londoner, found success in 1955 when he adapted his own fantasy novel, *A Kid For Two Farthings*, into the hit film of the same name directed by Carol Reed who had previously directed their mutual friend Orson Welles in the landmark film noir *The Third Man*. Welles, who made his stage debut at Dublin's Gate Theatre in 1916, was a regular visitor to renaissance man Mankowitz.

Like many stellar tax exiles that would follow, Mankowitz came for the savings but stayed for the sheer love of the place. Looking back in 1991, he said that when he'd arrived more than two decades earlier, "The notion was that I'd reduce the amount of work I was doing. If I didn't have to pay tax I wouldn't have to work so much. And then, I don't know, we just stayed on and on, getting more and more related to the place." Shortly after settling in West Cork, and for reasons best known to himself, Mankowitz accepted an offer to become Honorary Consul of the Republic of Panama to Ireland. He admitted that the diplomatic post paid minimum wage but he found it highly amusing and a little flattering that he was asked.

Chapter 2

PETER SELLERS' KILDARE HELL, ROBERT SHAW'S MAYO HEAVEN

"This is the nearest point on earth to heaven. When I go, I hope it will be from here."

– Robert Shaw on Tourmakeady

TWO YEARS after the arrival of Wolf Mankowitz came Peter Sellers, the lead man in Mankowitz's Bond spoof *Casino Royale*. Shortly after settling in Ireland, Sellers appeared on the nation's flagship TV programme *The Late Late Show*. He ran through a dazzling array of comic characters which had everyone in stitches until the host Gay Byrne asked, for a second time, why Sellers had recently moved to Ireland. His playfulness evaporated and he shot back, "I'm not going to answer that. You're trying to get me on the tax dodge." His sensitivity on the subject was down to the fact that wealthy tax exiles were generally unpopular in his native Britain, but for his Irish audience that night Haughey's tax exemption was no dodge, but an honourable means of supporting the arts.

Sellers was a good buddy of John Lennon who had worshipped

him since his radio days, and latterly an acolyte of Swami Vishnu Devananda who had stood on his hands in Skerries to drum up publicity for Sid Rawle's fantasy island circus. The actor, who'd reached the UK Top 10 long before Lennon, was born in Dublin in 1924, and again in Portsmouth the following year. It sounds like a line from *The Goon Show*, the zany radio showcase that made him a star, but it's true.

Sellers' English parents, variety actors, were touring a show in Ireland when the first Peter was stillborn. The one who would find global stardom was born a year later and registered as Richard Henry, but given the name Peter in family circles after his older brother. It was a fitting start for a man described as a chameleon, a cypher and a mimic, whose entire life was a mish-mash of characters to the seeming exclusion of any personality of his own.

Sellers arrived in Ireland directly from a stellar send-off party attended by Princess Margaret, Warren Beatty and a host of other A-listers, and appeared to miss the bright lights immediately. With his new wife Miranda, an English socialite and It Girl, he settled into his 18th Century stately home, Carton House in Maynooth, behind five miles of high walls. The couple had been alerted to the imposing Georgian mansion by Blake Edwards, the director of the hugely successful *Pink Panther* franchise which starred Sellers in possibly his best-loved role as the bumbling Inspector Clouseau.

The year before the movie star and the socialite arrived, Edwards and his superstar wife Julie Andrews had lived there, with Rock Hudson also resident on the grounds of the location for the movie *Darling Lili*. Sadly for Sellers and Miranda, the isolated great estate quickly proved a disastrous lifestyle choice for a restless actor with a low boredom threshold. During the couple's two years in Ireland their marriage suffocated and disintegrated, leading to a divorce in 1974. While Sellers would accuse his wife of repeated infidelities, he was distracting himself with drink and drugs, sometimes shared with his admiring Goon-fan pal John Lennon who once told him, only half in jest, "Showbiz people need a form of relaxation. It's drugs or exercise and drugs win hands down."

Desperately bored in his enforced tax banishment and stuck in a crumbling marriage, Sellers was an easy mark for the shameless self-publicist Swami who chose Ireland to launch his latest hairbrained stunt in September 1971, exploiting the tragic troubles in the North.

The *Associated Press* reported, "An Indian yogi from the Montreal area and movie actor Peter Sellers swooped down from the clouds in a multi-coloured plane today to 'bomb' Belfast – with peace leaflets. The most unlikely pair to arrive on a peace mission to the battle-scarred Northern Ireland capital, they circled overhead in the yogi's two-seater aircraft before touching down.

"They set off to sing peace chants in the riot-torn Roman Catholic Falls Road district. Sellers, 46 today, and Swami Vishnu Devananda, 42, said they would try to meet Protestant leader Rev Ian Paisley and Roman Catholic Bernadette Devlin, British Parliamentary representative for Mid-Ulster. Sellers, who now lives in the Irish Republic, has been studying yoga for three months. Swami Vishnu Devananda said his trip is the first stop on a five-month tour of world trouble spots. He will fly on to Europe, Pakistan and Vietnam."

Sellers' time in Ireland was as unhappy in its own, pampered, way as the sufferings of the hippies abandoned by Sid Rawle on Dornish. His movies of the period were poorly received by the critics and at the box office, while his marriage was heading straight for the rocks. He had suffered a near-fatal heart attack in 1964 and his destructive, reclusive lifestyle behind the thick walls of his Irish retreat did nothing for his fragile health. Sellers and Lennon died within six months of each other in 1980.

While Sellers came to Ireland in a forlorn quest to escape both the taxman and the pressures of superstardom, his fellow actor Robert Shaw found the freedom he craved far from the bright lights. That was until the money ran out, and it kept running out. Shaw was a pop culture icon twice over, first as the man-mountain assassin out to kill James Bond in 1963's *From Russia With Love* and then a dozen years later as the salty, scene-stealing sea-dog Quint in the movie that changed movies forever, *Jaws*, the very first summer blockbuster.

The Irish language documentary, *Jaws, Deoch & Deora* (*Jaws*, Drink & Tears) does a wonderful job of capturing Shaw's love affair with the rural townland of Tourmakeady and the community's heartfelt love affair with him. One legacy of that great romance is a chat with his Irish-speaking grandchildren.

In 1970, desperate to evade the clutches of the British taxman, Shaw and his second wife Mary Ure drove up and down every lonely boreen west of the Shannon before coming across Drimbawn House, a handsome Victorian pile on 75 acres rolling down to the shores of trout-filled Lough Mask in 1970. The stately home was in a bad state of disrepair and the muscular actor took a hands-on approach to renovating.

According to his third wife Virginia Jansen, "He said if there's a shack at the end of this avenue we must buy it. I absolutely love this place." An interviewer for *The Irish Times* wrote, "He pitched in with a corps of workmen to fell trees and move boulders and proceeded to carve out an authentic family domain."

An Oscar-nominated actress best known for her starring role in *Where Eagles Dare*, playing opposite Richard Burton and Clint Eastwood, Mary Ure died in 1975 from an "accidental" overdose of barbiturates and alcohol according to the coroner's report. At the time of her death Shaw was still married to the actress, although they were no longer living as a couple.

The following year he married Virginia Jansen who had been secretary to Shaw and Ure for several years. Shaw had adopted Ure's son from her marriage to the playwright John Osborne and now adopted Virginia's son from a previous relationship. When Victoria gave birth to their own son, it brought the total number of children Shaw supported to 10.

A gifted Shakespearian actor, Shaw frequently cited this ballooning brood as the reason he took film roles that he knew were beneath him. For instance, he found it impossible to turn down the hefty sum of $100,000 for six weeks work as a drunken Irish priest on the spaghetti Z-movie *A Town Called Bastard* in 1971. He later reasoned, "Money isn't the sole reason. But I do seem to spend more than I earn. And it takes a lot of money to raise these children of mine." Veronica reflected, "The movies were mostly because he had to pay the school fees. He'd have liked to have been writing books but he had eight, nine children. Ten children in the end and the school fees were huge. He did enjoy doing his films when he got good ones, but he needed the money."

Shaw said, "I don't spend much on myself, maybe a drink. And I like to travel and stay at really fine hotels. I have an interest in fast cars, and I now have a Mercedes 450SL, but it's not like before, when I drove Rolls-Royce convertibles and Aston Martins. Of course, the tax situation in Britain is impossible. I wake up in the middle of the night, frequently, with pain and humiliation and a great deal of shame at some of the work I've done in films. And I would do a good movie any day, regardless of the money. Unfortunately, there aren't many, and… if you are not successful now and again, nobody asks you to be in any movies at all. For years the studios would say, 'Shaw's pictures make no money, he's not an international star.'"

When the BBC visited Shaw in his Mayo hideaway in 1970, they found him downcast and forlorn. He lamented, "You know bloody well that in a few years' time you'll be dead. And so what? In my case there might be nine books on a bookshelf that nobody's reading anymore. I know that a lot of people look upon me as successful and when I complain they say, 'How dare you complain! What's he getting so angry about?' But from my point of view, I don't feel so successful at all. Of course failure always makes one reshape one's pattern. What is sad in life is the people who have genuine talent who failure beats, who failure knocks into the ground. No, failure isn't going to knock me into the ground until I'm too tired. That's what I'm going to fight against – exhaustion!"

The situation was turned on its head and any sense of exhaustion was banished when he energised *Jaws* with a rare raw power and emerged as a star reborn. The movie's director Steven Spielberg paid tribute to the sheer force of Shaw's fated drunken sailor, singling out Quint's account of the real life shark attacks on the survivors of the USS Indianapolis that sets up the film's spine-tingling finale. Spielberg said that Shaw's first reading of Quint's speech, which Shaw had rewritten, "devastated the set". The director confessed that, "The effect was so overwhelming that it threatened to capsize everyone prematurely. We had to do it again, with more restraint. In terms of the finished film, the reading was even better because Bob was imposing more control over his emotions."

Shaw took the role of Quint for the big payday it would bring, despite thinking it was "a silly concept". His neighbours in Tourmakeady were delighted for him. In fact, his neighbours would have got wind of the news ahead of even Shaw's close friends.

The actor's phone number was Tourmakeady 20 which was a party line shared with three other households, which meant that his neighbours could listen in. They knew even before Hollywood what Shaw's next movie was going to be and how much he was being paid for it. For instance, before *Variety* could report the story, the regulars in the pubs surrounding Lough Mask – including Maire Luke's, where not a word of English was spoken – knew that the script for *The Sting* would be arriving by courier any day now.

Shaw sent his kids to the local primary school and when the school was forced to close for repairs he opened up his home for lessons, turning his gym into a classroom. His local watering hole was Paddy's Thatch Bar which he would access by rowing from the pier at the bottom of his garden. He was a familiar sight pulling pints behind the bar of Paddy's where he'd buy rounds for everyone as a means of keeping the sessions going long into the night. One local reminisced, "He was a star, someone you could talk about to other villages. We have a big actor living here in Tourmakeady and sure down the road there was nothing but sheep."

He became loved because he threw himself wholeheartedly into becoming part of the community and downplayed his wealth and fame. He bought cattle and had a five-hole golf course built which he opened to the locals. His wife Virginia testified that he always loved to get home to Ireland, but that after three weeks his money worries would return to haunt him and he'd be on to his agent asking what was available.

In August 1978 Robert Shaw was driving Virginia and their toddler Tom back from Castlebar where he'd picked up a parcel. A short distance out of the town he told Virginia he felt unwell. He pulled over, said he had to throw up, began choking and fell into the shallow grassy roadside ditch. Virginia rolled him back onto the road where he groaned, "I think I fainted". A car stopped on the quiet road. Virginia recognised the driver and screamed at him to "get Doctor Brown". The driver grunted that Shaw had "drink taken" and drove on. Virginia knew in her bones that he wasn't going for the doctor. Another car pulled up and again Virginia knew the driver. This time she was certain he would fetch the doctor. When the doctor arrived he told Virginia to find the nearest phone and call an ambulance. She and the ambulance arrived back on the scene together and she pleaded to go with her husband. The doctor told her he was already dead.

In 2008, on the 30th anniversary of his death, a stone memorial was unveiled by the people of Tourmakeady in honour of their favourite adopted son, Robert Shaw. Virginia was there with many members of his family. She told the large crowd, "He was a wonderful person. He was fun, generous, naughty, drank too much and loved his children."

A neighbour later remarked, "What we put on his memorial stone was that he was a man who lived here, not a man who died here."

His youngest, Tom, said, "There's not a day goes by that I don't see some reference or think of him. Because his image is out there all the time, still. For a long time I thought it was some elaborate tax dodge, that he was living in South America and would make himself apparent to us once again." Family and friends recalled the actor describing his Mayo sanctuary as "the nearest point on earth to heaven", telling them, "When I go, I hope it will be from here."

Chapter 3

NO COUNTRY FOR YOUNG MEN, OR WOMEN, OR FRANK SINATRA

"There exists the duty to supply instruction that can tranquillise the adolescent."

– Archbishop of Dublin John Charles McQuaid

THE HOSTILITY which built against the hippies of Beatle Island was not unique to Ireland. Sid Rawle's ragged band fetched up in the north Dublin village of Skerries days after they'd been run out of London by a large squad of police who baton-charged their Piccadilly squatters camp, renamed Hippiedilly for the occupation. The military dictators of Greece were far from alone in enforcing a ban on long hair and rock music. Young people and alien pop culture has always met with a wary reception from established orders the world over, but the conservative Irish Establishment – 'Official Ireland' – had made a special mission of wiping youth culture and pop music from the face of the nation.

The first rulers of independent Ireland were themselves very young men, many in their thirties and some even in their twenties. At the top of their fanciful agenda was to achieve a self-sufficient, Irish-speaking, 32 county all-island state. Although young in age, their attitudes were deeply rooted in tradition. The Free State's first Justice Minister, Kevin O'Higgins, was proud to boast that the country's new rulers were "the most conservative-minded revolutionaries that ever put through a successful revolution". He and his colleagues were zealous puritans determined to forge a spotless Gaelic state insulated from the wicked ways of foreign cultures. They took power near the start of the Roaring Twenties, the Jazz Age, when a frivolous new youth culture was sweeping a weary world, seeking pleasure and relief after the horrors of the Great War. 'Jazz' was a four-letter word they despised and feared.

For these Catholic ultras, tranquillising adolescent urges was the magic trick to moulding the right type of citizen. The first step was to build a Fortress State which in many ways resembled the fascist Total State which Mussolini was attempting to establish in Italy. In the days before invasive commercial air travel and television, a State could grip a monopoly on technology and communications within its borders and build walls to keep unwanted ideas out. In this spirit, Ireland's first film censor James Montgomery happily declared, "I know nothing about films but I do know the Ten Commandments."

Mussolini used repression and terror to achieve his Total State which he described as "all within the state, none outside the state, none against the state". With the Irish people still nursing the deep wounds of a brutal and bitter civil war, the new rulers were committed to taking a peaceful and civic-minded approach to unifying a society where Protestants knew their place and non-Christian faiths kept their heads down. Even tourists would be kept under a watchful eye. When Billy Butlin opened a camp in Mosney, Co Meath, which welcomed hungry holidaymakers from ration-starved, post-war Britain to a land of plentiful steak, butter and sweets, the authorities inserted a church into the plans and refused a drinks licence in case "bottle parties" in the chalets would lead to occasions of sin.

A big plus in Official Ireland's bid for splendid isolation from the wicked outside world was their physical isolation as an island, apart from the shared six northern counties that remained British soil. Five months after independence, the Irish Free State staged the first Brexit, which in this case meant exiting British rule.

On 1 April 1923, the partition of Ireland became a concrete reality when the southern government erected a hard border with the six counties. The Free State published a list of "approved" cross-border roads to be manned with customs checkpoints. In order to raise revenues and protect local manufacturers, the cash-strapped administration published a long list of goods that would be subject to stiff new import duties from 1 April. It all happened in such a rush that many took the start date as proof of an April Fool's joke. That was wishful thinking.

The importation of some goods was banned outright, with the authorities warning of "severe penalties" for anyone caught bringing in extracts of tea, coffee, chicory or tobacco. Other prohibited imports included dogs, guns, cocaine, heroin, and foreign editions of books and music. The ban on foreign music imports was aimed squarely at the young people's catnip, jazz.

A decade later, a steady trade in smuggled jazz records had developed in Ireland, and with the arrival of talking movies – starting purposely with *The Jazz Singer* – even the censor himself admitted that keeping the ears of Irish youth entirely safe from primal rhythms was beyond him.

In early February 1934, Dublin Corporation debated the hot issue of the day – the call to stop mongrel jazz music from debasing Ireland's pedigree culture. The Gaelic League took the lead. The Chairman of a League meeting in Leitrim decried jazz as "something that is borrowed from the language of the savages of Africa and its object is to destroy virtue in the human soul".

Jazz was seen by hardline nationalists and Catholic clerics as a conspiracy to capsize noble Christian civilization, and Leitrim, in the heart of rural Ireland, took up the cudgel. A rally in the village of Mohill attracted 3,000 protesters brandishing placards saying 'Down With Jazz' and 'Out With Paganism', while five patriotic bands played edifying native airs and marches. *The Leitrim Observer* warned its readers not to "disgrace the heroic saints and martyrs of our race", adding that Christendom would "rush forth again to expel the last and worst invader – the jazz of Johnny Bull and the n****rs and cannibals".

The young democracies of Europe were still fragile experiments and no one knew how long they might survive. Mussolini, Stalin and Hitler were forging societies based on strict deference and obedience, with Franco shaping up to subdue Spain in a murderous coup. Both of Ireland's larger parties sprang from authoritarian Sinn Féin roots and were zealously bent on reimposing a social order where everyone knew their place. Especially the women of Ireland, who had been largely forced back into their box after taking a lead role in the struggle for independence.

But, only a decade into their grand plan, the ex-revolutionaries were confronted with the stark reality that keeping out the big bad world was easier said than done. The post-war demand for fun and freedom had translated into a boom in spectator sports, cinemas and dancehalls. The economy was on its knees and a new generation was growing up, one that treasured Hollywood movies and jazz music as colourful escapes from their grinding everyday lives. The alternative offered by the Church and State authorities was chaste austerity and a wet blanket thrown over any and every fun activity deemed un-Irish – which was nearly all of them.

With economic emigration to the United States and Britain at epidemic levels, jazz discs and sheet music reached Ireland from ships' crews who were forever coming and going. The wireless was the pinnacle of new technology in its day. Nobody knew where it was going, and that scared the hell out of the authorities. When a national radio service was being set up, all agreed with the Dáil deputy who said, "The matter that will be transmitted should, in my opinion, be carefully revised from a moral and national standpoint. We do not want the minds of our youths contaminated with some of the stuff that the youths of other countries have been imbibing." Jazz culture was a genie that would not be put back in its bottle, but that fact was lost on the more misguided zealots who clung to a heartfelt belief that if Irish could be reinstated as the only spoken language, the people would be saved from Hollywood, smutty jazz lyrics and the English tabloids because they wouldn't be able to understand them.

The very personification of jazz was the glamorous flapper, as played on the big screen by Clara Bow, the It Girl of the 1920s. The founding document of Irish independence, the 1916 Proclamation, had very specifically referred to men and women as equals in its opening line. It also affirmed women's suffrage, mandating that the new Irish democracy would be elected by both men and women. This was discarded by the men now running the country, who ruled by virtue of the fact they had fought for independence. But they had not fought for the independence of young women in any shape or form, and certainly not for the leeway to shorten their skirts, bob their hair and gyrate to jazz. With the rapid global spread of the typewriter, by the 1920s Dublin had its share of typing pools – regimented sweatshops which nevertheless brought a deluge of young women into the workplace and provided them with spending money of their own. Freed from the captivity and drudgery of domestic service, these young followers of fashion were commonly derided as "shopgirls and typists". The new ruling class feared and loathed everything about them and they were sullied from the pulpit, the political hustings and in print as painted harlots and potential homewreckers. Upholding the adage that revenge is best served cold, the State would wait until 1937 to put into law that the only legitimate role for a woman was as a home-maker, as dictated in a new Constitution drawn up by Taoiseach Éamon de Valera in cahoots with Archbishop John Charles McQuaid.

Somewhat prematurely, *The Irish Times* in 1928 ran a feature under the wishful headline 'Reported Death Of The Flapper'. It wrote approvingly, "Gone is the flapper. In her place has come the young woman with poise of soft-toned and correct speech, soberly dressed and without closely cropped hair." As the paper proclaimed the last rites for "these hard-boiled little things with shaved necks", readers were reminded, "Her hair resembled that of a Hottentot, her skirts ended about her knees, she sneaked her brother's cigarettes and swore like a trooper. She chewed gum – great wads of it – vigorously and incessantly. Her make-up was as crude as a clown's."

When the flapper did disappear shortly afterwards down an evolutionary *cul-de-sac*, it was due to changes in fashion rather than any efforts of Official Ireland, including a Radio Éireann ban on adverts for cosmetics. The national broadcaster refused to carry any commercials for lipstick, blusher or eyeliner lest these would inflame the passions of male listeners. And when young women did change their style in the 1930s, they remained avid in their love of all things jazz and the silver screen.

The term 'dance music' or 'race music' covered swing, jive, 'hot' music and anything sung by a crooner. Almost no black music was played, which meant those banished included Bing Crosby, Glenn Miller, Benny Goodman, and pop's very first teen idol, Frank Sinatra. They were cleansed from Irish broadcasting in 1943 when, as one newspaper put it, "An official 'taboo' has been placed on dance music at Radio Éireann. The brake has been applied gradually and the small number of dance music records broadcast recently will be the last."

The biggest name banished was Sinatra, whose screaming, swooning Bobby Soxers following mobbed his every appearance. A few years earlier, this official radio taboo on jazz wouldn't have bothered the young people of Ireland in the least as most relied on Radio Luxembourg for their pop. But by 1943, the jazz-hating Nazis had commandeered the station for propaganda broadcasts by Lord Haw Haw.

It was during those darkest days of the Emergency – World War Two to the rest of the world – that visions of a culturally pure Irish-speaking Ireland and the elimination of foreign influence seemed most within touching distance. Parents who could afford it were packing their children off to new Gaeltacht summer camps that were springing up across rural Ireland. Here, kids were forbidden to speak a word of English while experiencing an edifying exposure to Irish music, dancing and verse. The censorship of newspapers intensified, removing anything that would infringe Ireland's neutrality. The same applied to movies. The classic *Casablanca* was banned twice, the first time because its anti-Nazi outcome was deemed dangerous to the state's neutrality, the second because lovers Humphrey Bogart and Ingrid Bergman were not married.

When the Dáil reconvened in the autumn of 1943, Labour's Dick Corish praised the "improvement" in Radio Éireann as a result of the taboo imposed over the summer. He said that if the Irish people had been subjected to "crooning and jazzing" for too much longer "we would have had very little music in this country within the next generation". Corish said next up on the programme of cultural purification was to banish "these supposed variety artists" that were letting down standards.

"Some of them have been trying to ape British comedians who would not be listened to on an Irish stage." Instead of subversive stand-up comedians undermining the State's cultural masterplan, he wanted homegrown, "magnificent violinists and singers and other artists".

He had especially in mind Jimmy O'Dea and Maureen Potter, who gently jibed politicians like Dublin's perennial, Lord Mayor Alfie Byrne. O'Dea nicknamed Byrne 'The Shaking Hand Of Dublin' and told a joke about a cyclist up in court for failing to signal a turn. The defendant said he'd been afraid to put out his hand in case Byrne shook it. This type of disrespectful humour went down like a lead balloon with the entire political class who took a lofty view of themselves and their mission to revive the mythical land of saints and scholars. An abject failure to fruitfully engage with the distrusted field of comedy remains a sore point with TV licence payers into the 21st century.

Established in 1922, the year of Irish independence, Walton's Music Store was for decades the physical embodiment of the State's anti-pop, musical purity policy. The Walton's Programme on Radio Éireann – a fixture of Irish broadcasting until 1981 – would sign off with the friendly instruction from host Leo Maguire that "if you do feel like singing, sing an Irish song". As music stores went, it was the Head Prefect, the teacher's pet. If you wanted the latest swell hit by Elvis or The Beatles, best go somewhere else. For pop kids of more than one era, the sound of the Walton's Programme jingle – a patriotic marching dirge that blasted through every kitchen in Ireland each Saturday lunchtime– was emphatically *not* music to the ears. If truth be told, it was the ultimate vindication of the old adage that the definition of a gentleman is someone who can play the accordion, but doesn't.

The freedom fighters who had taken power at the start of the 1920s were very young and very idealistic. The average age of the first cabinet was 35. At the outbreak of WW2 in 1939, it was 48. By the time of the listless 1957 general election for control of a country on its knees, that average age was 65. Distrustful of the young generations coming up behind them, and desperately anxious to freeze their revolution in their own safe keeping, the Young Turks of 1922 had grown old clinging on to power. In this they had been greatly aided by the so-called 'safety valve' of youth emigration. While the vast majority had fled the economic stasis of Ireland in search of work, this forced exodus had also handily removed generations of potentially rebellious malcontents who might have challenged the stagnant status quo.

As the 1973 general election approached, Fianna Fáil had been in power with just two short breaks for 35 years on the trot, prompting one commentator to take issue with the party's self-description, noting, "They look less like the Soldiers of Destiny and more like *Dad's Army*." Dragging out their distrust of the country's youth to the bitter end, the Fianna Fáil government set a quickie date for the poll, which meant they beat the introduction of the new electoral register which would have given the vote to 140,000 over-18s for the first time. Out of time and ideas, they lost anyway.

No-one in their wildest dreams could have imagined that 14 years later the same party would be returned to power feting Ireland's musical youth – dollar signs in their eyes – as "our greatest national asset".

Chapter 4

THE SHOWBANDS: AN IRISH SOLUTION TO AN IRISH PROBLEM

"My voice comes out very flat on tape, but singing's a lot better than shovelling gravel for a living."

– Jim Tobin of the Firehouse showband

THE OPENING lines of Derek Dean's autobiography, *The Freshmen Unzipped*, shockingly capture the unsteady relationship between pop music, drink and the taxman in the Ireland of the '60s and '70s. Dean was the charismatic frontman of The Freshmen, a showband that entered local legend when, playing support to The Beach Boys in 1967, they blew away their road-weary heroes with a set entirely comprised of Beach Boys covers.

Walking down Dublin's Grafton Street one afternoon, Dean was approached by a stranger armed with "a litany of amazing facts about The Freshmen". They dropped into Davy Byrne's pub and the singer started his usual day's boozing. As the stranger rattled on, Dean's alarm bells began to ring. He recalled, "This was no ordinary fan. Not only did he know the venues we were doing, but he was also clued in about the crowds we were getting." Then it dawned on him, "It's the taxman! The bastard is about to land me with a gigantic bill!"

Several double vodkas later, now certain this was a set-up, Dean lunged at the stranger, grabbing his throat and snarling, "Who the fuck are you? Where are you from and what do you want from me?"

Released from Dean's grip, the shocked and gasping stranger blurted out, "I've been drumming with the band for the past three weeks. I was speaking to you only last night in Cavan and said I'd meet you today for a drink."

Gifted, gutsy, and unprepared to churn out any old rubbish, The Freshmen came closer than any other showband to achieving rock credibility. (Although The Royal Showband could point out that The Beatles played support to them in 1962 and Elvis came to see their Vegas residency.) After he was sacked for his excessive ways, Dean's mercurial bandmate Billy Brown landed 'Single Of The Week' in the ultra-hip *New Musical Express* and became a staple fixture on John Peel's impossibly cool radio show. The Freshmen were good and, in the thriving black economy that was the showband circuit, they were raking it in. Dean wrote, "It's lovely having your pockets stuffed with big rolled-up bundles of notes... Instead of washing clothes, I'd buy new ones." In the showbands' heyday it was not unknown for the top stars to blow a small fortune flying to London to take in one of the many hit movies banned by the Irish film censor.

To paraphrase a future Irish Prime Minister, Charles Haughey, who built an impossibly lavish lifestyle on dodging the taxman, the showbands were "an Irish solution to an Irish problem". The problem was that for many top touring acts, this remote island clinging to the edge of Europe was just too out of the way to bother with. In relation to British acts there was the further complication that the busy twin-island touring circuit which had existed before the Great War had been dismantled first by Irish independence and secondly by Ireland's neutrality in WW2, which had caused great resentment in Britain and further isolated the smaller island.

The advent of the showbands provided the solution to this Irish problem. Groups of talented homegrown musicians were recruited to learn off the British and American hits of the day and they would reproduce them live at hops which, in rural areas, would attract dance crazy kids from 40, 50 or more miles distant. By the early '60s the crowds and the cash had grown so massive that chains of giant ballrooms the size of aircraft hangars were springing up across the land, which meant the promoters could attract top international stars. Big names like Chubby Checker, Little Richard and Jim Reeves (with mixed success) as the Irish scene evolved separately from the rest of the world into an oddball musical Galápagos.

One popular touring act was Desmond Dekker and The Aces, who had chalked up one of the earliest reggae smash hits in 1968 with 'The Israelites' at a time when Dekker's protégé, Bob Marley, was unknown beyond the pair's native Jamaica. But this Desmond Dekker and his ace Jamaicans were not who they claimed to be. They were a bunch of English lads recruited by an unscrupulous promoter on the assumption that most Irish people had seen so few black people that his doppelgangers would be accepted unquestioned as the genuine article. That assumption proved correct. The fake Aces toured the ballrooms several times, going down a storm.

Sometimes a global superstar would be faced with a half-empty hall because a showband was playing up the road. The showbands scheduled their year by the Catholic Church calendar. Rolling in cash on the home circuit, they rarely ventured abroad apart from the 40 days of Lent when Ireland shut down and they decamped en masse to Britain. There, they shared the same tour buses, motorway cafes, pubs and stages with top British and American acts like The Beatles, The Stones, Smokey Robinson, Little Stevie Wonder and The Supremes. They were generally treated with respect for their energy and musicianship, if not for their entire sets of cover versions. Sometimes this friendly respect may have been overegged. Many years after the event, Eileen Reid of The Cadets suggested on Irish radio that the US-style military uniforms worn by her group when they toured with The Beatles in the early '60s may have inspired the Fab Four's outfits for *Sgt. Pepper's Lonely Hearts Club Band.* Or maybe not.

Derek Dean's assault on his imagined taxman was prompted by a belated Revenue crackdown on the brown envelope culture of the ballrooms. Even though it was common knowledge that the showband business was very probably Ireland's biggest and most profitable industry, Revenue paid it little attention until there was a bitter falling out between one big star and his management. The singer squealed to Revenue about his manager's loose relationship with the tax laws. The taxman was agog on hearing of the true amounts being generated and undercover agents were dispatched across the land to investigate.

The swizz they uncovered worked like this. A band would draw 2,000 punters to a gig. The official receipts would show that 1,200 paid in. The door takings from the other 800 would be divvied up between the venue promoter and the band's manager. After the squealer squelt, tax officials began turning up at halls armed with clickers to do a headcount on the audience going in.

A couple of top promoters fled the country rather than give satisfaction to the taxman. Around the same time, the manager of The Big 8 tried to rustle up some publicity by putting out a yarn that the band were thinking of buying a Vegas casino. The story generated lots of column inches as intended. What the manager didn't foresee was that by greatly exaggerating the band's wealth he'd attract the prying eyes of the Revenue.

Not only was Ireland at the very end of the line for visiting entertainers, who usually got off a stop or two earlier, but it was also at the end of the supply line for vinyl, the petroleum-based goo from which records were made. Until the business model changed in the 1980s, Irish pressing plants manufactured the hits of the day from master imprints supplied from Britain and America. The Irish pressings had always been inferior to imported copies, but with the first global oil crisis of 1973 things went from bad to worse and Ireland's physical isolation meant it literally got the bottom of the barrel. Shortly before the OPEC (Organisation of the Petroleum Exporting Countries) oil embargo made a bad situation even worse, the Capitol Showband thought it worthwhile going to the extravagance of recording several tracks of high sound quality in a New York studio for release as singles in Ireland. But when they touched down in Dublin, customs officials demanded import duty on the master copies. Faced with a stark choice between stumping up the tax or surrendering a year's worth of planned singles, the manager decided to keep the money.

By and large, the managers, agents, promoters and ballroom owners were jumped-up, foot-in-the-door salesmen with country accents. One of the brashest and most successful, Jim Hand, had cut his teeth going door to door flogging everything from washing machines to bibles. In general, these managers and promoters cared nothing for music and very little for their musicians who were expendable and readily replaceable.

Two of the main reasons they had to be readily replaceable was because life on the showband circuit was fraught with danger, with long late-night drives on narrow winding roads a cause of countless deaths and serious injuries. The most eminent figure to emerge from the showband scene, until Louis Walsh overtook him in fame and fortune, was Albert Reynolds, the tee-total owner of a string of ballrooms who would become leader of his country. Paddy Cole of The Capitol related how, when heading back to Dublin after a show had been cancelled, he called in at Reynold's pub, the Longford Arms, where he knocked back several brandies.

Reynolds was not known for his largesse – Joe Dolan once remarked that the ham sandwiches he served his performers were so thin "you could read the *Irish Press* through them" – but the promoter bought Cole a large brandy to chase the several he'd already downed. When the musician arrived at his girlfriend's flat in Dublin around midnight, he was unable to speak. The flat's occupants poured coffee into him until he was sober enough to be propped up behind the wheel of his customised Volkswagen Beetle, the flashy car of choice of the biggest ballroom stars who would line up at dawn on Rathmines Bridge for a spot of drag racing before the police got out of bed. Cole described how the final stage of the sobriety process involved "driving around the city in my VW with all the windows open, trying to catch a breath of fresh air".

In stark contrast to the vast majority of the population, the top musicians could easily afford luxury holidays in the sun. It was in Italy that 21-year-old Derek Dean took his first mouthful of a substance that would almost destroy him. His first sip of wine turned into three-and-a-half bottles and a blackout. A pattern had been set that would lead to a half-strangled drummer and far worse.

Before ever drinking, Dean had almost wiped out the band by driving into an unfortunate horse. When the drink took a grip, he recalled, "There were nights when I would leave Kerry and wake up halfway to Dublin, still behind the wheel, and wonder how I'd ever got so far. I wouldn't remember whole journeys and despite vowing to myself that I'd never repeat this madness, the very next night I'd do the same again."

The Guards might have upped his life-expectancy, but they "would stop the car and, on seeing it was a band, they'd tell you what bands were on the road and ask if there was any chance you'd have a drop in the car. I left many a checkpoint with a huge sigh of relief and an emptier bottle of vodka."

The drunken carnage on the winding potholed roads was one factor in Robert Ballagh's reluctant decision to quit at the top. The bassist with The Chessmen told himself he must be crazy to walk away from the bright lights and the big paydays, but he had two compelling reasons.

"It was a very dangerous game because of all the car crashes," he recalled. "My friend Paul Williams of The Greenbeats was killed. Another friend, Keith Donald (later of Moving Hearts) was badly injured. When people leave bands they always say it's down to musical differences, and it was. But my differences weren't with the band, but with the Irish public. Playing around Dublin we knocked out good rock 'n' roll. In rural ballrooms they just wanted country 'n' Irish. At the end of one gig I realised I hadn't liked a single song we'd performed so I said, I'm out of here!"

Ballagh sold his bass guitar and amp to a young up-and-comer called Phil Lynott and took his leave of the showband game like Van Morrison, Rory Gallagher and others before him who felt they had more to offer than joyless regurgitation. Morrison quickly got fed up playing sax on the sidelines of The Monarchs. Making a quiet exit, he founded the beat combo Them, penned the timeless garage anthem 'Gloria' and caught the coattails of the British Invasion of America. Guitar supremo Rory Gallagher's exit was anything but quiet.

In the mid-60s Teilifís Éireann had two pop programmes. *The Showband Show* showcased Irish acts doing inferior covers of The Beatles, The Kinks, Dusty Springfield and so on. A straight lift of the BBC's *Juke Box Jury*, *Pickin' The Pops* featured slightly fewer showbands interspersed with new releases from the US and Britain. Mistrustful of youth culture, the TV authorities decided that if they were going to have a pop show, there should be a responsible adult somewhere in the room. And so *Pickin' The Pops* recruited a middle-aged academic, Denis Franks, "professor, revue artist and lecturer in Shakespeare", to keep the kids in line. It was on *Pickin' The Pops* where Gallagher decided to step out of line. His band, The Impact, were supposed to cover Buddy Holly's maudlin 'Valley Of Tears' but when the moment came, on Gallagher's signal they launched into a gritty rendition of the Larry Williams R&B classic 'Slow Down'. The panel and the programme makers were taken aback, but there was nothing they could do but let the band play their angry racket to the end.

Another top showband figure, Jim Conlon of The Royal said it best of all when he declared, "I quit showbiz because of my utter contempt for my own musical performance."

In addition to their own dedicated shows on TV, the showbands were very well served by friendly radio disc jockeys and the showbiz correspondents of the national and local press. They also funded several magazines dedicated to bigging them up as stars on a par with Elvis and The Beatles. Looking back on his days as a record plugger, the producer of the Oscar-winning *My Left Foot* Noel Pearson mused, "RTÉ and all the newspapers were very corrupt in the early '60s. There was huge payola. Most of the records played on the radio were played through 'little gifts'."

Spotlight magazine was the in-house organ of the showbands.

The Capitol's Paddy Cole testified, "If you didn't take ads you didn't get write-ups. If you featured on the front cover you had to take so many ads." When The Capitol fell out with the people at *Spotlight*, all mention of the band was wiped from its pages. A truce was called in the financial interests of both parties, which involved a *Spotlight* hack writing a flattering piece on the band for one of the newspapers.

Before he hit the jackpot writing Johnny Logan's Eurovision winner 'What's Another Year', Shay Healy edited *Spotlight* for a stint. One of his tasks was to do the horoscope. He confessed to me that this amounted to cutting out the horoscopes from the British girls' magazine *Jackie* and rearranging them on the page from issue to issue, so that last week's Aries became this week's Taurus and so on. A lovely man, and the goalie in our midweek music-biz kickabouts, a grinning Shay also admitted to me, "I never took money to bend the truth or the *Spotlight* charts. You had to bend the charts anyway because you'd never have the figures. You tended to favour people you liked."

Shay would likewise never accept money for giving an act favourable coverage, but he would accept payment for writing press releases for bands. These gushing press releases would then appear verbatim in *Spotlight* under an assumed name. He told me with a chuckle that he would buy English magazines such as *Screen Gems* and *Melody Maker*, pull out quotes from the latest Elvis interviews, stitch them together and recycle them under a headline such as 'Elvis Talks Exclusively To Shay Healy In His Graceland Mansion'.

From the mid-70s the ballrooms saw a steep nosedive in their fortunes. The dance mad generation of the '60s no longer had the stamina to jive for five hours straight, and the youthful dancers who might have replaced them were instead flocking to the disco, which did very nicely without the expense and hassle of hiring live bands. So the showbands and their loyal fans migrated to new, purpose-built cabaret venues and hotels. Paddy Cole quit The Capitol to found The Superstars, which evolved the frenetic dance band into a more laid-back experience with a focus on soft jazz and Country 'n' Western, which in turn evolved into a zombie sub-genre called Country 'n' Irish.

The undisputed King of Country 'n' Irish music was Big Tom McBride. This was confirmed as a fact in 1977 when, in the wake of Elvis Presley's death, a single entitled 'Big Tom Is Still The King' shot to No 1 in the charts.

Big Tom had drifted into the music game after giving up on hard labour, like his stable mate Jim Conlon of The Firehouse who memorably confessed, "My voice comes out very flat on tape, but it's better than shovelling gravel for a living." McBride had stints as a farm hand, laying cables, picking tomatoes and erecting hay sheds. It took him just three minutes crooning a bashful 'Gentle Mother' on Teilifís Éireann's *Showband Show* in 1966 to melt the hearts of rural, conservative, Catholic Middle Ireland, and he found stardom tapping a vein of maudlin nostalgia for a picture postcard land of pretty Omagh girls, sorrowful mothers, candles in windows and welcomes on mats.

Peddling songs like 'Old Rustic Bridge', 'Old Love Letters' and his signature tune 'Back To Castleblayney', Big Tom drew regular crowds of 3,000 and more to shows in Ireland and Britain. In the 1970s one showband source estimated McBride's earnings at £150,000 a year when the average wage was £15 a week, much of it earned playing to lovelorn Irish nurses and navvies in the ballrooms of romance in London's Kilburn, Cricklewood and across the English Midlands.

The cabaret scene which superseded the ballrooms was popularly known as 'the rubber chicken circuit' after its staple diet. Second only in popularity to Big Tom were Paddy Cole's

Superstars. Cole reflected, "That's where I learned what show business was all about. It's not about getting a standing ovation in The Capitol, when they would have cheered even if we'd played 'Baa Baa Black Sheep'. Show business is about going out on your own and trying to entertain people while they are eating… That was a new challenge."

The frontwoman of The Superstars was Twink, who'd cut her teeth in the ballrooms which involved changing in filthy toilets and generally living it rough on the road. For women like Twink, the cabaret scene provided much improved creature comforts, so that a lot of the squabbling now lay in musical differences. Twink explained to me that while she wanted to sing 'quality' material like 'Evergreen' and 'Pearl's A Singer', the band leader would generally rule it out, telling her, "Twink, it's too fuckin' sophisticated. The punters won't understand it."

He did eventually give in on 'Evergreen', partly because it had a nice flute solo which would showcase his talents. Mountainy men would write to Twink with requests like "Would you come down if I sent you the train fare?". Her friend Maxi, of the all-girl group Sheeba, got one letter saying, "I've been a great fan of yours for many years, though not of your singing. I read somewhere that you like tall, skinny men. I'm a tall, skinny man and if you'd like to meet me please sing the Everly Brothers' 'Let It Be Me' the next time you're playing town." (In fact it was Twink who liked tall, skinny men.) After one TV appearance the girls of Sheeba, who represented Ireland in the 1981 Eurovision Song Contest, received a fan letter saying, "I've got a big farm. I'd like to marry the one in the middle. Are you interested?"

Grasping that chicken-in-a-basket cabaret was the way of the future, Albert Reynolds decided to give it a go as he planned his exit strategy from the stand-up ballrooms. Taking on board a well known publican as a business partner, the pair scoured the greater Dublin region for a suitable new high-end cabaret venue. The partner came up with the perfect spot, a small hotel in the north Dublin village of Malahide. The partner put down a deposit of £1,000, but the pair ran into an apparent brick wall trying to get the full purchase price from the banks. Then, out of the blue, Reynolds found £33,000 and bought the premises for himself. The partner, who'd found the perfect venue, was left to lick his wounds and reclaim his £1,000 deposit.

Reynolds converted the hotel into a state-of-the-art cabaret venue with the latest sound system, kitchen galleys and comfy seats. With a seating capacity for 1,000 people, the enterprise was christened The Showboat. The Showboat went ahead full steam for a short while until issues with the licence got into a tangle. Those licence issues became immaterial when the venue was razed to the ground in a fire in the summer of 1970. It emerged that Reynolds had taken out an £83,000 insurance policy on the building he'd bought for £33,000. Pressed on this by a journalist when that fact came out, he responded inscrutably that The Showboat had been "definitely underinsured".

As he diversified away from the dying ballroom business, one of Reynolds' early projects was a bacon factory in the Liberties area of Dublin. Not long after The Showboat went up in flames, a mysterious fire forced the closure of the factory and the lay-off of the staff. Happily the blaze coincided with a move by the government to rationalise the pig industry, allowing Reynolds to take advantage of a compensation scheme for surrendering his bacon export licence.

By the mid-70s the 'classic' showband era was dying on its feet. The ballroom business remained strongest in the border counties, even after the Troubles erupted in the North. Some unscrupulous managers and promoters even took advantage of the worsening sectarian violence to add a new entry to their book of dirty tricks, phoning in hoax bomb scares to venues and forcing the cancellation of shows by rival bands. Far worse was a stunt devised by the members of at least one band to break the tedium of cramped van journeys, and told to me in shame many years later by one of the guilty parties. As they drove home from gigs at the crack of dawn the yobs would keep an eye out for early risers cycling along deserted country roads, perhaps to get the cows in for milking. They'd overtake the cyclist and a couple of bends later they'd stop the van. One of them would kneel on the roadside facing the ditch, and another would produce a starting pistol and – just as the cyclist arrived on the scene – would 'shoot' his victim in the head, execution style. As the victim slumped to the ground one of the gang would point at the horrified cyclist shouting, "He's seen us – get him!"

This obscene 'joke' was retired when the whole showband scene reached a tragic turning point in July 1975. The Miami Showband were approaching the border on their way back south after a gig when they were flagged down by a man in uniform, flashing a light. They presumed him to be a British soldier. They were told to get out of the van and more 'soldiers' lined them up with their hands on their heads. Two of these 'soldiers' acted like they were searching the back of the van. In reality they were planting a bomb intended to go off further down the road. As well as killing the band, the explosion would provide 'proof' of Loyalist claims that the southern showbands were a front for smuggling Republican arms into the North. The intention was to make all southern showbands 'legitimate targets'.

The bomb went off as the disguised Loyalists were planting it, killing two of them. Their accomplices opened fire on the musicians, killing three and critically wounding one. Another survived by playing dead and escaping in the confusion. The

Miami massacre sounded the death-knell for the showband era and turned the island of Ireland into a no-go area for international acts.

It spelled the end for the bands, but not for their managers, agents and promoters. Most were still young and energetic, many were rich. They'd tasted success and now they looked for other routes of advancement. The biggest venue owners and band managers wielded significant clout in their communities as employers and patrons, so a significant number turned to politics as a natural follow-on. One of the biggest and most powerful ballroom owners, Albert Reynolds, would become the leader of his country at the head of what became known derisively as "the Country 'n' Western wing" of the largest party, Fianna Fáil. In time, Reynolds would be overtaken in fame and fortune by a graduate of his own ballrooms, Louis Walsh. Described at the start of the noughties by one English newspaper as "the man who owns the UK's No 1 slot", Walsh would orchestrate the revenge of the showbands on a world that had thought them safely consigned to the dustbin of history.

Chapter 5

PUNK REFRESHES PARTS THAT OTHER POP CANNOT REACH

"1977 has been the most exciting year for rock 'n' roll since tax exile became fashionable."

– Tony Wilson, founder of Factory Records

FOR TWO years following the Miami showband massacre, Ireland was shunned by virtually every international touring act of note. But new life was restored to the country's moribund music circuit from a source that seemed entirely at odds with the largely rural and deeply conservative country that was Ireland – punk rock. Punk and New Wave acts who were barred from many venues across their native Britain discovered an unknown and entirely unexpected new audience in Ireland's pop kids.

Bars and clubs threw open their doors as the pub rock circuit which had sprung up in Britain over the previous decade arrived in Ireland, re-establishing a British Isles touring circuit that had vanished since neutral Ireland and wartime Britain went their separate ways in 1939. Almost overnight, from the summer of 1977, acts famous to Irish youngsters from *Top Of The Pops* were playing down their street in Dublin, Belfast,

Cork, Limerick, Galway and the back of beyond. In addition to energising a lifeless Irish music scene, punk and New Wave provided an entreé for Irish acts into the UK charts and, by the close of 1978, Dubliners Bob Geldof and his Boomtown Rats were sitting pretty at No 1 on Britain's flagship music show. This recognition helped rouse a new Irish generation from a listlessness that seemed to hang in the air.

From the outset, Church and State had attempted to banish all glamour bar that of the Virgin Mary, our missionaries abroad, solemn parades to honour dead freedom fighters, and the manly skirmishing of Gaelic games. Every youngster was conditioned to believe in Irish exceptionalism – meaning that they were morally superior to every other race on earth. Except that the lived reality of most young people didn't tally with this state-spun glamour, and successive generations struggled with poor self-image and low self-esteem.

Punk arrived at a time when, outside of sports, being in a band was one of the very few social outlets for young Irish people. There were no smartphones, no Game Boys, no home computers and very often no jobs. The old cliché that the only way out of a dead-end life was to become a footballer or pop star had a real element of truth – although generations of youngsters were diverted from a potential football career in England by Gaelic games which were compulsory in most schools while un-Irish 'foreign' games were outlawed.

Inspired by the DIY ethic of punk, countless youngsters bought cheap instruments and formed bands having seen with their own eyes that international success was achievable. This was an ambition the showband managers had actively discouraged in their acts which were raking in large fortunes at home and their owners didn't want them getting ideas. The managers, promoters and venue owners did all they could to protect their dying industry from the onslaught of punk, New Wave, power pop and every other class of "foreign rubbish" which might dent their earnings and hasten their demise. When RTÉ's first pop station went on air to combat the thriving pirates, the powerful showband lobby cried foul that the newcomer was playing original hit records by the likes of Rod Stewart and The Police when there was a perfectly good showband cover version gathering dust.

Forging an alliance with the nation's self-anointed moral guardians, the dons of the showband mafia mounted a noisy picket outside the Montrose home of the national broadcaster on the day that the second national TV station launched in 1978. The object of their fury was that RTÉ 2 was to feature a live re-broadcast of the BBC's *Top Of The Pops* which they feared would kill their golden goose. They were right.

The very next week after the protest, local heroes The Boomtown Rats were rubbing it in their faces on the chart showcase with 'Like Clockwork' and just weeks later Bob Geldof was back again, this time gleefully tearing up a poster of John Travolta and Olivia Newton-John whom they'd knocked off the top spot. Abroad, the Rats were regarded as a lightweight pop combo whose mouthy singer had blagged them onto the punk bandwagon. At home, by virtue of winning approval from Britain's hippest influencers, they were installed as the authentic voice of 'Young Ireland'.

To hammer home their newfound status, the Rats booked Dublin's Leopardstown Racecourse for a celebratory homecoming gig. The city fathers, supported by the political class and the plain clothes morality police, responded with 'not in my backyard'. Objections were swiftly lodged and District Judge Frank Johnson nailed his starched colours to the mast. Refusing a licence, he said, "I have to take into account the behaviour of fans of these concerts elsewhere. They have been sent to the Isle of Wight and other places where there is nothing to break." The Rats appealed to a higher court where the cultural chasm between the two sides was laid bare when counsel for the objectors, Peter Sutherland, perhaps with Led Zeppelin in mind, quizzed a witness, "Van Morrison, I take it, are a group."

The Rats lost and their grand homecoming gig was cancelled mere hours before curtain call. Geldof's poison pen revenge was the withering hit 'Banana Republic', which damned his homeland as a "sceptic isle" suffocated by "police and priests".

The Dubliner's scathing put-down provided an Irish counterpart to Johnny Rotten's snarling protest against England's "fascist regime" on 'God Save The Queen', a song which was widely believed to have been usurped from its rightful No 1 slot by a scandalised British establishment in cahoots with the BBC.

One year after the break-up of the Pistols Johnny Rotten – now answering to his birth name of John Lydon – was due at Dublin's Project Centre with his successor band, Public Image Ltd (PIL). Landing the chief Sex Pistol was a major coup, and he was loved all the more for the fact that he identified as a proud Irish renegade who just happened to be born in London by a roll of the dice. PIL had been booked to play Dark Space, a groundbreaking two-day festival of living art installations and cutting edge music at Project Centre. Founded in the mid-70s to showcase visual artists and trad/folk musicians, the Project had become a hub for the punk and post-punk movement.

By the close of the decade, Project Arts situated in Temple Bar in the derelict heart of the city would become one of the green shoots of Ireland's creative and cultural revival, not to mention the physical rebirth of the capital itself which radiated out from Temple Bar's cobbled laneways. The Project nurtured a dazzling cluster of talent including U2, Hollywood star Gabriel Byrne, director of the breakthrough Irish Oscar-winner *My Left Foot* Jim Sheridan, and the playwright and best-selling author Peter Sheridan.

The younger of the Sheridan brothers, Peter reflected, "The music was really the generation coming behind us, but myself and Jim came from music. We formed a garage band in the mid-sixties. I was learning the guitar and Jim couldn't play anything so, in classic fashion, we put him on bass. We were in a band before we got into theatre. In 1971 we did a rock music version of 'Oedipus Rex' which featured 'The End' by The Doors as a running theme. The music kids coming behind us took over, but there were people who straddled music, theatre and poetry. We brought over music poets like John Cooper Clarke and Linton Kwesi Johnson to the Project."

Put together by the Sheridan brothers and performance artist Nigel Rolfe, Dark Space was to serve notice that Ireland was ready to shake off the cobwebs and rejoin the modern world. Nothing like it had been attempted before, but when PIL signed up others were quick to follow including The Undertones, The Mekons, Throbbing Gristle and the cream of the local talent led by U2 and the Virgin Prunes.

Adding to the merriment, the line-up included jugglers, fire-breathers, circus acts, street poets, vintage rock and reggae movies and vegetarian cuisine. Sheridan said, "Dark Space was the sort of event we would have liked to go to because we were deeply interested in the music. Bands that were alternative and groundbreaking, like the Virgin Prunes, were deeply attractive to us."

So when PIL pulled out, it hurt like "a kick in the teeth", according to Peter. He told me, "It felt like the future was about to arrive in Ireland. We were taken up with the notion that Dark Space was supposed to state that the time had come for the young people to take control of the culture and here we were, betrayed by the people we thought were the most radical and we just wanted to ask them the question, 'Why won't you come? Why have you done this to us?'"

So Jim Sheridan flew to London in a fit of pique and tracked Lydon to a once grand house in Chelsea subdivided into a warren of dilapidated apartments. When he pressed the buzzer marked 'Lydon' he was confronted by a burly man blocking his way. The clamour brought Lydon onto the stairwell where a shouting match turned into a short bout of handbags. Outnumbered, Sheridan suggested they talk it out over drinks in the pub next door. He didn't persuade Lydon to change his mind, but he did return to Dublin with a good yarn for the front of the *Evening Press*. The day after the newspaper hit the streets, Dark Space sold out.

The following year, 1980, John Lydon arrived in Dublin for a visit he quickly regretted. If the Boomtown Rats' encounter with a hostile judiciary was the phoney war, the artist formerly known as Johnny Rotten brought them eyeball to eyeball with the real thing. In town for a gig by his brother Jimmy's ramshackle band, 4" Be 2", Lydon was stopped in the street and asked for an autograph by a fan who offered to buy him a pint. The pair entered the Horse & Tram on Eden Quay where the barman refused to serve them. There was a skirmish and when the dust had settled and a policeman intervened, Lydon had a court appointment pencilled in for the next morning. This was all grist to the mill for the singer who went to the gig, drank late into the night and showed up in court on time the following morning. So far, so routine. Until the judge fixed bail at £250 but then refused to accept it from three Lydon associates who offered to hand over the ready cash there and then.

And so Johnny's rotten reputation got him locked up for the

weekend in Mountjoy Gaol while a thug arrested for a hammer attack at his brother's gig walked out of court on a bond of £50. In court the following Monday a barman from the Horse & Tram, referring to the accused repeatedly as 'Rotten', claimed the singer had used foul language when he and his now vanished accomplice were refused service. Lydon countered that he was making a peaceful exit when "I got smashed on the back of the head. My response to the punch was to look around and then *that* happened." Here he indicated his bruised cheeks. Lydon's solicitor put it to the barman that he'd "completely over-reacted", thumping his client in the eye after going at him "stripped for action". The barman denied this, though he did agree that he forcefully punched the punk icon in an unspecified part of the body "above the shoulder".

The judge dismissed Lydon's version of events. He launched into a speech, described by London's *New Musical Express*, as a "customary, smug, highbrow sermon", underlining his duty to "protect the citizens of the city" from "this sort of thing". Passing sentence, the judge lectured Lydon that there was "a lot of indiscriminate behaviour in Dublin by people with drink and without drink taken, who go around looking for trouble". He was tempted to give punk's panto villain six months in jail. However, his soft streak had gotten the better of him so it would be just three months behind bars in Ireland's most notorious prison. The Irish representative of Virgin Records became the fourth person to have their offer of bail turned down while the case went to appeal. The judge finally relented when the Virgin rep produced a letter from his bank manager vouching that he was solvent. John Lydon was on the next available flight to London.

John Lydon's brief incarceration allowed him, in his own mind at least, to become Johnny Rotten once more. By the time he came to pen his autobiography, *No Irish, No Blacks, No Dogs,* his brush with the Irish law had gained more embellishments than the *Book Of Kells.* His English lawyer's "upper class twitty voice" had antagonised the judge. At one point, he claimed, a brand new BMW had been put up for bail. Asked for an Irish address he'd given that of his uncle in Cork. But "they wouldn't accept that, and went on a tirade about 'damned kulchies' which is what Dubliners call people from the country."

Newspaper reports of his arrival at Mountjoy noted that he was given a hero's welcome by starstruck fellow prisoners who even struck up a chorus of 'Anarchy In The UK' with amended lyrics. This didn't suit his narrative however, so in his version of events he was saved from a fate close to death at the hands of hostile hard chaws only by the warders' sadistic decision to make an example of him. This they did by stripping him naked, hurling him onto the slates of the exercise yard and hosing him down with freezing water. This convinced the other jailbirds that he must be okay. Then, as a one in a billion chance would have it, Mountjoy's Saturday night movie, *The Great Rock'n'Roll Swindle*, opened with a performance by The Sex Pistols. Only at this point did his fellow inmates finally twig that they had amongst them one of the most recognisable persons on the planet. His new best friends were a tough bunch.

"IRA, UDA, psychopathic murderers, the lot," he said. Presumably the IRA and UDA men had hidden in the toilet cubicles when all paramilitary prisoners were moved from Mountjoy seven years earlier.

The lily-gilding didn't stop there. His cellmate was a jewel thief who'd been captured when a brick he had thrown at a window had bounced back and knocked him out. Lydon's sleep was disrupted when, according to the singer, "In the middle of the night two warders decided to come in and beat me with truncheons. You know the way they do. 'Your blanket isn't straight!'" He was saved by the protests of other prisoners roused from their slumber. But he still felt uneasy. Neither the Republican or the Loyalist killers knew what to make of him. "I'd lost both ways because of my English accent and my Irish name."

"I learned to be vicious pretty quick in that environment," he recalled. He'd have had to learn very quickly indeed, since he was behind bars for just under 48 hours. No, scratch that, "I was locked up for four days – felt like four years... My father flew into Ireland from London the day I was released ... My father's hotel room was searched by the police for IRA weapons and fugitives."

And finally, to John Lydon's appeal against his three-month jail sentence, despite the actual facts of the matter, the singer vividly recalled facing a stone-faced judge the day after he was freed from his terrifying two-days in Hell. "The years were going by in front of me. Five. Ten. Fifteen. I was scared." Having learned valuable lessons about the workings of the Irish judicial system, Lydon had dumped his twitty English lawyer for a well-got native legal eagle. This proved a shrewd move. "He said to the judge 'Hello sir! How are you doing? I'll see you later on. We'll have a game of golf!' Those were the first words out of the guy's mouth."

Ripping yarns, Rotten memory.

U2 would shake up the Irish music scene just as explosively as the Sex Pistols had across the water. When the Pistols effed and blinded their way through their infamous TV interview with Bill Grundy, their manager Malcolm McLaren was crestfallen, believing their career was over before it had properly begun. According to guitarist Steve Jones, "He was terrified". McLaren reverse engineered the narrative so that the incident became just part of his brilliant masterplan for the group

In stark contrast to the Pistols, U2 had a manager who really did have a masterplan. Paul McGuinness had selected them as his 'Baby Band' – footloose kids with no wives, kids or day-jobs – who'd be free to follow his scheme for breaking the lucrative US market. Stripped to basics, that plan consisted of playing the same places over and over and over again, until the natives realised how good you were. The same basic model had paid huge dividends for the bands of the First British Invasion like The Animals, The Hollies, The Yardbirds and many others. In 1979, the First British Invasion of the States was recent history, occurring only 15 years earlier. Since then, the Atlantic had widened into a vast musical chasm of style and taste, and no-one in their wildest dreams could foresee there would be a Second British Invasion just around the corner. But McGuinness's grand plan for U2 didn't require the heft of any mass movement behind it, just single-minded hard slog and it began with winning over the kids of the Dandelion Market.

While Phil Lynott was greatly loved and Geldof greatly admired, they were older than their fans, not by much in the greater scheme of things, but when you're in your teens, a five or 10 year age difference can seem a chasm. U2 were the same age as their fans, and only as older as a slightly older brother to the younger fans they actively targeted. Every Saturday and Sunday an oasis of colour lit up the drabness of dreary Dublin. It was Dandelion Market on what is now the Stephen's Green Centre and it screamed youth. Like a great oriental bazaar its stalls and kiosks sold everything your parents wouldn't like. It had slashed punk t-shirts, hippy joss sticks, a zillion posters, badges, belt-buckles, lava lamps, miles of vinyl and far-out stuff like Bombay Mix, Patchouli Oil and tattoo parlours.

For the youth of 1979 the Dandelion Market *was* The Social Network, and from very early on U2 had shown an uncanny knack for networking. The previous year – before Paul McGuinness had come on board – the managerless outfit had eagerly stalked Boomtown Rat Gerry Cott and rock god Phil Lynott, fearlessly pressing the *Top Of The Pops* regulars for advice and any leg-ups that might be going.

Not only was the Dandelion the country's biggest Mecca for teens and twenty-somethings, which could deliver the ambitious band's target audience on a plate, but it offered access to school kids too young to see U2 in pubs and clubs. U2 didn't come up with the idea of playing afternoons in the grubby carpark. But unlike all the other pub bands struggling to conceal their disdain at wasting their Saturday afternoon there, U2 treated the draughty concrete cage as if it were Madison Square Garden and they were Led Zeppelin in their pomp.

There were maybe 60 avoiding the puddles of standing water in that dank car park for U2's first show. By the last there might have been 600. With the passing of time, the number of punters who claimed to have been there approached six million.

Chapter 6

FRANCIS ROSSI: THE ROCKER WHO SET THE BALL ROLLING

"People in England ignore each other. But people in Ireland would come across this long haired dickhead walking around the roads of County Clare and people would say, 'good morning' and they'd often stop to talk. No-one wanted to shag you, but that was fine."

– Francis Rossi

THE ROCK star who set the ball rolling on Ireland's influx of rock exiles was Status Quo frontman Francis Rossi. What started out as a tax year beyond the grasp of the British taxman became a much longer stay, during which he played a key role in alerting the wider pop world to Dublin's newly opened Windmill Lane Studios, a hidden gem just an hour from London.

He brought his bickering band to Ireland and they rediscovered some of their old camaraderie, recording two UK Top 5 albums in Windmill. This vote of confidence by a top rock act gave the studio a calling card to transition from local trad and folk bookings to a pop proposition with global reach. In the years that followed, Windmill would attract some of the biggest acts in pop history including The Rolling Stones, David Bowie,

Kate Bush, AC/DC, Metallica, The Spice Girls, Ed Sheeran, Depeche Mode and Kylie.

Looking back smiling on a life in crisis more than four decades ago, Rossi reveals that he was desperately in need of a safe refuge from the endless in-fighting of his bandmates and a marriage speeding towards the rocks.

"David Oddie, one of the Irish guys in our management, said, 'Why don't you go somewhere for a weekend to write?' Go to Ireland or somewhere nice. So me and my co-writer Bernard Frost went to Dromoland Castle in County Clare and stayed writing there for a while. Pretty soon after I got back to England the issue of taking a tax year came up and I said, 'I'll go to Ireland, to Dromoland Castle. The place suits me'. The pair divided their living arrangements between Dromoland for writing, and Jurys Hotel in Dublin for access to recording studios.

"A little while after I returned to Ireland, Bernie arrived. We wanted a studio in Dublin to write songs and we found this woman called Elizabeth Gernon who at the time was in partnership with the promoter Pat Egan. Elizabeth found us a little studio called Trend on Lad Lane in the city centre. I had a great feeling of freedom in Ireland at that time. I knew the divorce was coming up so I was very happy to be in Ireland singing with Bernie. The vibe in the band was beginning to go.

"I remember Niall Stokes (*Hot Press* editor) came over to see us in Essen and our band truck slid down a hill and straight into a brand new Peugeot. Caused a bit of a problem. Our man Colin Johnson was bringing Niall on a tour of our hotel. My wife was there for some reason. Our bassist, Alan Lancaster, was playing chess with one of our tour people. Our drummer, John Coughlan, was trying to get some sleep. And Colin was walking Niall through this and I remember him saying, 'It's amazing how well they get on and how they're still the best of friends after all these years'. Then all of a sudden this almighty row breaks out between Alan and John right in Niall's face!

"I don't know where the rest of the band lived at that time. I think John was in the Isle of Man and Alan was in Australia. I've no idea where Rick Parfitt was living. One day Rick said he was coming over when I was in Dromoland and I went to meet him at Shannon Airport in this beaten-up old car that we tried to wreck while we were here. We'd ride up and down the country bashing into things.

"So I went to pick him up at the airport but nothing, no-one's come through, and his flight's gone. Then this private plane comes in and I'm looking at it and there he is. He fell out of the plane drunk.

"He stayed for a spell but not for too long because things were beginning to get fractious between Rick and I, and Rick and everybody and myself and everybody. That saddened a lot of people but you have to understand that we were young boys when we started out. Myself and Alan formed a band at 12 or 13, John Coughlan joined soon after and Rick was only 16 when he joined. So, you grow up, you become successful, but you grow older and everyone knows that you're a different person in your thirties than you were at 18. That's what happens to a band and you all end up resenting each other for whatever reasons and that's just natural. And then each one of us begins to think that he's the reason the band is successful.

"What happened with Rick and I is that various wives and girlfriends start to tell each other this and that, also the management realises that Rick and I were so close when we were younger that they're not going to get anything past us, and so you had to get in there somewhere and separate that closeness. And that's what slowly started to happen. Various people got in between us and it was inevitable where it would end up. We were so into each other that I don't think it was fair to Alan and John and whoever the keyboard player would be, because Rick and I were inseparable – all but shagging. So I can see how that was an affront to everybody else."

Rossi's wife Jean gave birth to their third son Kieran at the beginning of 1979 and shortly afterwards walked out of the marriage, taking the kids with her. The break-up persuaded the singer to make Ireland his full-time home for a tax year which would go a long way to putting his chaotic finances in order.

He recalled, "A few days later (after his wife and kids had left him) I was back in Ireland. I was close enough to London that my children could come over for visits. I was still able to enter the UK for up to 60 days in a year so that also made the transition easier to manage. I really rationalised the whole thing, laid it out in my mind as a marvellous step to take. I thought by being in Ireland I was escaping the worst of my problems. In fact, they had only just begun."

Rossi was happy in his own mind that his Irish exile would break up his 'coke brothers' double act with Rick Parfitt, but in its place his own coke use escalated – something he rationalised as a coping mechanism for the twin trainwrecks of his family and band lives.

Known as the rock star's party drug of choice, cocaine for Francis Rossi became a solitary habit. Describing his time in Ireland as a "permanent midnight", he confessed, "While I was tax exiled in Ireland, my coke habit had grown out of all proportions. I'd be locked away smoking dope, snorting coke and hiding from the world." But while his extended Irish tax holiday was filling his coffers, his spiralling coke habit was blowing a big hole in his finances. Hole-in-the-wall banking was very new to Britain and Ireland and strictly the preserve of the rich, of which Francis Rossi was one, to judge by appearances anyway.

But towards the end of his time in Ireland he was spending more on drugs than the ATMs would give him, which meant he had to go into the bank, join a queue, and personally withdraw wads of cash over the counter. Even though the bank staff knew he was the famous pop star from the telly, consumed by the paranoia that goes hand-in-hand with coke, he believed that the scale of his withdrawals made him a figure of suspicion. This led him to start driving from town to town seeking out bank branches he hadn't used before, or at least not for some time.

The Irish rebirth of the band a couple of years earlier seemed dim and distant, as the quarrelsome quartet slipped into another creative and commercial trough. As he lamented many years later, "Having three of the four members stoned out of their minds on coke and booze definitely made things 10 times harder than they were already." Regrouping in Ireland to record those two albums in 1980 had pulled them out of their tailspin, and Dubliner Bob Geldof would issue a repeat prescription when he gave them the surprise call to do his Band Aid single and open the greatest show on Earth, Live Aid.

"We were lucky. I think it was insecurity too that made it last that long because I don't think any of us were particularly good musicians. Rick became a very good rhythm guitarist but once he got to that level he didn't want to expand on that to get any better.

"Things were starting to change in the band, and living in Dublin away from all that was heavenly. Me and Bernie would go to Trend seven days a week, and you'd find out that today was Sunday just after lunch because the toilets in the area would all flush at the same time. *Phowwah!* There was a broken sewer pipe somewhere under or beside the studio. We'd have to go outside and stand around to allow for the stench in the studio to clear. But it was a great time because we were very prolific. At first,

Elizabeth was booting us around every day 'cos we couldn't get hotels. Then we got two first floor rooms in Jurys and we lived there side by side for around six months and it was just great.

"There was a real buzz in Dublin at that time (late '70s, early '80s). The city was slowly coming back to life after the mass emigration of Irish youths that had been happening for years. It was on its way up again. Subsequently all that Euro money helped Dublin out and helped Ireland out, but I have a fond, fond memory of the city and the Irish at that time."

Destined to become a Mecca for hot pop stars, the Pink Elephant nightclub in Dublin's city centre was only opening its doors at the time, meaning the sole option for a very late night drink was Leeson Street with its seedy strip of basement wine bars. This was not where you'd ever find the teetotal Rossi.

He explained, "When we were in Dublin, Bernie and I would work in the studio all day until around six, eat, have a joint, and then we'd start writing or playing and singing something that was to be done the following day. It wasn't like a chore and that's what we did. So I can't think if we ever went out on the town. I wouldn't go to a club. I don't like clubs. 'You're saying a club's got music? Yeah. It's got women? Yeah. It's got lights? Yeah. – I've been there!' Clubs aren't fun unless you're a drinker, and I was never a drinker until some time in the '80s when we went out with Queen to a Mexican restaurant in Montreux, Switzerland. Before that I was happy to stick to lemonade." His tee-total lifestyle was abandoned overnight after that Montreux meal with his fellow tax exiles. Queen ordered endless pitchers of tequila margaritas, so sweet it could have been lemonade. Honeyed margaritas were immediately installed as his "new favourite pastime – after coke, obviously".

Rossi recorded that drastic and damaging shift in his autobiography, *I Talk Too Much*, writing, "Back in Ireland, getting the landlord of the pub to make you up a pitcher of tequila margarita was not always an option – read never – so I would get them to mix me a tequila and orange, a tequila sunrise." The spirit measures quickly became doubles, then trebles, then quadruples, then straight quadruples with no orange juice.

On a trip to the bar he would down maybe three straight quadruples trying to look casual, then order a fourth with a dash of orange for colour which he'd bring back to his mates at the table. In order to come down from the manic coke and booze highs, he now developed a dependency on the powerful tranquiliser Mandrax, also known as quaaludes, which was readily available on prescription from upmarket doctors with stellar client lists. He told me, "I drank a load of margaritas and became a drinker for a while from writing 'Marguerita Time' (1983) to around 1987. Other than that, I was completely anti-social and I had no desire to go anywhere."

He recalls arriving back in Ireland after trips abroad.

"I would get off the plane and get out into the street, and the smell of coal fires burning reminded me of being a kid again in England. I *loved* being in Ireland! I lived for a long time in Dromoland Castle and then I moved up to Dublin and lived for a long time in Jurys while we recorded the two albums. I was happy being in Jurys. I knew everybody. I knew the staff. And they had the Coffee Dock. It was one of the only places in the world that was open 23-and-a-half hours a day. They only closed it for a half -an-hour so they could throw out the tramps. I was really fond of the place. I would go in and order beans with cheese on toast. It was the first place I ever had that. Then we'd have a cheese omelette with fried onions. The Irish do the best fried onions on the planet."

Dublin at the start of the '80s had two restaurants that charged notoriously eye-watering prices for haute cuisine, Le

Coq Hardi and the Mirabeau, but Rossi never darkened the doors of either.

He recalls with a chuckle, "The Coffee Dock had a posh section. One time we went into the posh side and our producer Pip Williams ordered something with sautéed potatoes. The food arrived and the waiter put the dish down in front of Pip and as he was walking away Pip called him back and said, 'Excuse me. I ordered sautéed potatoes' and the waiter said, 'Aren't they salty enough for you, sir?'

"There was a very good Indian restaurant on the one-way system over where the Dáil is, and we were in there one day with Pip again and he asked the waiter,'What's the meat curry?'

'Meat sir, meat.'

'What meat?'

'Meat sir, meat.'

'I know it's meat, but what meat? Beef? Pork? What is the meat?'

So the waiter goes off and comes back with a great big tin with 'Meat' written on it."

Settled back into Ireland for the long haul, Rossi abandoned the basic equipment and rank odours of Trend when he was introduced to the all mod cons on offer at Windmill, recently built on the city centre quays. Highly impressed, he summoned the rest of the band to Dublin and the re-energised combo recorded the back-to-back hit albums *Just Supposin'* and *Never Too Late.*

"That was a funny one," he says. "The management wanted me to make two albums there without telling anyone in the band. As I said, the band was going all a bit pear shaped. But they came over and it all came good. A Windmill engineer said one day, 'There's a little band next door that I'd like you to see' and I said, 'Nah' and I kept putting it off until one day they were in and he said, 'Will you have a look and perhaps you'd like to do something with them.' And it was U2. I must admit, I went, '*Weh*... I don't see it.' That's where I think you're a certain generation, and the next generation's coming through and I'm thinking I just don't get it.

"But there was another Dublin band I produced there called Tokyo Olympics. Their frontman was called Paul McGuinness, which was a bit weird. I quite liked working with them. That was fun, but because by now I'd fallen in love with Elizabeth I was just so happy being in Ireland."

As the writer and singer of Status Quo's 1968 worldwide debut hit 'Pictures Of Matchstick Men', Francis Rossi had been living the rock 'n' roll highlife for 10 years before fetching up in Ireland. Did he find Dublin at the end of the '70s a tad shabby and down-at-heel compared to all the world-class cities he'd stayed in?

"I don't know," was his short answer. "I was young and I loved being there, but when I think of Dublin back then I think of Jurys, and I think of Dromoland. Because they both catered for Americans there was a standard in those two hotels, whereas when I stayed in the Shelbourne and any of the others – fucking hell! As much as they were okay, we wouldn't stay in those ones because they didn't have a decent shower. Jurys and Drumoland had proper American shower heads and American bathroom fittings so I was happy there."

He wasn't so happy one night when he was downgraded from his high-priced hotel room to accommodate a visit of the permissive society to the west of Ireland.

"In Dromoland myself and Bernie Frost would share a room with two single beds. There were lots of flies because it was in the country, so we'd lie on the beds with wet flannels and smoke a joint – I didn't drink at that time – and we'd throw the wet flannels at the ceiling to kill the flies. One time the manager told me, 'Sorry, Mister Rossi, we'll have to move you to another room because Burt Lancaster is coming to stay'. I said, 'Me move for Burt Lancaster? That's fine!' But Burt Lancaster was a grumpy fuck. Frostie asked for his autograph and he just printed Burt Lancaster. He just wasn't interested. What was interesting was that Burt Lancaster turned up with two women, but there were only two single beds in the room we'd vacated for him."

A year or two after Rossi ended his stay in Ireland, which ran on long after his obligatory tax year expired, the five members of Def Leppard moved in for a tax year of their own, which again lasted long after tax laws dictated. The band's frontman Joe Elliott told me that, aside from the cash savings, life in Ireland was attractive because it was like a foreign country but reassuringly familiar.

Rossi agreed, "There's a warmth in Ireland that is just endearing. I couldn't have felt more at home there than anywhere. I did spend time in Amsterdam and a very similar thing struck me about there. They're very friendly, very warm people, and you can get hash. They could get the same British television stations as in Ireland, so it was a toss up between both places but being in Ireland was a great period of my life.

"When I first moved to Ireland, to Dromoland, I used to go out walking along the country roads or around Ennis, and everyone you passed would say good morning to you. Now I'm not saying it wasn't like that in England when I was a kid, but progress brings regress or digress, and people in England ignore each other. But people in Ireland would come across this long haired dickhead walking around the roads of County Clare and people would say good morning and they'd often stop to talk.

"No-one wanted to shag you, but that was fine. Frostie and I would go out to the fields around Dromoland Castle after our evening meal and play acoustic guitars, and six or eight cows would come up to us and just stand there watching us strumming and singing.

"I remember taking one of my young sons to Sunday mass while we were staying at the Castle. There was an Irish-American lady who put on a prayer service in a room at the Castle to save the lazy fuckers from going to Mass but I brought my son to a church down the road for the last mass of the morning. Mass is about an hour in Dublin, but in the country the priests flew through it – 'Blah-blah-blah-blah Amen, go in peace!' Fucking hell, how did he get through it that quick? And the moment the priest was finished the men would dash out the door and up the road to the pub. It was magic!"

One Dubliner who could occasionally lure him out of his hermit's cave was Phil Lynott, who could often be seen holding court in the capital's hippest pub, the Bailey, off Grafton Street. Phillo would remark that the great thing about Ireland was that the world's biggest stars could walk down trendy Grafton Street and no passer-by would turn a head. It was a highly dubious claim but everyone knew what he meant, Francis Rossi included.

"That's what it was like! I knew Philip and we knew Philip's mum Philomena years before we knew him. She had a service digs in England. Philip was one of the nicest blokes I ever met. It's so sad he became a heroin addict. I remember being pulled up by the police in Dublin one night in this Suzuki jeep I'd bought from Bernard. And the policeman said, 'You haven't got drink in you, do you?' I said 'No' and he said, 'I pulled Philip Lynott up the other night and he was pissed as a fart, but I couldn't arrest Philip, could I?' A few years after that nasty showband incident, when he'd formed Thin Lizzy, we got to know Philip really, really well. Philip for years didn't touch hard drugs, didn't do anything heavy. I remember we played Dalymount Park in the summer of 1979. We've all heard the Irish jokes about the thick Paddy, but that gig gave us a thick English joke, 'Have you heard about the English band that spent a quarter of a million pounds on lights to play in daylight?' We'd spent a quarter of a million and were forced by the local by-laws to play the whole show in broad daylight. We were all leaving the gig, me to go back to the country and the others to go back to England and our road manager was carrying Rick to bed. Rick had sat with some of Lizzy in a room and had what must have been some heroin in something because Rick had this cigar and it burned clean through to the bone on his fingers and he didn't feel anything."

Rossi's most precious memory of his time living in Ireland is of the birth of his daughter Bernadette, the treasured offspring of his love affair with Elizabeth Gernon, the dynamic promoter who'd found him splendid Dromoland Castle and smelly Trend. The love affair ended, he says, because "after Bernadette was born Liz was too busy with our daughter to give her big baby – me – all her attention". But the precious memories of the birth of his Irish daughter will always remain, though in a decidedly foggy way.

"I got to the hospital when Bernadette was born and I went out with Adam Clayton and we got so badly drunk I've no idea what happened that night except I lost a car. Me and Adam looked all around for it but couldn't find it. I have no idea how I got back to Jurys that night. I never went back to look for the car, and the police never sent me a thing about where it went. Only in Dublin…"

Chapter 7

TEMPLE BAR & THE REBIRTH OF DUBLIN

"We were digging out the basement rooms of the studio and had filled about eleven skips at this stage. Suddenly there's an Uzi machine gun pointed at my head. 'Get down, get down! It's the police!' They thought we were digging a tunnel to the Central Bank nearby."

– Paddy Dunning, founder of Temple Lane Studios

IN MARCH 1985 Bob Geldof returned to Dublin for a civic reception to honour his fundraising feats with the all-star Live Aid single 'Do They Know It's Christmas'. The complacent grins of the good burghers evaporated when the singer suddenly unleashed a blistering broadside. Angrily rounding on his audience of civic leaders he laid into them for their abject dereliction in their duties as custodians of the city's heritage and wellbeing.

Blaming his hosts for gross misrule, the singer thundered that the place of his birth had been "brutalised" by bad planning and no planning, and that its inhabitants in turn had been brutalised by the "shambolic mess" all around them.

He continued, "When a city is being destroyed by its custodians, what are the people who live in it supposed to think? The brutalisation seeps through, in the increased use of drugs, which is epidemic in this city, the street violence and the rudeness that is almost everywhere. And I'm sorry if my image clashes with the tourist image, but that's what I've seen. It's very nice to come home and it's particularly nice to be honoured in this way, but please stop destroying Dublin. And, please, bring back to this city some of the life and beauty that was there when I grew up, and make it somewhere that's nice to come home to."

And he wasn't done. "The city has been destroyed. It *is* being destroyed. I do think it's a result of political corruption. I do think it's the result of appalling architectural standards. It was one of the most pretty cities. Dublin is epidemic with regard to heroin. Its street violence is still bad and this isn't something I just think now. I was working with the Simon Community when I was 15 and I saw it then, but it's getting worse. If Dubliners – who should be proud of their city – know this, they should be aware that they can stop this destruction."

One man had already dedicated himself to stopping the destruction. Geldof took his lead from a just published book by *Irish Times* journalist Frank McDonald. *The Destruction Of Dublin* only just about made it onto the shelves after the publishers faced down several legal attempts to have it suppressed. McDonald's *exposé* opened a can of worms on the graft, bribery, corruption, sharp practice, golden circles and fathomless ignorance which had turned the centre of Dublin – once the elegant Second City of Empire – into a dismal, dangerous wasteland. The cobbled mediaeval streets of Temple Bar on the south quays of the Liffey – the heart of the city's Viking foundations – were now scheduled to be flattened for a sprawling new transport hub. Despite mass public protests, the precious nearby Norse-Gaelic Wood Quay site had been drowned in concrete to make way for two towering civic office blocks for the very same custodians raising their glasses to toast Geldof.

Admiringly dubbed "a prick in the fat arse of municipal pretension" by Geldof, Frank McDonald had been logging the sad decline of the city for some years. He told me, "It went back to the time I was a sub-editor in the *Irish Press* in the early 1970s. I'd be cycling home in the early hours after the late shift and I just noticed that Dublin was literally falling to bits. Vacant buildings, derelict sites. Nobody was writing about this so I started writing about it."

When he moved to *The Irish Times*, the paper's editor Conor Brady put him to work on an investigative series entitled 'Dublin: What Went Wrong?' Huge reader feedback meant McDonald had hit a nerve and he quickly followed up with another series that delved deeper into the murk. This new series, 'Derelict Dublin', shone a light on Temple Bar as the blackened heart of a city that was struggling to keep up the pretence that it was a going concern, never mind a European capital worth the name. McDonald's report card, headlined 'Dereliction And Decay In The Shadow Of The Central Bank', gave Temple Bar a damning F-Grade. There were, however, some tiny green shoots if you looked very hard. The first proof that the city's oldest streets might be brought back to life was Project Arts, a renovated factory that had hosted the Dark Space extravaganza and nurtured a cluster of future world-beaters. Right around the corner another bright cluster would come together in Temple Lane rehearsal studios.

When Peter Sheridan and his brother Jim opened Project in 1975 as part of a group of like-minded creative types, the idea was to challenge the stifling status quo in the arts, in the cosy consensus of a tame media and in society itself.

Peter said, "I think that sometimes a group of people come together and they become a magnet for a whole rake of people around them. Project became a magnet for so many people doing different things who were determined to get their voice heard but had no means to do it. Project made that possible for people across a range of things, initially as a gallery for artists who had no other space available until Colm Ó Briain created a space for a lot of the young turks. But I don't want to view this through rose-tinted glasses.

"There was a lot of fighting. The visual arts people didn't want any drama productions in *their* base. And we drew in a lot of music people from very early on because of Nigel Rolfe who knew everything that was happening in music in Britain which I knew nothing about. Because of Nigel I brought over people like John Cooper Clarke, Linton Kwasi Johnson, Roger McGough.

"I still remember Linton on stage singing, 'Inglan is a bitch, there's no escaping it. Inglan is a bitch, there's no running away from it.' He was speaking for England's black people and John Cooper Clarke for the people of the north of England. We hadn't seen this before and they were giving us English voices saying what we were saying about the Britain of that time and its attitudes towards Ireland, towards us. All of that energy was filtered in Project."

Anger was the energy coursing through Peter Sheridan as he dashed through the laneways of Temple Bar in a last desperate search for the punk poet Cooper Clarke who had failed to turn up for his debut Project performance where a full house grew increasingly impatient. Phone calls to his management in London came up blank. Ditto inquiries to Aer Lingus and his hotel. There was no sign of him in the few pubs that bothered to open on Sunday evenings in the lifeless quarter.

At 8.30pm Sheridan had to face the packed audience and tell them the star attraction was a no-show and they could collect their ticket money on the way out. Panting and wiping sweat, the promoter crossed the road to the bar of the Clarence Hotel and there was Cooper Clarke skulking in a corner supping a pint. "I wanted to kill him," Sheridan recalled, but instead he bundled the poet onto the street, shouting at the departing audience to come back, the show would go on. And so, making no apology to the half-full house for the debacle he'd caused, the unsteady poet launched into a 90-minute *tour de force* remembered by Peter Sheridan as "electrifying poetry at one hundred miles per hour".

With showcases from U2, The Virgin Prunes and their post-punk peers drawing young crowds, and dissident plays with soon-to-be Hollywood big noises Gabriel Byrne and Jim Sheridan putting bums on seats, Project was the epicentre of a new life force that would radiate out from Temple Bar to the rest of the jaded city and from there across the entire land. U2 and The Prunes made up the Lypton Village collective, with the former styling themselves as power pop and their other half embracing theatrical art rock. Peter instinctively saw more promise in the latter, saying, "I didn't think U2 were the best of the bands that were around, but I certainly thought they were different in the sense that they were one of the few bands that were really conscious of their image. Most bands went on stage wearing what they'd put on that morning. U2 had the appearance of a band that dressed up, which to me meant they felt slightly middle class. They didn't have the working class edge of The Atrix or The Blades. They felt like a slightly posher version of that. I wouldn't dislike them for that but I didn't see them as a groundbreaking band who were about to go viral. I've missed great actors as well. I've auditioned and turned down people who turned out to be really good and became international stars, I won't say who to save their blushes and mine. You don't always make the right judgement call."

Peter doesn't share the darker memories of others who walked the winding alleys with extreme caution after nightfall, apart from a stabbing outside a U2 show inflicted by "bad people" from the same north Dublin neighbourhood who "pursued" the band everywhere they played.

"The police were down and there was a follow up. That's as much as I remember of the bad stuff. Stuff happened. Phil Chevron (then of Ireland's first punk band, The Radiators, later of The Pogues) wrote us a great song for a play called 'The Ha'penny Place' that Jim wrote and I directed. When we did 'The Ha'penny Place' we wanted to include a group of homeless kids so we put the word out that we wanted real homeless kids to come in and audition for us, and they did. Three or four of them were in the show, and one of them was a fella who had the letters L.O.V.E. tattooed onto the tops of his fingers. About a week after the show finished I got a phone call from the police asking if I knew a kid with L.O.V.E. tattooed on his fingers, and I said yes, a young actor, and they told me he had died. So some bad stuff did happen but I never got the sense that the street was a dangerous place."

Little flurries of nightlife began to return to the abandoned quarter, not always to the liking of the inhabitants of the sleepy hollow. Now one of Dublin's premier tourist pubs, The Norseman was the slumberous hideaway of three men and a dog. Peter recalled, "The Norseman at the time was run by these two elderly gentlemen and it was a very quiet business because Temple Bar was deserted. But when Project started to happen and we began to attract audiences the pub became very popular and the two guys were freaked out of their minds that they couldn't cope with all these increased numbers coming into their bar, and they used to beg us not to put on things.

"They'd be saying to us, 'Oh, you haven't got a thing on Sunday night, have ya? Would ya not give us a Sunday off?' They were freaked by what was starting to happen because the Project and the Norseman were the only two places in Temple Bar open after 8.00pm. There was literally nothing open in all of Temple Bar. Then the Granary pub opened next door. (*The tolerance of the Granary's bar staff for suspiciously youthful looking drinkers made it an instant hit.*) Then things started to happen in Parliament Street and the surrounding areas and the place started to gain traction. Phil Chevron's lyrics for 'The Ha'penny Place' went something like

'Something's rotten in the whole of Dublin town. Something's going on that isn't going round. Every door we come to they say mum's the word … keeping secrets in.'

"It was probably the first song written about Temple Bar."

Whether the future Pogue or the Sheridan brothers knew it at the time, there were secrets being whispered at the highest levels of government about what to do with the rotten borough that was Temple Bar. Once again Ireland's endlessly pliable tax laws would play a part in shaping the country's future.

Campaigning journalist Frank McDonald kept a close ear to the whispers. He recalled, "The whole of Temple Bar was earmarked for a giant transport hub which would link all the bus and rail services in a one stop shop. To that end the State transport company, Córas Iompair Éireann/CIÉ was buying up as much property as it could lay its hands on so that it owned 60% of the entire block. Unlike Dublin Corporation who pulled down buildings as soon as they acquired them, or let them go derelict, CIE let them out on short leases at affordable rents for all sorts of ventures from rock rehearsal studios to comic stores to everything. And with that initiative CIE created the monster that would devour it.

"In February 1986, a group of citizens deeply concerned about the plan to bury Temple Bar under a giant bus station, held the Dublin Crisis Conference in nearby Christchurch Place. It began with an opening address by me, as an activist for Dublin, not a journalist. We packed the hall for the whole weekend and got the Taoiseach, Garret FitzGerald, to come along to make the closing address. And six months later the government published the Urban Renewal Bill providing tax incentives for designated areas including Temple Bar.

"A general election was called in February 1987 and we followed up with a reconvened meeting where the party leaders turned up, including Garret FitzGerald and Charlie Haughey. We had prepared a detailed manifesto for the city. Haughey arrived like a mafia chieftain surrounded by heavies. The journalist Olivia O'Leary was chairing and I prompted her to raise the issue of Temple Bar. She asked Haughey directly what he'd do with Temple Bar, and he responded that Temple Bar was one of the most historic, most traditional parts of Dublin and he wasn't going to let CIE near the place. I think it was probably a spur of the moment promise on his part.

"Haughey took over the leadership of the country at that election and, with relentless prompting from the Temple Bar regeneration lobby, he eventually came through, setting up a State agency to oversee the development of the area as Dublin's cultural quarter, aided by a package of lucrative tax incentives. It flattered Francophile Haughey's deep vanity to be seen as the patron of a bohemian Left Bank to mirror that of Paris.

Describing the newly tax-enhanced precinct as 'a distinctive part of Dublin frequented by young people, attracted by the unique ambience of the area, where art and cultural activities have begun to flourish spontaneously', he told the Dáil that the regeneration 'will make history in the life of this city' and pledged that 'this old and well-loved part of Dublin will be restored to prime condition, which it deserves'.

"Of course, Ireland being Ireland, politics being politics and Haughey being Haughey, this cultural and architectural rebirth was only half the story. Shortly before Haughey unveiled the Temple Bar Renewal And Redevelopment Bill that would seal his legacy as the visionary saviour of the city's heritage, the Taoiseach dispatched his general factotum and the government's press secretary, P.J. Mara, to tip-off certain wealthy individuals about a big new profit-making opportunities about to come up."

Like his boss, Mara believed he was untouchable, and the pair taunted their detractors by hiding in plain sight. When asked by *Hot Press* what his greatest ambition was, Mara answered, "Never to be found out." And his biggest fear? "Being found out." Like his boss, Mara would eventually be found out as a tax cheat by judicial inquiries. One of those favoured with a hot tip from Mara was the Dublin publican Martin Keane. Long after the event, Keane boasted to *The Irish Times* that Haughey's sidekick had given him the inside track over pints at the Shelbourne Hotel's Horseshoe Bar, a favourite spot for Ireland's high rollers to wheel and deal.

"Mara said if you've any money, go down there and spend it," Keane told the paper. "Then Haughey came in for a pint. I asked him if the Temple Bar thing was correct. That's effing right, says he." Generous tax breaks would transform Temple Bar from a blot on the landscape to a licence to print money.

Activist Frank McDonald takes up the story. "Armed with this insider information, Keane bought a Victorian building on the corner of Fleet Street and Anglesea Street —now Oliver St John Gogarty pub — as well as Bloom's Hotel, and became one of the multimillionaire oligarchs of Temple Bar."

Keane didn't do anything in exchange for this blue-chip nugget, gifted to him out of the blue over casual drinks by the country's leadership, but a few years earlier McDonald had exposed the existence of a proactive golden circle of politicians, developers, property speculators and even the trusted property editors of the national press in *The Destruction Of Dublin*. He named names wherever he could, in the full knowledge there would be ferocious blowback. The first legal threat arrived on the publisher's desk as the first print run was arriving in the warehouses for distribution. It came from Karl Jones, the property editor of McDonald's own newspaper, *The Irish Times*.

McDonald recalled, "I had named Jones in the book as a member of the Grand Canal Syndicate of property speculators, along with other prominent figures including his opposite number at the *Irish Independent*. Jones was acting for the whole group of speculators. The editor of *The Irish Times* had given Jones sight of an advance copy of my book which had been provided for review. There was an emergency meeting of my lawyers and those of the publisher, and they said we don't have enough evidence to go to print. So I got on to a source of mine in the High Court and they dug out pure gold, not only proving the existence of the Grand Canal Syndicate but naming its members including Karl Jones. So we had them cold. The book came out and it caused quite a sensation because it was the first time anyone had drawn together what had been going on in the city since the 1950s."

The Destruction Of Dublin did indeed cause a sensation, exposing a long-running scandal in which the State-sanctioned vandalism of the capital's cultural heritage was just the plainly visible tip of the toxic iceberg. And so the No 1 bestseller flew out of the bookstores – never to be replaced. Four decades on, well-thumbed copies of McDonald's charge sheet can still be booked out of Ireland's municipal libraries and fetch high prices on eBay, but *The Destruction Of Dublin* never went to a reprint. Why?

"The book wasn't withdrawn," McDonald explained, "but it was never reprinted because there were a couple of legal actions which were more an irritation than a real problem because although we lost two of them, they didn't involve awards of huge sums of money. But some money was paid out, and that had a chill effect, and years later the publisher Fergal Tobin used to say we never made a penny out of that book, but I'm still very proud of it. I didn't make a penny either, and I feel the same."

Much like Project founder Peter Sheridan, McDonald believes that a new lifeforce took form in and around the city's original timber hut birthplace and radiated outwards. Coming from a younger generation that would tap into that energy and unleash it in an exuberant chain reaction, Paddy Dunning founded Temple Lane rehearsal studios in 1983, a year after McDonald's scathing *Irish Times* report headlined 'Dereliction And Decay In The Shadow Of The Central Bank'. It was the close proximity of his fledgling studio to the nation's new Central Bank, an oversized slab of concrete dropped into the winding mediaeval warren, that would bring the full force of the law slamming down on Dunning and his mates.

Dunning tells the tale of an incredible personal journey that begins with pilfering unwanted carpets from rubbish skips and leads to rolling out the red carpet at his stately country pile for superstar houseguests including Michael Jackson.

"At the start of 1983 I was in a band, Liaison, and we were rehearsing six days a week in my rehearsal studio at the back of the family house in Walkinstown. It was the suburbs and there were complaints to my mother from the neighbours about the noise, so I had to look for another rehearsal space. Next door to us Last Chance, who would become A House, were rehearsing, and just around the corner Something Happens! were doing the same. There were lots of bands but no rehearsal studios, apart from maybe Litton Lane which no start-up band could afford. So my search for a suitable space brought me into town and we found this amazing warehouse on Temple Lane.

"CIE was buying up buildings all over the area with the idea that they'd flatten the whole place for a huge transport hub. While they were waiting for the wholescale demolition to take place, they leased out the buildings for peppercorn rents to people like me. The idea behind this was to make some small rental income while preparing the ground for the huge redevelopment, and then throw out the tenants when the site was shovel ready."

Paddy was alerted to the potential of the derelict quarter by Aidan Walsh, an eccentric self-made businessman who wore a white Stetson hat, sported an Indiana Jones style bullwhip, and harboured a genuine passion to establish a music centre in the locality. The business relationship between Dunning and Walsh soon disintegrated. Dunning concentrated on building his Temple Lane rehearsal complex while Walsh opened the neighbouring Eagle Studios.

Unfortunately, the strict security measures Walsh imposed on his clients tended to jar with their laid-back rock 'n' roll ways. The musicians were issued identity documents and warned that failure to produce the correct papers would result in a fine or some other unspecified punishment. Walsh responded to the strained customer relations with even stricter security measures, introducing a system whereby two halves of a torn photo had to be matched up before patrons could gain admittance to their rehearsal space.

Despite their occasional differences over the years, Dunning and Walsh remained good friends. Dunning even became a fan when Walsh released his debut album on the British indie label Kaleidoscope, home to the pioneering shoegazing hipsters My

Bloody Valentine. *Aidan Walsh & The Master Plan – The Life Story Of My Life* would boldly go where no band had gone before, featuring surreal gems like 'Eating And Drinking With Women' and 'Have You Ever Given Money Away?' Bringing to bear his inside track on the workings of the Temple Bar property game, the latter's lyrics warned against handing any money to the government, "*because they only give it back to their pals*". He followed up the line "*I spent four grand*" with "*not in one go*". The addendum, he explained, was in case the Revenue might mistakenly think he had piles of cash worth investigating.

Walsh's ambitions for the redevelopment of Temple Bar extended far beyond those of CIE, the government, or any lobby group, stretching out beneath the Liffey riverbed. He would use his new media celebrity to brainwash a young generation into becoming his 'happy slaves'. These workers would build the Underwater City of his dreams which, like his rehearsal studio, would run on strict house rules. The first rule was, "You'd be barred from making love in the Underwater City. We'd be very strict on that to keep the numbers down. If you come to the city, you never die. You'd be 2,000 years old and you wouldn't know it. When the world blows up the Underwater City becomes a flying saucer and leaves the Earth. There'd be about three million people on the flying saucer – it would be a big one. There'd be two of everything – two Guards, two priests, two doctors. Animals? There might be one or two. And I'd be the master of it. Master of the Universe."

Meanwhile, back on Earth, Paddy Dunning and his pals were grappling with spades and sledge hammers to turn their own vision into a bricks and mortar reality. Dunning said, "To build our studios we had to first clear out the warehouse, build walls and fill all the cavities with sand. Then we soundproofed them with carpets we got from skips outside Switzer's (Ireland's most fashionable department store), who were throwing them out."

Neither Switzer's nor anyone else paid a blind bit of notice to this redistribution of resources under cover of darkness, but an early start on a quiet weekend caused a red alert.

Dunning vividly recalls, "We were digging out the basement rooms and had filled about eleven skips at this stage. Suddenly there's an Uzi machine gun pointed at my head. 'Get down, get down, this is a raid! It's the police.'

"They thought we were digging a tunnel to the Central Bank nearby. Like I said, we'd already been at it long enough to fill eleven skips, so why did it only occur to them now that we were planning a bank job?"

My band were amongst the first in the door when Temple Lane opened its doors in 1983. Like just about every other garage band, we'd discovered that rehearsing even one night a week turns good neighbours into an angry mob beating on your parents' front door begging they put a stop to the torture, or else …

Paddy Dunning was behind the reception desk almost every evening, taking future bookings and cash with a friendly smile. And if you were a fiver short this time, you could get him next time. The rooms themselves were found in a warren of narrow caverns, and so thick was the sound-insulation of carpet and sheet-wood that even on the coldest nights you'd be quickly down to a t-shirt. A rudimentary coffee dock followed, providing a busy hub for bands to exchange introductions, banter, ideas and sometimes band members. There was nowhere like it.

Building this buzzing meeting place from the foundations up was hard toil, but workaholism was part of the atmosphere.

"By the mid-80s we'd have a 100 bands a week coming in," Dunning recalled, "rehearsing in shifts for either a day session or an evening session. First thing in the morning we'd hoover the rooms ready for the day bands and when they finished we'd clean up again for the next lot. We had what seemed like every band in Ireland there – In Tua Nua, Sinéad O'Connor with Ton Ton Macoute, The Waterboys, Light A Big Fire, Bagatelle, Aslan, Blue In Heaven. When they were looking for the cast of *The Commitments* they recruited from Temple Lane, including Glen Hansard who was there with The Frames. John Cooper Clarke and Mike Scott hung out in the café on the first floor.

"There was an amazing level of creativity with all these bands in the same space. It was electric. Everything was positive. All the bands would show up on time. We were all industrious. No-one ever turned up drunk. There was an amazing work ethic. Everyone would get the work done and then party. We'd get the money at the end of the night and go to the pub with the cash in a briefcase. We'd work out what was needed to meet the next day's bills and put that aside. Then we'd spend the rest. We'd go to the Bailey for a few drinks then on to the Pink Elephant with the briefcase full of pound notes and when the Pink closed on to Suesey Street until five. And then we'd be back into work at 8.30 the next morning to hoover all the rooms ready to do it all again."

The nearest pub to Temple Lane was the same Norseman which had been brought back to life by the patrons of the Project, despite the pleas of its put-upon owners. By the mid-80s, The Norseman's small cadre of old timers had decamped to The Foggy Dew just around the corner in a bid to flee an invasion of leather clad wannabees with gelled up mullets. It was to no avail. The Foggy Dew would be next, then the refurbished Temple Bar, until the whole place, seemingly overnight, was overrun with trendy fashion victims. For Paddy Dunning and every one of the 100 bands who filled his studios every week – mine included – this could only be a good thing.

"When we started up, the whole place was derelict. It was a landscape of broken windows, no street lighting, no eaterie. Even though all the streets were so narrow and winding, buses would fly up and down the cobblestone laneways. People like us were starting to occupy the vacant spaces. Artists were coming in. There was the Project. But even as the area started to become vibrant it was still in a state of decay because you could only do up stuff with pennies. There was no real structural work being done because we weren't allowed to make improvements because we didn't own the buildings. It wasn't until around 1991 that we were able to buy the buildings and really make changes."

One of Dunning's many regulars touted to be "the next U2" were Aslan, who could rehearse during the day by virtue that they'd decided that having jobs would hamper their chances of making it as a band. Speaking to me in 2019, the late Christy Dignam reasoned, "Today the pressure is on youngsters to get a job or, if they can't get a job in Ireland, to get out of the country and get a job in Australia or England or America. When we were starting out people felt no shame about not having a job. You weren't being pushed into a job because there usually wasn't a job there. Economic stability wasn't a big deal if it wasn't an option. The great thing about that situation was that your parents allowed you to rehearse your music. To this day I believe a recession is good for music. It frees people up but it fires people up about the injustices going on in the world. It's healthy in that way."

Long after that recession of the 1980s had passed, the lives of Christy Dignam and Paddy Dunning crossed again when the singer – brought to death's door by a spiralling heroin habit – sought respite in the now prosperous Dunning's country home, Grouse Lodge in the midlands. Described by Dignam as "an out-of-the-way place with apartments, a recording studio and a big old mansion house", it was just the tonic to get him back on his feet. He recalled, "I didn't bring anything. No methadone, no anything, just cold turkey. Paddy and his wife Claire would come over every day, though for the first week I was so sick I don't think I ate anything. I did cold turkey and after a couple of weeks I was okay to start up my life again. The following year Michael Jackson and his family took the mansion for the whole summer. He must have heard I liked it."

Looking back, Paddy Dunning is in agreement with Dignam that a happy confluence of time and place brought together unemployment and the work ethic in agreeable co-existence. Paddy reflected, "Music was a catalyst for a whole generation of people. It built their character. There was huge unemployment but we all found music as a way to living a happier life. Music was something heartfelt, something that we loved. And I don't take that for granted, because some people go through life without ever finding that something that they love and they're passionate about."

Dunning believes that the seismic waves of change rippled out first from the heart of the old city. "It was the musicians who rehearsed and recorded here. From their base here they went to every corner of the country, brought their art all around the land and then all around the world."

Chapter 8

STING, KUBRICK & FORSYTH ARE SENT PACKING

"Instead of the pleasure of popular success we were faced with the harsh reality of grey weather, bone-chilling damp, biting wind and bad food – all to beat the taxman."

– Police guitarist Andy Summers

FRANCIS ROSSI'S musically and financially rewarding tax year in Ireland sent the message to the rest of the pop world that the country was open for business. By 1980 The Police were one of the biggest bands in the world and were soaring steadily towards becoming the biggest. The time was right for a tax holiday out of the UK and Sting's marriage to the Irish actress Frances Tomelty gave Ireland an edge over competing destinations. Police guitarist Andy Summers tagged along as well, making camp in Cork while Sting took a grand old house in the tranquil Connemara village of Roundstone.

The pair's planned year-long break came to a premature end under the shadow of the gunman when the IRA hunger strikes, which began in late 1980, breathed new life into a flagging terror campaign to cleanse the country of high profile foreigners. They weren't the first to leave under duress.

In 1974, pioneering movie director Stanley Kubrick packed his bags and bade a hasty goodbye. The following year Liverpool and England footballer Kevin Keegan found himself on the receiving end of death threats. Even long-time tax resident Frederick Forsyth, author of blood-splattered blockbusters *The Day Of The Jackal* and *The Odessa File*, decided that disappearing was the better part of valour.

The roots of this renewed terror campaign against foreign nationals can be traced back very specifically to 1966, the year The Beach Boys and The Beatles really kicked off the era of peace and love with their respective mind-blowing masterpieces 'Pet Sounds' and 'Revolver'.

In the second half of the 1960s, Irish republicans, tapping a mood of patriotic fervour stoked by the Easter Rising 50th anniversary celebrations in 1966, began a campaign of ethnic cleansing against foreign landowners and their alleged native collaborators. The weapon of choice was a toxic mix of arson and murderous threats. The reporting of this strife made few lines of newsprint beyond Ireland. As the once moribund republican movement further reanimated in the 1970s, the provocateurs found that they could attract far greater international attention to their cause by menacing high-profile targets like celebrities and the heads of multinationals.

In the afterglow of the State's year-long Easter Rising celebrations, various self-appointed keepers of Irish culture renewed their fading efforts to keep it from being swept away by a rapidly globalising consumer society. The Irish language lobby group Conradh na Gaeilge (Gaelic League) fingered the State broadcaster RTÉ as one of the most blameworthy collaborators "because it has a duty to serve the people of Ireland and at the same time must serve the interests of the gods of advertising. This it cannot do." The accusers continued, "Our national identity is under fierce attack from the Anglo-American neo-colonialism and neo-imperialism which is attempting to gain possession of Ireland. This involves stamping out freedom – our people's freedom to be full Irish people." Angry Irish Ireland-ism was finding its voice again, having become a victim of its own success when, amongst other reforms, the newborn State made Irish compulsory for school exam certificates, entry into third level education and coveted public service jobs for life.

In early 1969, the Galway Command of the IRA, piggybacking on this new mood of super-patriotism, upped the ante with a warning to the Language Freedom Movement (LFM) that it was to quit agitating to free the people from the tyranny of compulsory Irish. The IRA branded the LFM not so much a movement as "a state of mind – the state of mind of the slave". The terrorist organisation claimed the LFM represented the "parasite" classes of Irish society: "Slum landlords, ground rent landlords, moneylenders of various kinds, solicitors, auctioneers and brokers."

Then came the chilling bit. "The IRA will not stand idly by while the fabric of the Irish nation is openly and deliberately attacked by the enemies of the people," it stated. "It will defend vigorously those who defend our nation and its language, and attack violently and relentlessly those who attack it."

The IRA had been dormant for years. Many dismissed the threats as the sabre-rattling of grumpy old men. Until four farms in Louth and Meath were set ablaze one night in early 1969. Three were farmed by Germans and one by a retired British Army officer. The IRA claimed responsibility. Shortly before the arson attacks, the Irish Republican Publicity Bureau released a statement confirming that it took a dim view of Germans coming over here and occupying farmland. It said, "We hereby advise prospective purchasers of land, fisheries, buildings or existing enterprises in Ireland, in their own interest, that the

Irish Republican Movement is concerned at the amount of such property that has and still is being acquired by non-nationals.

"Property acquisition is encouraged by certain Irish estate agents, some of whom even attempt to entice foreign purchasers by advertising offers of Irish property in the press of their countries, but such agents are in no position to guarantee security of tenure."

A few months later, in August 1969, the so-called Battle Of The Bogside exploded in the city of Derry. A three-day clash between nationalist residents and Loyalist marchers supported by a pugnacious police force, the confrontation is widely regarded as the spark that ignited three decades of murder and mayhem.

In the spring of 1973, the feted movie director Stanley Kubrick arrived in Ireland to film *Barry Lyndon*, a costume drama based on William Makepeace Thackeray's 1844 novel *The Luck Of Barry Lyndon* about a hot-headed Irish adventurer. A deeply neurotic auteur, Kubrick landed in Ireland nursing the psychological bruises from his previous cinema release *A Clockwork Orange*. The Oscar-winning adaptation of Anthony Burgess's novel had been a commercial and critical success, but it's graphic depiction of 'ultraviolence' had been scapegoated for a number of murders in Britain, to the point that Kubrick had taken the extreme step of withdrawing it from circulation himself.

Although Kubrick and his leading man Ryan O'Neal reportedly had a torrid relationship, shooting went well through to the end of the year, as the director infused an otherworldly luminescence into the natural beauty of Wicklow, Waterford and Cork, and the interiors of stately Powerscourt House. All the loveliness was sucked out of the project when the director and his crew got back to work after a break for Christmas 1973. On 30 January 1974, a scheduled day of shooting in Dublin's

Phoenix Park was abandoned when 14 bomb scares at strategic locations threw the capital into chaos. A few days later, a distressed Kubrick gathered his family and made haste for the ferry port of Dún Laoghaire. One version of the story is that a crew member relayed the message that booby-trap bombs had been planted on his shooting locations. Another was he'd been warned that if he didn't leave pronto under his own steam he'd be carried out in a box. He was on the next ferry to Holyhead in Wales.

The following year the threatmakers trained their crosshairs on a much sexier celebrity target, Kevin Keegan, the new poster boy of English football. In his 2018 autobiography *My Life In Football,* Keegan revealed that his one falling out with England manager Don Revie came in May 1975, before a fixture against Northern Ireland, when "a letter, purportedly from the IRA, was sent to the FA offices saying that if I showed my face in Belfast I was a dead man". A second death threat against Keegan was posted directly to the English FA. Ambitious, cocky and competitive to the Nth degree, Keegan would not be cowed. He wrote, "What if it was a hoax, as I suspected, and another player scored a hat-trick in my place?... And what if someone, possibly an opposition fan, realised what could be done and delivered the same threat to Liverpool before a big match?"

The Liverpool star persuaded Revie to play him in Belfast but, once there, he had a hard time "clearing his mind" and played poorly in a drab goalless draw. His reward was to be dropped from the starting line-up for England's next game against Wales. The young striker packed his bags and stormed out of the England camp. He later wrote, "After going to Ireland with a death threat hanging over me, an explanation was the least I deserved. I even started wondering whether Don had tried to use the IRA scare as an excuse to get me out of the team." A hostile tabloid press laid siege to Keegan's home – taking his manager's side – but Revie quickly forgave his talisman and shortly after promoted him to England captain.

Five months after Keegan faced down the IRA's exclusion order, the international spotlight again focused on a story which fed into the narrative that the sovereign Irish state was teetering on the verge of anarchy, a dismal and dangerous place ringed with barbed wire fences and big signs blaring Keep Out!

On 3 October 1975, Dr. Tiede Herrema was flagged down at a police checkpoint as he drove to an early morning meeting at the Ferenka steel plant at Annacotty, Co Limerick. The Dutchman, who was Chief Executive of the factory complex, gave his name to the Guard, who then whipped out a revolver and bundled the 54-year-old into a getaway car. A phone call to the Dutch embassy demanded the release of three Republican prisoners from Portlaoise Prison. Failing the release of the trio, the industrialist would be "executed" in 48 hours.

It quickly became apparent that the daring crime had been committed for mainly personal motives, adding to a perception at home and abroad that the Republic had descended into lawlessness to the point where even freelance terrorists now had the run of the country. The bogus Garda was rogue republican bomber Eddie Gallagher, on the run from the law north and south, and from his ex-pals in the IRA. Gallagher wanted his fellow terrorist and lover Rose Dugdale released from Limerick Prison where she'd given birth to their son 10 months earlier. Gallagher's young moll, Marian Coyle, also wanted the release of a buddy behind bars for IRA crimes.

The economy was already on its knees after six years of the Troubles and the hangover slump from the crippling 1973 oil crisis. The kidnap and threatened murder of Tiede Herrema, the boss of one of Ireland's biggest employers, quite apart from the personal tragedy, would surely send foreign firms packing and slam the shutters down on any future inward investment. The fate of the nation seemed to hang in the balance.

The Army and Garda focussed on the greatest manhunt in the history of the State, with soldiers posted at every port, airport and border crossing. After two weeks of trauma, the nation awoke on a Sunday morning to learn of a dawn raid by Special Branch detectives backed by snipers on a terraced house in the Kildare town of Monasterevin. A long stand-off had begun.

For 16 days, watched by the world, the siege dragged on in deadlock. Then, on the 17th day, Gallagher asked for headache tablets before throwing out his guns saying he feared he had meningitis. He was reunited with the mother of his child, Rose Dugdale, in Limerick Prison where she already had a cell. There in 1978 they became the first convicted prisoners in the history of the State to wed behind bars. Dugdale was released in 1980, 10 years ahead of her husband.

Just a couple of hours' drive in different directions from Limerick Prison, as Rose Dugdale walked free that year, Sting and Andy Summers of The Police were doing their best to blend in with their new neighbours, with differing levels of success. One of the few British New Wave acts to crack America, The Police had conquered planet pop and the dollars were pouring in. In her first budget shortly after coming to power a few months earlier, Britain's Prime Minister Margaret Thatcher had slashed the top rate of income tax from 83% to 60% but even that seemed like a muggers' charter to pop's nouveau riche. The solution recommended by pricy accountants was a year-long tax holiday spent resident outside the UK, and Ireland had all the advantages of language, *Match Of The Day*, *Coronation Street*, proximity to home and a light touch monitoring regime of jet-set comings and goings.

Almost four decades after settling in, on a return visit to Ireland, Sting reminisced fondly about his time spent in the Irish beauty spot. "My back garden looked out on the Atlantic. It was a beautiful place. We just sort of fell in love with it. We knew Peter O'Toole very well. He lived in Clifden and we were staying there. We found this beautiful house, surrounded by a sea wall with fantastic views of the mountains and the sea. We loved it."

While Sting's decision was to go west, his bandmate headed south. The Police's gifted guitarist however never really settled. In his 2007 autobiography, *One Train Later*, Summers painted a grim picture of killing time in Kinsale, Co Cork, where he bought a house overlooking the harbour for himself, his wife Kate and their young daughter Layla. After three years of trekking the globe, Summers couldn't adjust to the dawdling pace of life in rural Ireland. He wrote, "There was nothing to do but walk along the cliffs and gaze at the wild beauty of the countryside... Life seemed to be about the ability to make it through the next day, keep the damp out of your bones and just pass the long, grey hours." He found the scarcity of half-decent restaurants depressing, while even the vegetables in the shops were no better than "a shrunken row of brown things". Exile to Ireland, he decided, "felt like a booby prize" and the frayed nerves chafed at the couple's marriage, which would eventually end in divorce. "Instead of the pleasure of popular success," he reflected, "we were faced with the harsh reality of grey weather, bone-chilling damp, biting wind and bad food – all to beat the taxman."

Things went from bad to worse as winter drew in at the close of 1980, when IRA prisoners in the North's Maze prison went on hunger strike, demanding political status. The first fast ended after 53 days just before Christmas, when the strikers believed they had won concessions. When it became clear they had not, a second hunger strike began with Bobby Sands being the first to refuse food. Unlike the first revolt, the second strike was staggered, with new refuseniks joining at measured intervals in an effort to ratchet up the pressure on British PM Margaret Thatcher.

The pressure bounced off the self-styled Iron Lady. Andy Summers and Sting upped sticks. Recalling the tensions ratcheted up by the hunger strikes, Andy Summers revealed, "In the mornings, with the biting wind cutting through my clothes, I often removed the nails that had been placed under my car tyres and washed the graffiti off our wall, with its taunts about The Police and being British. Naturally enough, I was very uncomfortable with all of this. Over in the west of Ireland, Sting actually received several death threats. Eventually, we both left the country."

A compatriot of the Police men who fled a few months earlier in fear of his life was author Frederick Forsyth. The proudly patriotic Englishman repeatedly insisted that he knew nothing about Ireland's hugely beneficial artists' tax exemption when he relocated to his 18th Century mansion in the green and pleasant "garden county" of Wicklow, despite the fact that he and his wife had spent the previous year in Spain to escape the 80% income tax top rate imposed by Harold Wilson's new Labour government. For five years, Forsyth's white Rolls-Royce would be a familiar sight on the narrow winding hilly roads, literally stopping the traffic when he got wedged in a bohereen made just for donkeys.

He quickly struck up an unlikely and lasting friendship with Charles Haughey, the politician who had dreamed up the artist's tax scheme. Many years later Forsyth reflected that there was "not the slightest reason" why the pair should get on, "but we did. As a passionate republican, he had little time for the English, or anything British, but seemed to make an exception for me." He elaborated, "To his political enemies he was relentless and vengeful for any slight or ill-turn. When relaxed over a dinner table, I found him an amusing rogue. And he was certainly a rogue." In the fullness of time Haughey's enemies would be vindicated, not only about his relentless vengeful streak, but about the culture vulture Finance Minister's lifelong creed that only little people pay taxes.

Within a few years, Forsyth's unlikely friend rose to the top job in the country. In his first TV state-of-the-nation address, Haughey haughtily warned, "We are living way beyond our means. We have been borrowing enormous amounts of money, borrowing at a rate which just cannot continue." As he preached this belt-tightening, Haughey himself had just started repayments to reduce his bank overdraft of £1.1 million, a staggering sum at the time.

The fact that Haughey didn't become Taoiseach until two months after the visit of Pope John Paul II in September 1979, was lost on the master of spy fiction when he recounted how Ireland's prime minister sought out his security expertise to protect the Pontiff's life. Forsyth wrote in his autobiography that, "Hardly had he got the top slot when Ireland received Pope John Paul II on a state visit. Over the pine kitchen table, Charlie put to me a pretty odd request. He said he needed a monograph to present to the cabinet on security – he was terrified of an attempt being made on the Pontiff while he was in Dublin. I suggested it was out of the question for His Holiness to be in mortal danger – in Dublin, of all places – and that the British Government had a dozen security experts with years of experience. He countered that he would not turn to London, but that the Garda had no experience of this sort of thing. He needed the techniques that had kept de Gaulle alive. There was nothing for it but to do what he wanted."

Raking through the mountains of in-depth research he'd put into *The Day Of The Jackal*, Forsyth composed a report for the government "stressing the difference between close-up protection against the madman and the hazard of the long-range sniper". Haughey never told Forsyth whether his expert counsel had been put to cabinet, or whether Haughey had tabled his own plan, "or that of some anonymous ace known only to him". Happily, the Pope's visit went without a hitch, and maybe the government *had* taken a page from his *Day Of The Jackal* advice because, as Forsyth recalled, "I noticed a few snipers from the Irish army perched on the rooftops scanning all the windows opposite".

Haughey was Minister for Health at the time of the Papal visit, so unless the Health portfolio covered thwarting assassins, Forsyth's recollections may be untrustworthy. What's not disputed is that in 1980, he, his wife and their two Irish-born baby boys fled back to England in fear of the IRA campaign to scare away high-profile foreigners. The decision to leave already made, Forsyth called into the Taoiseach's office to let him know in person. "He was horrified and asked me to stay," he said. According to the fiction king, Haughey even offered to make him a Senator in a bid to change his mind. It was no use. In prose that echoed Johnny Rotten's account of his stay in Mountjoy Prison, Forsyth told how, as the two shared a parting hug, "doors popped ajar as open-mouthed senior civil servants looked out to see their premier draped around a Britisher, never seen before, or since".

Days later, the author received one last phone call from Haughey. "It was to give me his word that not a single IRA man in the country would dare raise his hand against me or my family. The only way he could have known that was if he had given a flat order to the army council of the IRA. Not many men could have done that." And especially not the leader of the enemy state the IRA was sworn to destroy.

Unlike Frederick Forsyth and his bandmate Andy Summers, Sting has always been reluctant to dwell on his departure from Ireland during a time of emotional turbulence, always preferring to accentuate the positive. When asked in 2017 if IRA death threats had led him to up sticks and get out of Roundstone, the singer was circumspect, answering, "Not really – it was uncomfortable. Nonetheless, people were wonderful." With some understatement he added, "It was a time of the hunger strikes and it was difficult to be an English Catholic in the Republic."

A fellow English Catholic taking a tax break in the Republic was Francis Rossi. Looking back on his time in Ireland, he told me, "I was completely unaware that there was anything like that going on. Maybe Sting and Andy Summers had a home and rented a place. I lived in Jurys Hotel and I didn't go out, so I was the bloke in the hotel room keeping a low profile – not on purpose. I wasn't consciously keeping a low profile, that's just what I'm like."

While his Irish sojourn left Andy Summers with a sour taste in his mouth, Sting departed with an enhanced grasp of the nuances of a sundered country, and a suitcase full of new songs for the band's next album *Ghost In The Machine*. The hits he penned in Roundstone included 'Every Little Thing She Does Is Magic', 'Spirits In The Material World' and 'Invisible Sun'. The latter was the lead single from the album in Europe, addressing as it did the conflict in Northern Ireland with a video shot there to match. The band's distributors in the USA and the rest of the world released the frothy 'Every Little Thing' as first choice 45 in preference to Sting's solemn meditation on war and peace.

When The Police briefly reunited for Amnesty International's Conspiracy of Hope tour in 1986, with U2 as co-headliners, Bono would join the trio to sing along on 'Invisible Sun'.

The hunger strikes ended, heightened hostilities and xenophobia ebbed back to what passed for normal. Word quickly spread down the showbiz grapevine about this great spot for a tax holiday.

They didn't even have to leave their own time zone. Everything in Ireland happened in real time GMT. Unlike Sting and Andy Summers, however, the new arrivals had no plans to seclude themselves in splendid isolation along some wild Atlantic way. This was a new generation of millionaire superstars – freshly minted by MTV and Smash Hits for the younger brothers and sisters of Police fans. They were here to keep close tabs on back-in-the-swing London, to write, record, rehearse and party in style – and Dublin was gearing up at breakneck speed to meet all those needs.

Chapter 9

THE SECOND BRITISH INVASION OF IRELAND

"If ourselves, Spandau and Frankie were living in London we wouldn't know each other, but here we're all like foreigners abroad, so we've struck up good friendships. When we played football against Dermot Morgan's Showbiz XI, me and Steve Norman were like Gary Lineker and Peter Beardsley up front."

– Joe Elliott, Def Leppard frontman

IN THE early summer of 1986, a celebrity football match took place in Dublin between Dermot Morgan's Irish Showbiz XI and a Rock Exiles selection featuring members of Def Leppard, Spandau Ballet and Frankie Goes To Hollywood, three juggernauts of the so-called Second British Invasion Of America. Six decades after expelling its British overlords, Ireland had got itself a new English colony and, far from being scorned and shunned by the natives, these newcomers were admired and adored, even if everyone knew they'd only come for the tax breaks.

Irish football itself had a rebirth in 1986. Very soon the team's travelling supporters – now lumped with U2 as "our greatest ambassadors" – would open a second front on Ireland's charm offensive to the outside world. The newly appointed manager of the national team, Jack Charlton, an English World Cup hero, would invoke an arcane "granny rule" permitting foreign-born players with Irish grandparents to line up for the Republic. This paved the way for a second influx of English and Scottish star talent, individuals destined to become infinitely more admired and adored than the fugitive pop colonists. Players like John Aldridge, Ray Houghton and Mick McCarthy would be loved and hero-worshipped.

A barricade of stubborn Irish isolationism was stormed from within and without in the 1980s by an alliance of restless youth and unruly new media. The fall of Ireland's wall happened in parallel to the great disruption that capsized the Soviet Union, whose rulers had uncorked the twin genies of '*glasnost*' (openness) and '*perestroika*' (restructuring). Romanian legend has it that the banning of the TV soap *Dallas* was the final nail in the coffin of the brutal Ceausescu regime, but for shorthand, we can boil down the catalyst of change to "MTV culture".

A remarkably similar revolution happened in Ireland, where the state's traditional control of the broadcast media was overthrown just as a tame, sleepy print media suddenly grew claws and started asking questions that had not been asked before. This was Ireland's *glasnost*.

What we can call MTV culture came to Ireland long before it reached continental Europe. It arrived here at the same time and at the same pace as it reached Britain, the wellspring of most of what was good on America's hip new channel.

When MTV launched in the USA in August 1981, it was only available to a tiny audience of cable viewers. Despite its small-time beginnings, its producers were brimful of confidence that they were making history. To leave viewers in no doubt that this was a momentous event, the new station blasted off with footage of the first Moon landing as a sonorous voice boomed, "Ladies and gentlemen – rock and roll!" The new era in broadcasting opened with 'Video Killed The Radio Star' by Buggles.

In fact, video didn't kill the radio star, but quite the contrary, as the new TV presence spread like wildfire, fanning new interest, creating new stars, and sending record sales soaring. The station's format of back-to-back pop songs was so simple and effective that RTÉ did a straight copy of it.

Starting in 1984, *MT-USA* ran for three hours each Sunday with a midweek repeat, with 'Fab' Vinny Hanley supplying breathless links filmed on the sidewalks of New York. *MT-USA*'s three-hour video block was unique in all of Europe. Even Britain had nothing like it, and Britain was the main supplier of videos to MTV in the USA.

Why Britain? Because in the early '80s, the North American music scene was like a giant oil tanker, incapable of turning around quickly enough to catch up with a video revolution moving at breakneck speed. The US sales charts and radio stations were still strictly segregated along lines of race and genre. The industry was so vast and cumbersome that the Billboard Top 40 moved at a glacial pace. In a perpetual state of near gridlock, the Top 10 hits could stay virtually unchanged for weeks on end. Pop music had become deadly dull and static.

The arrival of MTV would shatter the old model and inject a new fluidity, but to get rolling the new entity needed videos to fill its endless hours of airtime, and the vast majority of American acts were slow to grasp that they were in a new game. They didn't do videos, they didn't even understand videos. For British and Irish acts video was a natural evolution from the image-fixated New Romantic scene.

Much younger than most of their American counterparts, the

New Romantics were already dressed to impress and good to go. They instinctively 'got' MTV in a way the elder Americans just did not. MTV in the US was crying out for videos, anything would do. The British and Irish acts (well, U2) jumped gleefully into the gap, to the point where duff bluffers like A Flock Of Seagulls who couldn't get arrested in their homeland found huge overnight success in the States by dint of taking a punt and splashing 10 grand on a video. (An honourable mention is due to The Boomtown Rats' 1979 video for 'I Don't Like Mondays' which was well ahead of the game, though two years too early for the launch of MTV.)

From as early as 1983, the newly minted millionaires of the Second British Invasion of America were sending scouting missions around the world in search of safe tax refuges. The hideaway of choice turned out to be Ireland. It was a simple matter to jump on an aeroplane and pop home for dinner with the folks, or a few pints down the local with the mates without bothersome red tape. Strictly speaking, this island hopping wasn't allowed, but no-one on either side of the Irish Sea was keeping a tight watch.

A popular misconception of the time was that the new MTV millionaires were drawn to Ireland by the 1969 Finance Act framed by then Finance Minister Charles Haughey. Better known today as the Artists' Tax Exemption, this legislation did entitle creative types resident in Ireland to save a great deal on income from works deemed to be of artistic merit. The operative word there was 'resident'. In order to avail of the Irish scheme, foreigners needed to commit to living in Ireland for at least as long as it took for the money to filter through. This could mean a lengthy commitment.

Ireland's new colony of British tax exiles had instead arrived to exploit a piece of UK legislation they fondly dubbed 'The

Five-Year Trick', which involved spending one year out of a given five-year period outside of their native jurisdiction. By doing so, they could line up a row of loopholes in UK law to avoid surrendering a hefty chunk of their earnings. Ireland's light touch tax laws rolled out the red carpet. Any income brought into the Republic would be liable for Irish tax, as would any income the visitors made while living in Ireland, from an Irish tour for example. But a loophole in Irish law left the way open for loans to be taken into the country tax free. So that's precisely what Ireland's new English colony did. They supported themselves during their stay with loans sourced from abroad, thus legally avoiding tax on both sides of the Irish Sea.

Shortly after the Rock Exiles vs Irish Showbiz football friendly, I caught up with three stellar rock residents at their various Irish retreats: Holly Johnson, the frontman of Frankie Goes To Hollywood, was nearing the end of his tax-holiday year, spent in the quiet solitude of Borris House in County Carlow; Joe Elliott, the lead singer with the world's biggest heavy metal band, Def Leppard, had spent his year in Dublin, getting to know and love the capital city, and Alannah Currie and her fellow Thompson Twins had discovered Borris House prior to handing it over to the Frankies.

The Twins vacated Carlow to tour the world, which included playing the Philadelphia half of the Live Aid spectacular and returned to take up residence in a stately home outside Newtownmountkennedy in County Wicklow. They went off on another tour and came back again. This time when Currie and her band partner and boyfriend Tom Bailey returned to Ireland, it was with a view to buying a house in Wicklow. She told me their decision to set down roots was "an emotional thing", explaining, "I was pregnant after the last tour and we wanted to have our child in Ireland because it's a neutral country." The

Cold War by the mid-80s was getting molten hot and with it the possibility of nuclear strikes and mutually assured destruction (MAD). Sadly, Currie lost her baby not long after the couple moved back to Ireland, but there were other attractions that kept them in the country, though she made no bones about putting tax at the top of the list.

"You've got to strike while the iron is hot," she said candidly. "We paid enormous taxes on the income from our previous two albums, so we decided to spend a year in exile to capitalise on the success of *Here's To Future Days.*"

She continued, "Ireland is a good place for songwriting. People here are more familiar and more tolerant than anywhere else. They're great in that they don't get excited when they have pop stars living down the road."

Tom Bailey recalled how the Twins found out just how blasé the locals could be about pop stars. Explaining that they'd come back to Ireland for the splendid isolation as much as the tax incentives, he said that they increasingly found themselves drawn into village life. Alannah took driving lessons and signed up for circuit classes at the local gym. Tom recalled how the natives had a friendly way of bursting their pop star bubble. "We were invited to go down to the town's youth club. We thought it would be a bit of a gig, that we'd be signing autographs and all that. We dressed ourselves up in all the gear but when we got there it was a case of 'Okay, let's all play a game of rounders'. We were destroyed but it was great fun."

Frankie Goes To Hollywood took up the lease on Borris House when the Twins went off touring. In need of rest, recuperation and somewhere to protect their earnings after conquering the globe in 1984, the five Frankies spent most of 1985 in the Carlow mansion. Holly Johnson did anyway, while the others displayed a yearning for the work-in-progress that was Dublin's nightlife.

Reflecting on their year out of England, the frontman told me, "I think I enjoyed living in Borris a bit more than the rest of the band. They'd go off and do the Dublin nightclubs from Thursday to Monday, so we didn't write as many songs as we should have. I would have liked more work to have come out of it, but we were in a strange place, in a valley where the air was really heavy and it made everyone feel sleepy. I made a bit more effort to get involved in the community. My biggest activity was going down to a place called the Village Shop where I'd drink coffee with the ladies there. They were all lovely and they knitted us stuff. I think the nicest thing I got was a tea set, which was hand-painted by an old lady of 80."

During his stay in the happy valley, the singer struck up a close friendship with a local, Alice, who made terracotta pottery. On one occasion she informed Johnson that she had to spend the day out of town and had no-one to look after the shop. He good naturedly suggested that, having sold millions of records, the lads should have no problem shifting a few pieces of pottery, and so Frankie Goes To Hollywood, at the height of their global fame, became shopkeepers for a day in a little Irish village.

Johnston recalled, "The shop got very busy, but it was all kids coming in looking for autographs and not buying anything. After a while we got a bit pissed off and told them 'no more autographs unless you buy something'. So when Alice came back we'd sold dozens of cheap egg cups. She was very pleased!"

When I spoke to Joe Elliott in the middle of 1986, his band Def Leppard were the undisputed world heavyweight champions of what had become known as the new wave of heavy metal. Having steamrolled several times across the USA, the five-piece were looking forward to some down-time in their native Sheffield, until their accountants slapped a hefty price tag on going home.

"I'd love to say we came to Ireland because the grass was greener," said Elliott, "but it was for tax reasons initially, though we've found a lot to keep us here since then. We first came here in February 1984 for a stay of six months. We'd just spent six months touring the States and we were in the middle of a tax year so we couldn't go home. We're not one of those bands who, because they've had a slight amount of success, go to live in a mansion in LA."

So they headed instead for Dublin, where they awaited the cash rewards from their multi-platinum *Pyromania* album while living all together in a modest house in the suburb of Booterstown. They'd chosen Ireland on the advice of their Irish lighting engineer, Shay McMahon, who told them that Ireland's capital would be just like living in Liverpool, and that sense of being close to home proved the deciding factor.

Elliott reflected, "Dublin is as near culture-wise to England as it's possible to get. Everyone speaks English and drives on the same side of the road. You can get fish and chips here and the Guinness is great. As well as that you've got all the British TV channels plus two extra. RTÉ gets *Dallas* and *Dynasty* about four months ahead of Britain, so I get all the episodes video-taped and send them over to my mother. She loves that because she's able to tell all her friends what's going to happen next."

Unlike the Frankies in sleepy Borris, heavy metal's new world-beaters found Dublin conducive to knuckling down to the business of writing what would become one of the biggest albums of all time, *Hysteria*, which would sell over 25 million copies. Elliott explained, "We're one of those bands that prefer to sit down on a Guinness crate and write songs. We all like a bit of sun, but when it's cold and damp you feel more like working and you also get an earthier feel to the songs. We wanted to be close to England because we've always written in England

and we were a bit afraid of how it might turn out if we went and wrote an album in Los Angeles or wherever. That's not my scene. So I think it's worked out for the best."

The band members were particularly enamoured of the way Dubliners let them go about their business unhindered. "It's nice to be able to do simple things like walk down Grafton Street," he said. "We like to be treated like ordinary people and that happens here. We like to keep our star trips for the stage and the videos. As a capital city, Dublin is very small. You very quickly get to meet the people that you like, and you just as quickly weed out the undesirables. Because of its size, Dublin is full of gossip mongers – everyone knows everything about everyone else. In that way it's a lot different to London, where bands don't really have much contact with each other. Like, if ourselves and Spandau and Frankie were living in London we wouldn't know each other, but here we're all like foreigners abroad, so we've struck up good friendships. When ourselves and Spandau played football against Dermot Morgan's Showbiz XI, me and Steve Norman were like (Gary) Lineker and (Peter) Beardsley up front."

Taking off the rose-tinted glasses, the singer observed, "Things I don't like about Ireland include the fact that Dublin is reminiscent of the Champs-Élysées or parts of India because of the number of beggars on the streets. And you have to be very careful about where you park your car, because stealing them seems to be a hobby with many people. One of the worst things about Dublin is the number of places you can go for a meal that only sell wine. I like to have a couple of pints if I go out late."

Currie agreed, adding, "The clubs aren't very good and I can't find shops that I like."

The club that all the exiles agreed *was* very good – and the one that Ireland's new pop aristocracy made their hangout

– was the Pink Elephant. As for shops to lure the discerning pop star with money to burn... It's fair to say that the capital city experienced by the early colonists of the mid-80s was no New York, Paris or Milan. Touted as the most chic boulevard Ireland had to offer, the recently pedestrianised Grafton Street was condemned by one commentator who bemoaned the new trend for outlets ditching good established family names for foreign tack. He cited Kojak's, Purdy's (after Joanna Lumley's New Avengers character), Roots (after the US TV smash) and Roxanne, named for The Police hit about prostitution.

As the pathfinder for the new influx of MTV millionaires, Police chief Sting had been a familiar sight strolling Grafton Street at the start of the decade. The Dublin that Sting knew at the start of the '80s was the same one that the Spandaus, the Leppards, the Frankies and the rest came to know in the middle of the decade. Hollowed out for lack of investment, it seemed a city moving in ever decreasing circles. As Bagatelle sang in their monster hit 'Summer *In Dublin*', the Liffey really did stink like hell, assaulting passers-by with a foul stench, the result of unregulated factories upstream spewing out gloopy effluents that clogged the drainage and treatment works beneath the river. The quays flanking the Liffey resembled two rows of rotten teeth, soot black and full of demolished gaps. Urban decay blighted the city's heart which fell quiet after the pub chucking out apart from the barks of security dogs and the shuffle of winos.

Pedestrians shuffling from north to south across the Ha'penny Bridge found themselves in Temple Bar, a warren of winding cobbled laneways pockmarked by boarded-up windows, dingy, forbidding shops and poky, dark pubs which had remained stubbornly set in their ways since the 1960s, or maybe the 1860s. 'Men Only' signs had been outlawed for a decade, but they weren't needed to scare off the ladies from places like these dank, grubby dens smelling of stale booze, mildew and smoke, where pub-grub meant stale sandwiches garnished with dead bluebottles, and toilets were optional.

For some, this down-in-the-dumps Dublin of the mid-80s had a shabby bohemian charm. Def Leppard said a decidedly fond farewell in an advert they placed in *Hot Press* before departing on their 1986 world tour.

> *"So! Dublin, we're off and wish to express our thanks to all of you who have helped us along after the last 12 months. Special thanks to Windmill, the clubs, restaurants... all those who broke into our cars, stole our bikes and robbed our apartments. C'est la vie! Non? We will be back."*

The Thompson Twins had already come back, despite having had their misty-eyed visions of an isle of saints and scholars rudely shattered by the brutish intrusion of Ireland's '80s heroin scourge. Currie explained, "Our car broke down on the outskirts of Dublin and we found ourselves surrounded by kids who were smacked out of their heads. They were between the ages of about eight and 12. One of them, who was about nine, asked if we wanted to buy some smack. I can count the times in my life that I've been shocked but that really shocked me. I know lots of people who are, or have been, into heroin – but they're older people. You read about kids like that in the papers but it doesn't have much effect until you see it. When I was those kids' age, eight or nine, I was really intrigued with the world around me – but heroin just dulls you." The experience prompted her to write 'Don't Mess With Doctor Dream' which, sprinkled with Nile Rogers' production magic, gave them another hit.

Joe Elliott concluded our chat with a robust defence of Ireland's new super-rich English colony, saying, "I'm aware that we hold a privileged position here, and that because we're English we might arouse an amount of resentment from people who say 'they're only here using us'. But in return we're putting a fair amount into the Irish economy that we'd otherwise be spending somewhere else."

They did put a fair amount into the economy and competition for their stellar custom forced the local restaurateurs, hoteliers, nightclub owners and recording studios to raise the bar of what Dublin in particular had to offer.

But Ireland's colony of rock stars did more than that. They set the scene. They spread the word. They got buy-in from planet pop. They helped turn Dublin from a dreary backwater into a hip and happening capital city worthy of being called a capital city, and they did it before U2 turned all eyes on us with their 1987 masterpiece *The Joshua Tree*.

Chapter 10

FABLES OF THE RECONSTRUCTION: CENSORSHIP & THE CONDOM WARS

"Shatter! Shatter! Shatter! You're the fella that's going around shoving condoms down everyone's throats."

– Irate constituent to Fine Gael TD Alan Shatter, 1987

THE UNRULY spirit of *glasnost* sweeping Ireland's rising generation from the mid-80s brought with it a new sense of permissiveness, and the surge of a more permissive society presented a head scratching challenge for the traditional guardians of public morality, state-appointed and self-anointed. Time and again they got it wrong, and at times they could hardly be blamed, faced as they were with a bewildering new landscape of hitherto unavailable choices. For instance, by the time it was Dublin's turn to be European City Of Culture in 1991, the capital was the most cabled-up and satellite-dished place in Europe.

Commodified sex in Ireland was a lot like rock music – an underground entity that once had to be actively sought out had suddenly gone overground in open pursuit of a paying audience. The hunted had become the hunter. And the changed conditions produced a Cambrian Explosion of experimental forms, some of them bizarre. In a flash there was mud wrestling in the Midlands; a gauze-vested Dublin housewife with a feather boa and a tape machine who billed herself as Toni The Exotic Dancer; a lad from swinging London who went by the name of King Dick and a touring troupe of 'foxy boxing' women from England whose propensity for 'popping out' of their skimpy singlets drew big crowds across rural Ireland. Everyone was making it up as they went along, with cowboy promoters flinging anything and everything at a sexually awakening Irish public to see what would stick. In a disruption where no-one knew what was permissible any more, the gatekeepers more often than not erred on the side of caution, as in the case of the two-day wonder that was the affair of the lesbian nuns.

On a Thursday morning in September 1985, two lapsed Catholic sisters, Nancy Manahan and Rosemary Curb, confirmed in a radio interview that they would arrive the following day to plug their US bestseller *Breaking Silence: Lesbian Nuns On Convent Sexuality*. An appearance on the nation's flagship TV programme *The Late Late Show* was in prospect, although the producers had a policy of keeping its guest list top secret until transmission time. Horrified protesters jammed the switch of the national broadcaster, just in case.

On the face of it, this was all very odd. *The Late Late Show* had always been a safe house for gay celebrities and a few years earlier Gay Byrne had conducted a wide-ranging interview with an enthusiastic lesbian without so much as a *hurrumph* from the viewing public. But these were changed times. Here, at the mid-point of the '80s, the rancour of the divisive 1983 abortion referendum still lingered, while the battle lines were being drawn for a poll on divorce bearing down hard. A state of uncivil war was ratcheting up between Ireland's modernisers and traditionalists. And besides, lesbians were one thing, but lesbian *nuns*... Was nothing sacred?

Within two hours of the radio interview, Dublin customs seized 1,500 copies of the offending book from storage, even though it was not on the State's lengthy banned list. Unfortunately for the quick-acting officials, 3,000 more copies were already on full-frontal display in bookshops around the country in readiness for the ex-nuns' promotional visit. When the book's hasty seizure led the lunchtime news, customs hurried out an embarrassed announcement pinning the raid on an unidentified lone zealot. The impounded tomes were released from captivity, having now been "cleared by reference to a higher authority".

Upon their arrival in Dublin the next day, Friday the 13th, the nuns ran straight into another piece of jittery self-censorship. A press conference was arranged for 3.00pm that afternoon at a top city centre hotel. However, upon arrival there, the two women were told the room they'd booked was unavailable. No reason was given, it just wasn't. The ex-sisters, a gaggle of hacks, and half of Dublin's gay community were summarily dispatched to the sidewalk. There they loitered for some time. There was nowhere to go because it was the middle of Holy Hour, when the pubs shut from 2.30pm to 3.30pm to ensure indolent workers went back to the workplace after lunch. The Pink Elephant bar provided a makeshift press centre when opening time resumed at 3.30pm. Robbie Fox, proprietor of the Pink, recalled, "I can't remember who the organiser was, but it was some journalist who rang me and asked if we could do it at short notice. I said fucking sure."

At this juncture the action shifted across the Liffey to the High Court where Thomas O'Mahony, a solicitor and director of the previously unheard-of Christian Community Centre, was seeking an injunction to keep the former sisters off that night's airwaves. O'Mahony argued that if the *Late Late* appearance was allowed to go ahead, "it would greatly undermine Christian moral values in Irish society". Furthermore, he claimed, "The respect of the general public for nuns would be greatly undermined."

Justice Barr was having none of it. He couldn't even ascertain for certain that RTÉ were going to interview the renegade sisters that night. The case for a court ban was too little too late. The judge went on, "RTÉ have in the past interviewed leading homosexuals, giving them the opportunity to express their views and explain their..."

"Moral depravity, m'lud," interrupted O'Mahony.

Thomas O'Mahony was not finished. Hotfoot from his failed High Court challenge, he arrived outside the RTÉ studios at Montrose where the station's top brass had green-lighted the appearance, releasing a terse statement saying they were "satisfied that it will be presented in a responsible manner". In the hours before the show's 9.30pm start, O'Mahony, in the words of the *Irish Press*, "led the crowd outside the studio in reciting decades of the Rosary and in hymn singing".

The pocket-sized multitude in question consisted of the singing solicitor, a Fianna Fáil TD Michael Barrett, 80 civilians, several bullhorns and one portable Virgin Mary. Leaflets issued by Christian Community Action said the purpose of the high-decibel vigil was to persuade the national broadcaster "to desist from offending the Christian moral values of the Irish people by glamorising the heinous sins of Sodom and Gomorrah". One protester, Mrs Elizabeth O'Hanlon, who described herself as "a concerned mother of three", was worried that the item might put young girls off vocations. As protest callers swamped the RTÉ switchboard, several suggested that if *Late Late* host Gay

Byrne went through with this heresy, he might want to consider a new career in the United States.

The lesbian nuns show did go on and it was televised purgatory, a five way discussion radiating sleep-inducing sweetness and light, and lacking anything the protesters could mark down as lewd perversion, or the casual viewer could take as redeeming raciness. Leaving the studio under police escort, Gaybo revealed that since the prospect emerged that he'd be hosting the lesbian nuns on his chat show, "there have been several threats on my life, on my children, on my wife and on my home".

The next morning brought a predictable slew of 'Gay And Lesbians' front page headlines. By Monday, normal service had been resumed. "'No Moving Statues,' Says Bishop", trumpeted the *Irish Press*. It was the start of another routine week in inter-referenda Ireland.

Five months later, on the day before Valentine's Day 1986, the Censorship Of Publications Board banned Dr Alex Comfort's bestselling manual *The Joy Of Sex*. It was actually a re-banning. It had been originally outlawed in 1974 but the 12 year prohibition had lapsed. The renewal came as a big surprise to the Irish Family Planning Association who, unaware that it had been banned in the first place, had sold over 1,000 copies.

Pressed as to why the Censorship Board had renewed the ban, its Chairman, Judge Diarmuid Sheridan, insisted it was necessary to "protect adolescents". He said, "You put this book on an ordinary bookshelf. Imagine the effect it would have on a 13-year-old." He explained that if any citizen wanted to import a copy for personal use they could apply to the Minister for Justice. The sale and supply were banned, but not possession, and doctors could legally acquire copies on licence.

A few months after that, the same need to protect adolescents, specifically adolescent girls, was trotted out by RTÉ bosses as a painfully lame excuse for preventing one young woman from telling her compelling story. It was late 1986 and Mandy Smith was big news. The stunning 16-year-old had turned down the BBC's top-rated *Wogan* show and flown instead to Dublin to make her first ever TV appearance. Her screen debut was to take place on *Saturday Live*, hosted by Ireland's lady who lunched, Noelle Campbell-Sharp.

In the event, Smith ended up watching the show cooped up in her Gresham Hotel suite, surrounded by her hopping-mad entourage. The teenager hadn't come to corrupt schoolgirls or subvert the state or promote Devil worship. The cute party piece she'd prepared for the telly was to count to 10 in the first national language – Aon, dó, trí... – just like she'd learnt at the knee of her Irish granny.

Mandy Smith's personal life had exploded across the planet's front pages just a few weeks earlier with the revelation that she'd been seduced by parchment-faced Bill Wyman of the Rolling Stones. At the time the furtive love affair began she was a 13-year-old schoolgirl, while he was a tearaway 47-year-old grandfather. Some wealthy men move their mistress into a swisher class of apartment – Wyman installed Mandy into a snootier class of school. When the news broke, Wyman made a quick break for France while Britain's Serious Crime Squad quizzed Mandy and her Cabra-born mother Pat. As things stood, no charges could be brought against the wrinkly Lothario unless a complaint was filed, and three months on none had.

Noelle Campbell-Sharp had gone to a lot of trouble and personal expense to secure the most sought after chat show guest in the western hemisphere. Mandy and her minders had been jetted in, limoed about and given the five-star treatment at the Gresham. Everything was fine until a phone call came from RTÉ saying that Mandy was to be in her seat by 9.00pm.

Her Dublin-born manager Maurice Boland didn't understand. Why did they want her seated a full 30 minutes before the show was due to go out live? The voice at the other end explained that Mandy had been bounced from star turn to a seat-filler in the audience.

Boland explained forcefully down the phone who Mandy Smith was. "She's the third most famous woman in Britain," he thundered, pausing to let his words sink in. Something came back from the other end. Through clenched teeth he growled, "The Queen and Princess Diana."

Boland phoned the producer of *Saturday Live*, who told him bluntly that if he didn't like the new arrangement, he and Mandy could take the evening off. Shortly afterwards, RTÉ issued an official press release stating that Mandy Smith was "not important enough" to guest on the show.

Seething, indignant and bent on getting even, Boland took his troupe off to the Suesey Street nightclub on Leeson Street. They found the place strangely empty. It turned out that, forewarned of Mandy's imminent arrival, the bouncers had been extra rigorous in their application of the already strict door policy. They did, however, have express orders that one VIP was to be granted immediate entry. He was Fleet Street's premier stringer in Ireland, Tom McPhail.

And so it was that by Monday morning the British tabloids were having a great laugh at the expense of the prudish, backward, priest-ridden Irish. Campbell-Sharp's response was a let-down to those who expected her to rage hard against the moral cowardice of the show's producers. She said, "RTÉ got cold feet at the last minute. The production team decided against her. They felt she should not give a bad example to young teenage girls. And I had to agree that by having her on the panel we would perhaps be giving her some kind of support."

RTÉ Controller of Television, Joe Mulholland, cited, "a certain nervousness" about giving Mandy's life choices the oxygen of publicity. "We did not want to go into detail," he submitted, insisting that *Saturday Live* was "supposed to be a family show" even though it occupied a slot safely past the watershed.

The *Saturday Live* Lolita-gagging botch job petered out in an unseemly spillage of sour recriminations and disputed expense tabs. In 1994, Mandy Smith was back in Dublin to appear on Pat Kenny's *Kenny Live* which occupied the same slot as *Saturday Live* which had shunned her in that different country of the recent past. The first time around she was 16 going on 26. Now she was 23 going on 33, her vivacious girlish beauty given way to a cosmetically enhanced frailty. Her even Permatan and flawless skin couldn't mask a sad gauntness. She was still beautiful, but in a careworn fragile way.

I asked for her memories of that visit eight years earlier when she'd been shunted aside as a moral threat to Ireland's young girls. She recalled little, largely because she hadn't even gotten within three miles of the studio. Besides, as an anecdote, the "bad example" banning episode which would have been trotted out countless times by anyone living an ordinary life, wouldn't have made Mandy's Top 500. Since her *Saturday Live* non-appearance she'd launched a modelling career, had a hit record, developed anorexia, become a recluse, married Bill Wyman, split up from Bill Wyman, launched a TV presenting career and married the Tottenham Hotspur footballer Pat Van Den Hauwe. And as if all that wasn't enough to occupy her, her Irish mother was currently on a headlong course to marry Bill Wyman's son Stephen, 30 years her junior.

Initially "distraught" at that prospect, she now saw the funny side.

"If they get married, Bill will be my grandad," she pointed out delightedly. "Won't he hate me? Won't he *hate* me! I'll have the last laugh."

Patsy and Stephen did marry shortly afterwards. It lasted two years, roughly the same as Mandy and Bill's wedded union.

Smith dropped out of view for a few years in the '90s, but she hadn't been forgotten by Louis Walsh, who was looking for a pretend girlfriend for gay Boyzone star Stephen Gately. After the break-up of Boyzone, the top pop svengali boasted of how he'd "married" Mandy to Stephen.

That sham "marriage" lasted even less time than either of her two real ones.

Smith's run-in with RTÉ self-censorship in 1986 provided some comic relief during a long, hot silly season lasting years, when the nation's moral watchdogs went actively hunting for new things at which they could take outraged offence. After some years of relative neglect, condoms were thrust back into the spotlight.

In the summer of 1978, four months after rebranding themselves from The Hype to U2, the four young northsiders played their first ever benefit gig. The event at Dublin's Liberty Hall, organised by the Contraception Action Campaign, was to protest against the Republic's blanket ban on the sale or supply of condoms and contraceptives of any sort. U2 raced through their short set against a backdrop of roughly drawn cardboard banners with slogans saying down with this sort of thing. The political classes took no action to liberalise the laws while at the same time making no move against the growing number of family planning centres and market-stall spivs catering for a growing public demand.

For hardcore zealots, a looming AIDS pandemic was both a punishment from God and a Heaven-sent gift because it pushed sin and sinners back front and centre – and these zealots still had the clout to put the fear of God into Ireland's elected representatives. At the start of 1985 – with AIDS now sitting terrifyingly at the top of the public health agenda – Garret FitzGerald's Fine Gael/Labour government squeezed through a cautious law allowing the sale of condoms without a prescription to over-18s, but only by pharmacists. An English Labour MP, Joe Ashton, did nothing to heal Anglo-Irish relations which were close to breaking point when he taunted, "Remember, all you untrained Irish lads, the tin foil is not to be used in an emergency. It is only there to keep the product from perishing." Pledged to the principle of opposition for the sake of opposition, the Fianna Fáil party fought the new law tooth and nail. It was still a crime to advertise condoms.

The criminalisation of the condom had been high on the public morality agenda since the foundation of the Free State and once the most pressing issues of winning a vicious Civil War and establishing law and order had been resolved, the puritan government turned its attention to the twin social evils of drink and sex. New restrictive alcohol laws were imposed and widely observed in the breach. A blanket ban on all 'artificial' contraception met with far greater success, mainly because few Catholics had the faintest idea of what it was. In fact, so successful was the purge that even the mere mention of contraception quickly vanished from public discourse.

Looking back on the middle decades of the 20th Century, the comic novelist Mervyn Wall recalled, "The two words 'birth control' never appeared in any newspaper. It was thought indecent even by the editor of a newspaper to mention those two words." One of the final references before editors began heavily self-censoring was a Fianna Fáil deputy's condemnation of 'birth control houses', by which he meant the small family homes being built in the new suburbs to rehouse families being evacuated from the filthy, crumbling, overcrowded tenement blocks. The objection against these small, clean, modern units was that their lack of space for raising large broods of children forced parents into practising unnatural family planning methods. The self-imposed ban on the terms 'birth control', 'contraception' and 'condoms' remained very much the rule until members of the Women's Liberation Movement travelled to Belfast in 1971 and returned on the so-called Contraception Train, waving condoms blown up as balloons and daring the virtually all-male customs and police to confiscate their contraband.

The civil war over condoms raged throughout the 1970s, with Taoiseach Liam Cosgrave notoriously crossing the floor of the Dáil in 1974 to vote down his own government's Bill to legalise them. Defending his boss, Justice Minister Patrick Cooney told the House that buying condoms "implies a right to fornicate and in my opinion there is no such natural right". *Hibernia* magazine speculated that Woody Allen's 1972 comedy *All You Ever Wanted To Know About Sex (But Were Afraid To Ask)* had been banned outright for a short sketch featuring a couple unable to make love because both were sheathed in giant full-body condoms. The writer suggested that Church and State should surely have applauded the scene of foiled fornication.

In 1979, then Health Minister Charles Haughey pushed through his 'Irish solution to an Irish problem', allowing married couples to purchase condoms with a doctor's prescription, and then only for "*bona fide* family planning purposes", whatever that meant. Haughey insisted "this legislation opens no floodgates", which was true, although there was a trickle available to those who knew where to look. At the time of his Act, condoms were available from a tiny number of defiant family planning centres, under the counter at hippie markets like the one at

Dublin's Dandelion Green, and from a dispensing machine at University College Dublin.

By the start of 1987 there was an uneasy political consensus that a government public information campaign on AIDS prevention could no longer be avoided. One was drawn up with an advertising agency, then withdrawn because it needed to be "redesigned", then delayed for months as a general election had been called and the Fine Gael/Labour government feared the wrath of a conservative electorate. It was then watered down by the incoming Fianna Fáil government and finally given a launch with a *Late Late Show* special, entrusted to the country's safest pair of hands, Gay Byrne. From the start of the process to the end, the headline message remained the same, and it was one of total abstinence. The government's slogan was: 'Casual Sex Spreads AIDS'. Offering their advice while the campaign was still on the drawing board, the Catholic Bishops cautioned, "There is a grave danger that the promotion of condoms will give further encouragement to permissiveness and this in itself would contribute to a further spread of the disease."

By the time of the 1991 local elections, the hysteria surrounding AIDS had receded, but a generation of young adults grown immeasurably more assertive were now demanding unfettered access to condoms as a right. The most extraordinary contribution to the long-running condom debate of those years was provided by a previously unknown body called the Children's Protection Society, who allied themselves to a new party contesting the elections called the Christian Principles Party. "Compiled with eminent medical assistance", a pamphlet entitled '67 Reasons Why Condoms Spread AIDS' was distributed to every Dáil deputy and senator by the Children's Protection Society. One of the 67 reasons, given without any further explanation or supporting evidence, was, "The more condoms are sold against AIDS, the more AIDS is transmitted." Another of the 67 reasons was that, because not a single trader in the County Monaghan town of Carrickmacross sold condoms, the surrounding districts had "either Europe's lowest, or the world's lowest, AIDS rate, depending on sources".

Again, without bothering to provide any sources, the pamphlet concluded, "In a debate, the condom lobby would lose." Sadly for the Christian Principles Party, it was they who were the losers when the electorate had their say.

That same year, 1991, the hipster tycoon Richard Branson flew into Ireland for a court appearance after Gardaí raided his Virgin Megastore on Dublin's quays, seizing condoms being sold over the counter without a pharmacist in attendance. A sales assistant had been entrapped by a plain clothes detective posing as a sexually active young adult. The global publicity generated by Branson's personal appearance exposed Ireland's authorities to international ridicule and forced a rethink and, in 1992, the prohibition was relaxed to allow the sale of condoms over the counter to over-17s. However, vending machines were still outlawed.

After the law was relaxed *In Dublin* magazine sent out a reporter in search of condom machines in the toilets of city centre pubs and clubs. Only one could be found, which had proved a popular crowd-puller for some considerable time. The day after the magazine appeared, the venue was raided by police and the machine ripped off the wall. By 1994 condoms were on open sale in chemists, pubs and other outlets, but the publishers of the 01 Area Telephone Directory for the capital refused to list a phone number for the Condom Power contraceptives store in Temple Bar. Instead, the national phone company Telecom Éireann offered to list the store under the name Power Health Products, but the owners declined.

If any single device can be credited with bringing the walls of state control and censorship crashing down from the inside, it was the VCR, the video cassette recorder. The VCR brought about a revolution and its impact on Fortress Ireland was more subversive than just about anywhere else. Every place it went it was revolutionary in that it transformed viewing habits unchanged since the birth of TV. Prior to its arrival, all viewing was strictly in real time. If you wanted to watch the football or catch that soap cliffhanger, you had to be perched in front of your TV as it happened. Miss it and it was gone forever from a world where broadcasters and viewers alike believed that screening repeats was short-changing the public. Conferring the ability to record programmes in your absence and watch at your leisure, the VCR was a magical game-changer.

In some ways, the VCR was a foretaste of the internet to come. Suddenly, the consumer had a sprawling choice of content far beyond that provided by the information gatekeepers. For great swathes of Ireland, that sole content gatekeeper was the state broadcaster Teilifís Éireann, which had only added a second channel in 1978.

It could be argued that the VCR had a greater shock effect on Ireland than the internet as it brought the walls crashing down on an insulated, cosseted society in one great tumult, paving the way for racy satellite TV and uncensored web surfing. Thanks to the snail's pace roll-out of broadband, it took the internet 15 years to achieve anything close to full coverage in Ireland. VCR achieved 100% penetration in the blink of an eye. From Malin Head to Mizen Head the land was dotted with video stores before you could say "didn't that used to be a drapery?"

Another shared feature of VCR and the internet is that the lightning take-up of both had much to do with pornography, bypassing the age-old barriers purpose-built to meet the threat outlined by the Council of Irish Bishops in 1927. They had warned, "The Evil One is ever setting his snares for unwary feet. At this moment his traps are chiefly the dance hall, the bad book, the indecent paper, the motion picture, the immodest fashion in female dress – all of which tend to destroy the virtuous characteristics of our race."

And so it remained into the 1980s, with the Nanny State taking a firm hand in protecting the Irish people from themselves. While Dustin Hoffman and Anne Bancroft were picking up their Best Actor Oscars for *The Graduate* at Hollywood's 1968 gong gala, Irish cinema audiences were watching a version in which the seduction scene between the older married woman and the much younger man – the pivotal point on which the whole movie hinges – was ripped out to protect public morals. The '80s began with Irish cinemagoers denied sight of Monty Python's *Life Of Brian*, routinely voted the greatest screen comedy of all time. It had been banned upon its release in the summer of 1979 by censor Frank Hall who continued a system under which, of 50,000 films submitted for vetting between 1923 and 1970, 13,500 had been severely cut or banned outright. Most films were never submitted on the grounds that they stood no chance of getting past the censor.

This was the Ireland into which the VCR arrived, followed by a culture shock the likes of which the country had never seen. The big family-friendly chains like Xtra-vision and Blockbuster made staying-in the new going out for kids' birthdays and cheap dates, but that was the Disney version of a grittier reality. For every Xtra-vision there were a million grubby rental stores or newsagents with screened-off racks, supplying hardcore material that skyrocketed national levels of exposure to sex and violence from zero to a zillion with no soft middle ground. The '80s saw a growth in some urban enclaves of male-only Sunday morning pub 'stags', featuring scantily clad women gyrating to burlesque ditties. By the standards that were to overtake them, these rituals were a bit of innocent fun. The VCR pressed fast forward on Ireland's exposure to sex as much harder versions of the Sunday morning stag spread like wildfire. Out went the titillating cabaret of 'Hey Big Spender' and in came XXX hardcore, drawing a lot more salivating punters for the small spend to the publican of a five quid tape rental.

While the police and customs officials played a fraught game of piggy-in-the-middle, trying to second guess the shifting views of their political masters, the politicians themselves seemed frozen in the headlights of this juggernaut steamrolling across the land, partly because censorship had always taken care of itself, and partly because something was going on with their voters that they didn't understand and therefore required a lot of determined fence-sitting. The electorate were acting out of all previous character, so what was the shrewd political thing to do – something or nothing?

In the end, it took a storm of moral outrage blowing from Britain to get Ireland's rulers moving against the scourge of the 'video nasty'. Except the target here was not the pandemic of hardcore sex but the relatively tiny virus of ultra-violence as in the schlock horror of exhibit-A, *Driller Killer*. It seemed that in the mid-80s Ireland's political class were largely unwilling, or simply too embarrassed, to acknowledge that hardcore sex was the overwhelming market force at play. The evidence of 120 parliamentary debates on video nasties demonstrates conclusively that the politicians mostly didn't know what they were talking about. Two members of the Dáil demanded measures to "ensure that video nasties are never made in Ireland", seemingly unaware that the chances of this ever happening were almost certainly less than zero. Government TDs called on anyone who knew of anyone supplying video nasties to inform the local Gardaí, which would have shut down hundreds of hand-to-mouth shopkeepers in already crippled small town economies. Holly Johnson of Frankie Goes To Hollywood revealed to me that, during their tax exile year domiciled in stately Borris House, band members had a discrete delivery arrangement for hardcore videos with a rental store in nearby Kilkenny. Meanwhile, up in Dublin, one senator was whipping up public fears, without a shred of evidence, that exposure to video nasties was whetting appetites everywhere for "the so-called snuff movies".

A government committee on Crime, Lawlessness and Vandalism foisted much of the blame for all three blights in its remit on the video nasty. An RTÉ *Today Tonight* television special ratcheted up the hysteria, raising the unsupported prospect that children as young as six were being turned into future killers. At the same time rumours were doing the rounds that RTÉ itself was a major source of the porn craze. A production engineer was said to be running the station's tape duplication equipment at full pelt while he put in payment claims for out-of-hours work shifts. Irish troops returning from peace keeping duties in Lebanon were fingered as major importers of pirate tapes. Public figures were pressed to comment, with the playwright John B Keane memorably declaring, "I don't think the pornographic video is suitable for teenagers."

Precisely when the video nasty storm blew itself out, nobody clearly remembers, and by the time a four decade ban on *Playboy* was ended in 1995, nobody really gave a toss. The Ireland of 1995 was a very different country from the place of just 10 years earlier, even if *The Life Of Brian* stayed on the banned list. Appointed as the State's Film Censor in 1986, Sheamus Smith had a far greater understanding than the legislators that old models of censorship were no longer fit for purpose or even appropriate in a fast-changing world. During his 17 years in the post, Smith banned only 10 films and refused to cut any, arguing that it was the director's job to make cuts, not the censor's. Smith made it his task to classify films, not ban them, although the custom remained that the censor didn't have to give any reasons for decisions.

Smith's successor was John Kelleher, former Head of Television programmes at RTÉ, a successful independent filmmaker and a partner in the Windmill Lane consortium that established the national station TV3. Kelleher struck out the term Censorship and rebranded his operation as the Irish Film Classification Office. Crediting his predecessor Sheamus Smith with making a decisive break with outdated ways, he said, "It was my thing that in a mature society adults should be allowed to choose to view, or experience – subject to the law – anything that they want. So there shouldn't be someone saying you can't see this. What you do is you say, if you're under 15 or if you're under 12, you can't see this. So age-related classification was my thing and I introduced a new age rating, got a website going and gave consumer advice to parents. I also realised that it was no longer acceptable to make decisions on films without explaining the rationale, so the website served that purpose too. So that was what the role of film censor became. Like, this has got some horrifying scenes and your little girl Molly might be very scared. We commissioned a lot of market research and it was really gratifying to see that parents really welcomed this. Like can Johnny go to see this on his own, or if I take him will he be alright?

"So you handed responsibility over to the parents to decide on what their kids should be able to see, but as far as adults were concerned... I let in a film called *9 Songs* and I was quite proud that I okayed it. It was *really* explicit. It was just sex and rock ‘n’ roll. This couple were riding the arse off each other and they were going to concerts – it was one or the other for the whole film. But it was very well done. Michael Winterbottom was the director. It got a lot of controversy, but this came from the Legion of the Rearguard, the League of Decency, some group about the protection of the family and so on. So I went on the *Late Late Show* with Pat Kenny and this guy was seated in the audience and I was saying the things I’m saying now. It was embarrassing. He stood up to make his speech and he said *9 Songs* was disgusting and obscene, and Pat Kenny asked, ‘Have you seen it?’

‘No.’

“And seated right in front of him as he stood up to make his speech there were two young women who must have been in their early twenties and the look on their faces just said it all. They were modern Ireland and he was a relic of the past.”

Chapter 11

IN THE PINK – NUMBER ONE CLUB IN EUROPE

"It was all about nightlife. The place that we all remember was the Pink Elephant. We were doing a tax year, but at the same time we used to go to the Pink Elephant with Def Leppard and U2, so there was quite a little community and it was a good time."

– Spandau Ballet's Martin Kemp

An interview in the Bailey pub with Pink Elephant manager and gatekeeper Robbie Fox.

RF: We're sitting in the Bailey now and the Bailey was a big part of what I used to do. I used to go to pubs that I saw as feeder pubs to my club. The Pink kinda happened right here in the Bailey. When I went into the Pink first in 1980 it was a restaurant owned by Paddy Belton, who was Lord Mayor of Dublin at the time. The restaurant was called The Stables after the bar which was called Hunters. There were pictures of horses and hounds covering the walls. Paddy actually fitted out the restaurant with real stables, so you had big round antique tables in a stable stall. It was very upmarket, way ahead of its time for Dublin, even though it only lasted a year.

I was only 22 and Paddy Belton was an old man but very clued in. He took me under his wing and said, "What would *you* do?". Dublin at the time had just got into what were called fun bars, or disco bars. The first one, Rainbow, had opened off George's Street. I told Paddy that this would be a good idea, so we opened the Pink as a disco bar. It still operated normal pub licensing laws which meant it closed at 11.30, but we had a DJ and the first three we had were Tony Fenton, Tony Dixon and Henry Owens. They're all passed away now.

Belton also had the Central Hotel off Dame Street and being a politician, and being very shrewd, he realised that the Pink could sell drink an hour later if he had a restaurant licence – and he had just that because the place had been The Stables. So, The Pink became the first disco bar to serve alcohol until 12.30.

Up to that the only place you could get a drink after 11.30 closing time was Leeson Street.

In the '70s the clubs on Leeson Street charged jaw-dropping prices for paint-stripper wine with beer and spirits off the menu, officially anyway. The strip was the only place in town to party until dawn, to the point that there were ugly turf wars over lucrative burger stall pitches on the Leeson Street sidewalks.

RF: Every club on Leeson Street was a restaurant so they could serve wine until 12.30 provided it came with a meal. But over the years they pushed the serving hours back to three, four, five o'clock in the morning and then they stopped even doing food because no-one wanted it, so they became restaurants with no food. The Leeson Street clubs were all illegal, but we were legal when we opened, serving the extra hour after pub closing.

Move on another year or so, and delving into the legal situation Belton realised that we could get exemptions. Now exemptions at the time were only used for weddings and other formal functions, but it turned out there was no limit to the amount of exemptions you could get. When the Pink started up it was as a restaurant with a dance floor and every Friday and Saturday we'd get exemptions so that you could go to 2.30am – so for legal purposes every Friday and Saturday was a dinner dance.

At this point an Egyptian guy called George Sabongi came in as restaurant manager while I was general manager of the building. The Pink was a young people's restaurant, but it was still a restaurant, so I came up with the idea we should apply for exemptions every night of the week and the Pink became a nightclub. Belton was still the owner at this stage but political clout didn't come into it. He just used the laws that were there in ways that no-one else had actually thought about before.

Hotels in towns all around the country were doing the same thing but for some reason everyone thought that the law on exemptions only applied to hotels, but it didn't. It applied to anywhere that had a bar licence and a restaurant. Most pubs didn't do any food apart maybe from a sandwich and it wasn't worth their while installing a fully functioning kitchen for the few extra hours of late trading, and to be fair, most pubs had their money made by midnight when they could lock up and go home. Hence the uniqueness of the Pink Elephant.

The Pink became not just the most exclusive club in Ireland, but by the mid-80s was one of the most celebrated celebrity magnets in Europe. Was there a masterplan at play with a door policy that verged on cruel and unusual punishment?

RF: This was where I came in. The top floor back then was what was called a grill. The ground floor was a really good pub, and downstairs was the restaurant that became younger, got in DJs and became the Pink Elephant. We put a couple of pool tables into the top floor and it became an extension of the basement club. The question for me now was how do we attract a certain type of people – the right type of people?

We were lucky in that the ground floor bar had become a big hangout for Trinity College students, and Trinity at the time still had its reputation for being very elitist. The types of people going to Trinity were predominantly wealthy, or certainly from the right side of the tracks – let's put it that way. I befriended quite a lot of them and I came to realise that there was a whole section of people out there with lots of money to spend.

The Pink Elephant was quite small so I said okay – I don't particularly even now like the term 'exclusive' but I did target a certain type of people, people with money. Simple. I'm a businessman so I targeted people who would spend money. But by the nature of the job, and my own work ethic, I insisted on staying at the door and picking and choosing the sort of people I wanted in my club. And it wasn't all about whether they were going to spend, it was about whether they were 'cool' enough. I then began to look for certain people in a certain community in the city, and it was a much smaller city at the time.

So I'd come in here to the Bailey all the time and the Bailey was full of rock and rollers, including Phil Lynott. And if not here I'm in Davy Byrne's across the road and a few other places. I would make sure I was in those places, getting to know those people, rubbing shoulders with them and inviting them back to my club. And if it was, say, Phil Lynott, I'd have a private table ready for him. And that grew to the point where there would be four or five tables waiting for people to arrive. Let's hold a table for Phillo. Let's hold a table for Bono. And it wasn't all rock and rollers. It was across the line. So you could walk into the Pink and there'd be a fairly well-known politician here, and a business person there.

One very regular customer when he was an up-and-coming politician was (future Taoiseach) Enda Kenny, while one of my best customers from the world of business was Richard Murphy who founded the Xtra-vision chain of video rental stores (and was lionised as The Bionic Man Of Irish Finance in the business pages). And sitting in the corner would be Bono. So, the Pink Elephant very quickly became the number one club in the city. And the press obviously wanted to be part of that and by then, as the guy on the door, I was becoming the guy to know to get in the door. To get in you needed to get the nod from Robbie, which in one way was great but on the downside it meant that I had to be on the door every night of the week.

Then I started to study – I can't think of any other word than *study* – the social scene in Dublin, like who is who? I needed to know that that's yer man from the paper, that's the one from *blah blah blah*. Then there was the whole glamour element, the models, the people from the fashion scene that complete the picture. So now the Pink Elephant becomes a hub for the rockers, the businesspeople, the politicians, the models, all the cool people in the city. Move forward a couple of years and you have this scenario in England where all these rock and roll stars have big tax problems but if they can get out of the country for X amount of days those problems are solved.

The rules said that the tax exiles were supposed to stay out of the UK for a year, but several confirmed to me that a great attraction of Ireland was its light touch regulation and its Common Travel Area with Britain which allowed them to come and go at will and unremarked.

RF: I had them all here, Def Leppard, Spandau Ballet, Frankie Goes To Hollywood, Thompson Twins, Simple Minds, so many of them … And that's how it started. Yes they could hop in and out undetected, but great credit to Dublin, the more time they spent here the more they liked it here.

Take Def Leppard for example. They all loved Dublin so much that they all bought homes here. They lived here, they married here. I heard Tony Hadley from Spandau Ballet interviewed when they did a show here recently and the only thing he could talk about was Dublin and the Pink Elephant. All of the Spandau guys really took to Dublin and Dublin really took them under its wing. That all started around '84-'85 and it went on for four or five years when there was a spotlight on Dublin. Every magazine in the world was writing about Dublin. *The New Yorker* did a feature on how cool Dublin was and how it had become like New York, and they compared the Pink Elephant to Studio 54 which was the hippest club on the planet. Oh my God, my world was made!

Things got even better in 1987 when U2 released *The Joshua Tree* and it went to number one around the world. That increased the spotlight on U2 and on Dublin. I got a phone call from the stage in Basil, Switzerland, as they were walking off at the end of a show and they said, "Robbie, if we make it back to Dublin soon will you still be open?" I said, "I don't care how long you take, the answer is yes."

The journalist Lise Hand of the *Sunday Tribune* was there – Lise was a great customer – and I had an unwritten rule with journalists which was you don't write about what happens in the club or else you're not coming back anymore. I wanted the media in there as clients, not on duty. So it was okay to write that such and such a star was in the club, but not what that star was doing. It was a quiet Monday or Tuesday night when I got that call from Switzerland and Lise was leaving but I said don't go. An hour later two or three limos pulled up outside and all the boys got out and they were on a high after the show and I was so delighted, but they were even more delighted that I'd kept open for them. Lise got her story and it went *whoosh* all around the world. The club just went through the roof.

By the time David Bowie arrived in the Pink straight from his Slane show in 1987 the club had changed hands. Paddy Belton had died and Louis Murray had bought it from the Beltons. I was now a partner there because part of the deal when he bought it was that I would stay on with a one-third share in the business. The third share was Louis Murray's late business partner who was a nice guy but a bit of a socialite – he always wanted to be at the centre of the scene. He enjoyed the club and he liked to sit there at his VIP table with his bottle of champagne.

The thing was the club only had four private VIP tables and he was sitting at one of them and the place was packed when one of the doormen comes up to me and says Bono's here. I had a good relationship with Bono so no panic. I knew I could stall him, have a chat with him while someone's getting him a table. But the doorman hadn't said Bono, he'd said Bowie, and here I am staring at David Bowie getting out of his limo and there's no table for him. Now I panicked. I told someone to get downstairs and just get him a table.

Bowie had this minder who was straight out of Vietnam. He was dressed in khaki and he was nuts. He was watching everything and he was ready to pounce.

I had to tell the minder to calm down, don't worry, it's not that sort of club, he's safe here. So I get down the stairs with Bowie right behind me and there's my partner taking up one of the private tables with his usual bottle of champagne. I walked straight up to him and said, "Get the fuck off the table now!"

"What!?"

"Get the fuck off the table!"

I grabbed the bottle of champagne and handed it to a waitress and he moved. I put Bowie and his minder and whoever else at the table, but the minder was still on high alert.

"Get rid of them. Get rid of them. Get rid of them," he ordered me, nodding to a the occupants of nearby tables.

"Would you fuckin' relax. Do you want me to move them?"

"Yeah."

"No. Because that's Spandau Ballet. Fuck off, it's not happening."

Eventually he calmed down.

Another night around the same time, I arrived in on a really quiet Tuesday night to be told that Bono was in with a friend, so I went over to say hello and Bono was around the back, hush-hush having a pow-wow with Mick Jagger. Jagger had flown in just for the night to discuss something with Bono and my place was the place to meet.

Jagger's Rolling Stones bandmate Ronnie Wood was king of the pool tables both in the Pink and your successor club, Renards, during his many years as a resident of Kildare.

RF: I had the Baton Rouge restaurant up on Stephen's Green and I did an exhibition for Ronnie there of his paintings. Ronnie's a great artist. He said how much do you want for putting on the exhibition and I said I didn't want payment but I wouldn't mind one of those. So he gave me two or three paintings and they're on my wall at home. Ronnie was a great character.

Did your stellar regulars ever pass comment that Dublin in the '80s really was a dirty auld town where the Liffey really did stink like hell?

RF: I don't remember Dublin being filthy, even though there's no doubt it was. If you grow up in Mumbai it's Mumbai, that's the way it is to you. Looking back on it now you might have that opinion, but remember Def Leppard came from Sheffield and I don't think Sheffield was any better than Dublin.

Joe Elliott from Sheffield certainly took to Dublin very quickly. Around 1986 myself and Karla (Rhamdani, who later married Joe) started this thing called Miss Fun Pub. Paddy Belton still owned the Pink and because of the success of the disco bar there he decided to put a disco bar into the 10 or so other pubs he owned in and around Dublin.

I'd worked in the Sheaf o'Wheat in Coolock and the Towers in Ballymun and I told him this is not going to work in Coolock or in Ballymun. I told him the security would be a nightmare, but he said, "Ah, we'll give it a go anyway." So in an attempt to put these places on the map myself and Karla came up with the idea of holding Miss Fun Pub beauty competitions in each one of them. It wasn't considered politically incorrect at the time.

So we'd bring out the DJs from the Pink, Tony Fenton, Tony Dixon, whoever, and there were so many celebrities hanging out at the club I'd ask them would they come as a guest judge. And they were great. The Frankies would come with me, the Spandaus would come with me, Def Leppard would come with me.

So you'd go to your local pub in Ballymun and there would be Robbie Fox and top model Karla Rhamdani and Joe Elliott of Def Leppard. That's how Joe and Karla got to know each other, judging those beauty competitions. We lost the Spandau drummer John Keeble after one in Killiney. I was supposed to deliver him back to the Pink, which was where we always finished the night, but he'd just disappeared. We eventually found him in the car park snogging some girl he'd just picked up.

We drove back into town. This was before late night shops so the only place you could buy anything late at night was in a petrol station. So John said, "Robbie stop, stop, stop, I need to get some stuff." So he goes into the garage and comes out with a full box of crisps and a big box of Twix bars. And as we drove back into town, every time we stopped at a lights he'd open the door and give people crisps and Twix bars!

Joe Elliott got himself into Irish society very quickly, as did Sav (the band's founder Rick Savage). The other band members were in and out to England more but Joe and Sav got relationships here, bought homes and settled. Spandau not so much. They remained English. They'd go back and forth and their home was always England.

Holly Johnson didn't mix with the party crowd. I think he was in the club once or twice. But the other members of Frankie Goes To Hollywood were bonkers. Nasher (Brian Nash) the guitarist was a nut job, crazy. Himself and the drummer were real party animals. Some of the celebrities were wild but I never had a problem with any misbehaviour. This might sound like arrogance but we had so many celebrities in the club that I treated them all the same as everyone else there.

Obviously you might get them a table above someone else, but after that there was no real special treatment. They paid their way, they paid their bills. And Dublin being Dublin, people didn't bother them. I remember one journalist saying to me that even though we were impressed with them, being Irish we felt the best way to deal with them was to turn our back on them and pretend we didn't see them even though we wanted to stand next to them.

That's what the Pink Elephant was all about. But not only that, once you got in the door it was a community and everyone who was in felt an equal part of that community. Everyone went to the same loo and everyone wore black because that was the cool thing, so I would look out over the club on a Monday night and not see a trace of colour. Monday night was like a Saturday night because it was off-duty night for rock 'n' roll. It was the only night that rockers didn't work. The club would be packed and everyone's wearing black. Fast-forward to the actual Saturday night and all the models and hairdressers get their night off and there's colours everywhere.

It was put about that a secret tunnel had been constructed directly linking the Pink Elephant and Windmill Lane Studios.

RF: There was a close relationship between Windmill and the Pink. The sound engineers and anyone that worked late at Windmill was a regular at the club because there was nowhere else open when they knocked off. The Spandau people worked there. The U2 people worked there and they were all regulars at the Pink. And then there were the bands themselves. I was in Windmill Lane right through the recording of one of U2's albums. U2 would ring me and ask if I could bring them down some late night beers. Same with Def Leppard. Same with lots of bands.

There was no tunnel, but the two places were well-connected.

Chapter 12

IRELAND ROCKS AGAINST RACISM: THE THEORY TEST OF APARTHEID

"There are times I've gone with chicks who've been insisting that I'm not black! Well baby, I'm certainly not white! There is no way I can go grooving around South Africa."

– Phil Lynott

TOWARDS THE close of the '70s Phil Lynott was giving an English rock journalist a tour of his hometown. Inevitably, they fetched up at the capital's hippest watering hole, The Bailey, just off Grafton Street. They arrived to find all eyes on Bob Geldof, Ireland's newly crowned King Rocker. The talk between Phil and his Boswell turned to matters of colour, specifically the almost complete absence of it in Ireland's sameness of pale faces.

It went beyond that, Phil told the visitor, explaining, "There are times I've gone with chicks who've been *insisting* that I'm *not* black! Well baby, I'm certainly *not* white! There is no way I can go grooving around South Africa."

The English visitor asked, "Are there many other black guys in the capital, Phil?"

After mulling for a moment, Phil replied, "Oh, there's a few... there's... *uhh*... Dave Murphy." He nodded across the bar at musician Dave Murphy, the only other person of colour in a room of hundreds.

That reality was echoed a few years later, when *The Irish Times* Washington correspondent told a story against himself.

During a taxi ride in New York, the writer fell into conversation with his cabbie, who inquired if there were many black people in Ireland.

"Sure," replied the passenger, "There's Phil Lynott, and Paul McGrath... Chris Houghton... and, erm, Kevin Sharkey..."

"That many, huh?" replied the driver.

In place of a relationship with people of colour that was up close and personal, for decades the Irish cultivated one that was well-meant but distant, mediated through the legions of Catholic missionary priests and nuns stationed in Africa, Asia and South America. For the vast majority of ordinary Irish people, it was made present by the black babies box, which could be found on the counter of every corner shop, every drapers, every greengrocers and every church porch. In fact it was just about everywhere. Throughout the middle decades of the 20th Century the slogan, 'A Penny For The Black Babies' was as much part of the lexicon as 'Put A Tiger In Your Tank' or 'Vote, Vote, Vote For De Valera'. It was as if the black babies were the foster children of the thousands of Catholic priests and nuns out on the Missions in Africa, and that the decent folk back home were their fairy godparents.

The swaddling of the black babies by Irish society began in the 1930s as a proud but penniless independent nation fastened on one of the very few good news stories it had to tell – that of its Catholic missionaries who'd been active in Africa since the 1880s. It was something warm and exotic and noble to feel a part of. By the 1950s Ireland was going black baby crazy. Black babies were popping up as clues in *The Irish Times* crossword, top designer Sybil Connolly was using Black Baby Ribbon in her costly creations, and the exclusive Switzer's department store was selling 'Black Baby Dolls' for 23s 6d each.

In a 1954 trial of a 14-year-old Dublin boy, a judge remarked that it was "a nice commentary" on the times when he heard from a witness that some proprietors now had to chain their black babies boxes to their counters. The judge asked the boy why he had stolen the box containing almost one pound. When the youth replied that he'd simply wanted the money, the judge bellowed, "*You wanted to rob the black babies!*" Two years later a pair of Wicklow men were sentenced to two and three years of hard labour for breaking into a school and stealing coins to the value of one pound. The severity of the jail terms was linked to the fact they'd desecrated a black babies box.

Showing kindness and concern for people of colour from a safe distance of thousands of miles was one thing. In closer proximity the relationship was much less happy-clappy. In the 1950s a civil service report on "incidents of immorality" amongst unchaperoned young Irish jobseekers swarming to the English midlands landed on the desk of Taoiseach Éamon De Valera. It noted disdainfully that, "An Irish girl living with a coloured man had a baby by him."

As the 1960s rolled on, a great wave of decolonisation swept Africa, and word filtered back to Ireland that maybe the black babies box was starting to look like a relic of old-fashioned paternalistic colonialism, however well-intentioned. Perhaps more hurtful were the new Leftie jibes that all those pennies in all those boxes for all those years had never been more than a drop in the ocean when it came to fixing Third World troubles and that the main beneficiaries were the Irish people themselves who got to feel a little better about their own grey daily grinds.

Notoriously, in the '50s and '60s, it was not uncommon in England to see signs saying 'No Dogs, No Irish, No Blacks' outside rooms-to-let. Born in London to Irish parents, Johnny Rotten née Lydon chose this as the title for his autobiography. In Ireland, these exclusion orders were held up as rank examples of anti-Irish racism but a survey of Dublin landlords by *The Irish Times* in 1969 found that a great many would not offer accommodation to people of colour.

For this book, Francis Rossi recalled a shocking indictment of the casual racism endemic to generations of Irish society. On the receiving end was the teenage Phil Lynott. He said, "I stopped at Philip's mother's place one day with Rick to see her and she was going on about her son, and we were thinking 'Yeah, yeah, she's got a son'. But then we were touring Ireland in '68, '69, and this band were on before us – a showband – and the lead singer introduced the band featuring 'our new n****r on bass' and there was Philip stood there. I thought, 'Fucking hell!'"

Fast-forward a mere 15 years or so and while the black babies boxes had largely vanished from sight, the complexion of Irish society remained decidedly pasty. But African affairs didn't fade from Irish awareness – the focus just changed as a young generation found a new cause to channel their sincere will to do right.

In the autumn of 1985 a noisy war of words broke out between Ireland's pop kids and some of their musical elders over flagrant breaches of the cultural boycott placed on South Africa by the United Nations in 1980. Together with sporting, political, economic and other boycotts decreed by the UN, the cultural ban urged musicians and other performers to stay out of South Africa until the second-class status of that country's persecuted black majority was ended. The Irish Rugby Football Union

(IRFU), some top golfers, cyclists and others gleefully flouted the sporting ban, invariably trotting out the cynical cliché that "sport and politics don't mix". Amongst the cyclists to break the ban was Waterford's future world number one Sean Kelly.

Kelly and two fellow Irishmen were competing under false names and doing very well in South Africa's top race – sponsored by the leading Afrikaans newspaper – when they had the misfortune to cross the paths of the world's most famous celebrity couple. Elizabeth Taylor and Richard Burton were on a globetrotting honeymoon having just married each other for the second time, and the British paparazzi were shadowing their every move. One reporter took an interest in the five-man team competing for Britain and with a little digging exposed the true identities of the sanction-busters. The Irish cycling federation slapped a short ban on Kelly who was their best medal hope for the upcoming Montreal Olympics. The ban, through the inactive winter months, would have expired in time for Kelly to compete in Canada. It was only when cycling's world governing body learned of the violation that Kelly got the book thrown at him and missed his chance of Olympic glory.

It was the world of popular music, however, that sent over the greatest numbers of boycott wreckers. In 1981, for instance, Frank Sinatra took home almost two million US dollars for nine concerts, the largest of which was held at Sun City Casino, a massive entertainment complex located in the black reservation of Bophuthatswana. The apartheid regime made much ado about the fact that the rules of apartheid didn't apply to the Sun City venue for the duration of concerts, but since a single ticket cost more than a month's wages for the average black South African, the relaxing of the segregation rule was derisive window dressing.

In 1985 the UN published its updated blacklist of acts who'd breached the boycott. It featured Queen, Rod Stewart, Dolly Parton, Cher, Curtis Mayfield, the Beach Boys, Cliff Richard, Shirley Bassey, Ray Charles and Tina Turner plus many, many more.

By that year, clashing attitudes to the apartheid regime of South Africa had become a red line in Ireland's generation wars. Pickets outside Dunnes Stores supermarket outlets had been a familiar sight in Dublin city centre for a full year after a group of young workers had refused to handle South African fruit. One revered elder to address the issue from the picket line was future Nobel Laureate Seamus Heaney, who spoke under a banner which read: "You Buy Fruit And Diamonds, They Hang Poets". The country's elected politicians were largely unmoved, either content to turn a practised blind eye or actively kicking back at the uppity Dunnes troublemakers.

One vocal member of the government, Fine Gael's Alice Glen, a proud member of the World Anti-Communist League, spoke for many across the political establishment when she condemned the strikers' refusal to handle South African oranges as "depriving our old people of their Vitamin C". If the strikers expected support from the Irish Congress of Trades Unions (ICTU) they could think again. State papers released in 2016 show that the ICTU leadership felt the Dunnes workers were "way offside". The Labour Court agreed that the strikers were in breach of their contract of employment. Industry Minister and future Taoiseach John Bruton ruled out any restrictions on the import of apartheid produce because South Africa was "a hefty net importer of Irish goods".

It was another high profile elected representative, Senator Donie Cassidy of Fianna Fáil, who found himself caught up in a name-and-shame offensive against his showbiz associates Foster And Allen by the young whippersnappers of the Irish music scene.

As summer turned to autumn that year life was good for Mick Foster and Tony Allen. Conventional wisdom has it that the definition of a gentleman is someone who can play the accordion but doesn't. But Foster And Allen had never been cowed by convention, and their rich rewards were there for all to see. The pair had no fewer than three albums sitting pretty in the UK charts having three years earlier made an indelible mark on *Top Of The Pops* history by performing dressed to the nines like gift shop Smurfs in full leprechaun costumes. They were gearing up for yet another sellout Irish tour. The world was their pearly oyster.

The spark that detonated the powder keg that shattered their state of bliss was a scolding letter. The Irish Anti-Apartheid Movement (IAAM) wrote to the undynamic duo pointing out that their visits to South Africa "provided great assistance" to that country's white supremacist junta. The missive cited The Chieftains, The Dubliners and other entertainers who had turned down lucrative offers to play Sun City. By now, this was a pro forma letter familiar to the duo. The IAAM had written to Foster And Allen before. That body's Chairman, Dr Kader Asmal (later to become a minister in Nelson Mandela's first post-apartheid government) told the press that two previous appeals to the pair had yielded no response. This was hardly surprising. Foster And Allen were of the old school of entertainers, sports stars and businessmen who respected the fact that deals and ideals are like apples and oranges – one isn't necessarily better than the other, they're just different.

Contacted at a Tralee hotel, a bemused Tony Allen pointed out that Foster and Allen had no plans for returning to South Africa. This was true. The previous week they had announced details of their forthcoming world tour and the entire continent of Africa had been left out. In fact, they'd only just returned from an extensive South African tour a few months earlier and no-one had so much as raised an eyebrow.

But something had happened in those middling months of 1985. To use a phrase rarely if ever heard at the time, there had been a paradigm shift in the music world. Pop music had found its Manifest Destiny at Live Aid. Righting a wrong was suddenly now more intrinsic to rock 'n' roll than writing a song. As it happened, thanks to the on-your-street in-your-face moral bravery of the Dunnes Stores strikers, the young people of Ireland didn't need to look beyond their own doorstep for an eyesore of blinding injustice begging for a remedy.

As calls grew louder for his resignation from the Seanad, Senator Donie Cassidy took the opportunity to point out that – contrary to a widely held belief – he *was not* the manager of Foster and Allen. Up to the outbreak of hostilities, it had been widely assumed that Cassidy *was* the duo's manager, and in the annual *Hot Press Yearbook* for 1986 compiled just a few weeks later he would, as usual, be listed with his full consent as the sole "contact" for Foster and Allen, a listing he maintained in subsequent years.

Meanwhile, Tony Allen spelled it out again for those who seemed determined not to hear – Foster and Allen had *no plans* to revisit South Africa. Allen echoed many other acts who had played Sun City when he stressed that he "did not see any examples of apartheid on previous visits to the country". That casual utterance set Ireland's musical trendies alight with moral indignation.

Whatever the state of Allen's eyesight, the fact remained that Foster and Allen could state with absolute truth that they had no plans to return to South Africa. But that wasn't good enough for an upcoming generation of Irish performers who demanded that the pair must swear an oath to the UN never to go back until the pernicious apartheid regime was no more – signed in blood preferably.

This was payback time for the men waggishly dubbed 'Voerster and Outspan' by the rock critic George Byrne.

"It's a disgrace," fumed Donal Lunny of Moving Hearts. U2's Adam Clayton thought it was "absolutely clear why they shouldn't go". U2's hipness coach Gavin Friday proclaimed, "I wouldn't even allow a record of mine to be released there". The country's top radio DJ Dave Fanning employed the words "ignorant", "stupid" and "disgusting". Paul Brady – without furnishing any specifics as to why – found it "very hard to believe that a senator in Ireland could be entirely stupid".

Chris de Burgh declined to issue a blunt condemnation. Having played South Africa himself, he felt he knew "more about the situation than 99% of the armchair liberals who sat at home condemning apartheid". As Chris figured it, if they ever did decide to go back to Sun City, "Foster and Allen will be playing to multi-racial audiences, and even if that means only 2% blacks, it still proves that blacks are allowed in."

Foster and Allen were gearing up for a show at Dublin's Stadium when the storm blew up. Predictably, the fans filing in were harangued by protesters from the Irish Anti-Apartheid Movement. Those fans cheered loudly as a number of disruptive do-gooders who'd infiltrated the seats were flung out by the scruff of their necks. More precisely, it's probable that 85% of the audience cheered the ejections while the other 15% didn't even hear the heckles of the dissidents. A journalist once pointed out to Donie Cassidy that, in concert, the duo's vocals were far too loud in the mix. "That's deliberate policy," responded Cassidy. "We did a survey and found that 15% of Foster and Allen's audiences are deaf."

After the token rumble at the National Boxing Stadium, the

row between Ireland's young pop progressives and Foster and Allen fizzled out, without the pair taking the opportunity to swear an oath to the United Nations not to return.

The UN took due notice and when its 1986 blacklist of boycott breakers was published the following April, a copy was sent to Taoiseach Garret FitzGerald's government and the Irish media with Foster and Allen highlighted, along with several other Irish entertainers including Country 'n' Irish star Margo, Eurovision songwriting legend Phil Coulter, his partner the singer Geraldine Branagan (who'd finished fifth in the 1975 Eurovision Song Contest representing Luxembourg with a Coulter song) and Joe Dolan, a man lavishly introduced by the MC at one show as "The Mullingar Heifer, the Sun City Serenader, Aer Lingus' favourite passenger – the one and only Joe Dolan!"

Cheerfully upfront and unrepentant about his regular visits to the apartheid regime, Dolan once provided a surreal rebuke to his critics, saying, "The reason I went to South Africa is that when I was a young lad I used to collect silver paper and send it off to the black babies, and I always wondered what they did with it. So I went to South Africa to find out, and discovered they make money with it. So I took it back." He took a similar stance on calls – supported by the African National Congress (ANC) – for cultural, sporting and economic boycotts of Israel, although many Israelis would not have appreciated his boast that "I'm very popular in Israel because of my big nose".

Removed from the previous blacklist that year, 1986, were comedian Hal Roach and best-selling harpist Mary O'Hara who'd both taken the UN oath.

Just after the Foster and Allen furore, U2 were amongst a throng of top acts who took part in the recording of '(Ain't Gonna Play) Sun City' written by Bruce Springsteen sidekick 'Little' Steven Van Zandt. Other luminaries crowding the studio to send a message to South African President PW Botha included Miles Davis, Bob Dylan, Ringo Starr, Lou Reed, Keith Richards, Ronnie Wood and Pete Townshend.

The biggest act on the 1986 UN blacklist were Queen, who that summer embarked on their 26-date 'Magic Tour' of Europe, which would prove to be their last before frontman Freddie Mercury succumbed to the ravages of AIDS. It would also be the one where they belatedly put things to rights and gave a solemn undertaking that they would never revisit apartheid South Africa, albeit under threat of Irish protests on a far grander scale than the ones endured by Foster and Allen. Lord Henry Mountcharles, owner of Slane Castle, extracted the pledge as a precondition to the band's playing to 80,000 there that July, defusing a potentially tricky situation where the Irish Anti-Apartheid Movement had promised Queen a fierce reception.

"We won't be going back, not until the regime has ended," guitarist Brian May told the Irish media, before taking much of the good out of those good intentions by saying he harboured "severe doubts" as to whether observing the boycott was "the right thing". He was still of the view that "people's opinions get swayed by building bridges and not by building walls".

Just four months after his release from 27 years of captivity in 1990, Nelson Mandela visited Ireland where he accepted his Freedom of Dublin honour conferred in 1988. He met with the young Dunnes Stores strikers at a festive lunch, where he told the gathering, "In particular we remember the unprecedented stand taken by the Dunnes strikers, who for two-and-a-half years staged very effective pickets against the sale of South African goods in this country.

"We know the sacrifices they underwent. Some of them lost their jobs. What struck us most was that members of a labour movement so many thousands of miles away from us felt this sense of commitment to the struggle against racial oppression in South Africa."

Led by its youth, a new outward-looking Ireland had rocked triumphantly against racism. That was the theory test set 10,000 km away. The practical examination would begin with the mass immigrations of the Celtic Tiger in a decade to come.

Chapter 13

IRELAND'S NUMBER COMES UP: U2 & 'OUR GREATEST NATIONAL ASSET'

"The three great success stories of Irish society: The Blarney Woollen Mills, The Kerry Co-Op and U2."

– Broadcaster Liam Ó Murchú

IN THE autumn of 1989 I spent an entertaining evening with the ex-Sex Pistols Svengali Malcolm McLaren and the conversation inevitably turned to U2's conquest of the globe. As he lit his umpteenth cigarette, he mused, "There's something very good about U2, and there's something very nauseating about them. The nauseating thing about them is that they are great pretenders. But then again, pop culture *is* a great pretension. But they profer to be More Than."

McLaren's case in point was the band's sprawling double album, *Rattle And Hum*, where they placed themselves firmly and shamelessly in the pantheon of rock 'n' roll's all-time greats including Bob Dylan, The Beatles and BB King. The man behind the iconoclastic Pistols was having none of it. He looked back on the Live Aid extravaganza of four years earlier as the moment when the corporate music business finally and decisively seized back control after the twin disruptions to its business model of punk and the video revolution. A decade before Bob Geldof's 1985 global jukebox spectacular, in the year of 1975, fully 2% of all the records sold in the entire world were by one artist, Elton John, and that's exactly how the industry liked it, with the business determining what got stocked in the shops and what got played on the radio so that they could manufacture a limited range of material on a vast scale.

Over drinks in Dublin's Berkeley Court Hotel, McLaren reflected on the contradiction between Live Aid as the ultimate expression of rock as a force for DIY radical action in tackling a famine where the world seemed paralysed, and Live Aid as the ultimate expression of corporate control. He said, "I don't think records are any longer important as an instrument of change, simply because the world has become so corporate in its structures and attitudes that records are now less instructive than ever. They reveal very little that you don't already know. They tend most of the time to soften the blow of everyday life and are therefore not the guardians of evil they once professed to be, which made us all wake up in the morning and think it was worthwhile living. At least I did when I was 18.

"All those thoughts and practices are no longer part of it. They all seem to be coffee-table decorations or BMW muzak – they're not instruments for change, they tend to be accompaniments to everything. It's all a muzak world. Whether it's getting Pygmies up on stage with Peter Gabriel or Brazilians with Paul Simon, or it's the chains and the social injustices of the South Bronx – it all ends up sounding like muzak. To make records today, for me, is a contradiction, but I take it with a smile because no matter how much you feel it to be innocuous stuff, we are pleasure seekers and there is still a great deal to be gained emotionally from it.

We are seductive creatures. You still enjoy a good fuck. You still enjoy a good record. But we're not tearing down the world."

McLaren, as was often the case, was spot on – from a rest of the world perspective. Most of the acts showcased in the London and Philadelphia concerts enjoyed a big payoff with a surge of ticket and record sales, while the safe and reliable power ballad began a chart heyday.

But from an Irish perspective there was no obvious downside to Live Aid (that would come a year later). Billed by its Dubliner mastermind Bob Geldof as 'The Greatest Show On Earth', Live Aid caught the imagination of the whole world on 13 July, 1985. Live Aid was good for the starving masses of famine stricken Ethiopia. It was *really* good for an ailing Ireland at a time when the economy and national morale were both on their knees. The Irish dug deep to donate more per capita than any other country, prompting Geldof to recant his scathing indictment of five years earlier, 'Banana Republic'. Live Aid was a milestone moment in the life story of modern Ireland. In other words, Ireland 'won' Live Aid. It was the day mouthy Bob was upgraded to Saint Bob, but the real epiphany came around a quarter to six that evening, Irish time, when the whole world saw the future of rock 'n' roll depart the stage and that future was U2.

Even the corporate takeover of pop music worked at this critical time in Ireland's favour. The world's top entertainment companies were swallowing up their smaller rivals, asset-stripping them of the talent and expertise they wanted and spitting out the rest. At the same time, the planet's two biggest entertainment industries – music and movies in an age before computer games – were merging into what would become five or six monster companies by the mid-90s. Their product was culture and they were all engaged in a race to unearth new territories to mine and bring to market. In the '70s, Jamaica was mined out. With the rough edges knocked off his bumpy sound on the instructions of his record company, Bob Marley led a reggae revolution that swept the world. In the early '80s it was Australia's turn, starting with Mel Gibson's breakthrough box-office sensation *Mad Max* and the novelty faux-reggae hits of Men At Work. The Down Under craze hit its peak in the middle of the decade with the runaway success of *Crocodile Dundee* and INXS. Even by then however, the world was getting close to having its fill of all things Australian. This was brilliantly underlined in a 1995 episode of *The Simpsons* where on a visit Down Under, Lisa comes across a boarded up cinema with a sign advertising a Yahoo Serious Film Festival in reference to the actor/director whose 15 seconds of fame had long elapsed. Lisa says, "I know those words, but that sign makes no sense."

The fact was that the white European culture of Australia was a very thin crust stretched over 50,000 years of human settlement, all surface and no depth. Ireland, on the other hand, had layer upon layer upon layer of stories and songs and epic tragi-comedies to provide a relentless, insatiable entertainment machine with all it could handle and then some.

In other words, it was Ireland's turn, and U2 were precisely the right people in the right place at the right time to grab the chance for a place in the sun. Live Aid is as good a place as any to mark the beginning of that journey. Geldof caught flak for the fact that the only black musician on the Wembley bill was Sade. His response was that he'd picked the acts on the basis of their popularity. The glaring exception was his own Boomtown Rats whose 15 minutes of fame was by then fading from view. On stage, he declared, "This is the best day of my life." The Rats closed with 'I Don't Like Mondays' on the line "and the lesson today is how to die".

Those fortunate enough to be in the midst of their brief heyday that famous afternoon included Nick Kershaw, Howard Jones and Paul Young. Sting and Phil Collins played the first of several stellar double-handers, but many in Ireland were counting down to 5.20pm when U2 would take the stage. The Dubliners had packed out Croke Park two days running a fortnight earlier, but on the international scene they were still bubbling under. By 6.00pm they had come gloriously to the boil.

The Cold War was still sub-zero and President Reagan was threatening the USSR with his costly but patently preposterous Star Wars weapons system. U2 issued a statement condemning the huge spend on space junk while millions in Ethiopia starved. The hacks in the media tent chuckled and ignored it, but there was no ignoring U2's 14-minute rendition of Bad during which Bono plucked a girl from the crowd and made an electrifying connection between band and audience, even if it had to be strung out that long only because Bono couldn't find his way back up onto the stage.

Their performance underlined the flipside of Malcolm McLaren's reasoning on Live Aid. While he was on the money with his assertion that in one way, Live Aid was a crushing defeat for rock 'n' roll's refusenik spirit, he was also absolutely correct when he said that "they profer to be More Than". Possessed of boundless confidence from their very beginnings, U2 would never settle for bog-standard fame – they chased and captured what Andy Warhol termed 'Mythic Fame'.

U2 were the beginning of something, and in many ways the end of something. They were made to be the ones who would initiate Ireland's new relationship with the world. From the time they linked up with their ambitious manager Paul McGuinness they had set about confounding the small expectations of Irish music, first by taking on board a wily accountant, Ossie Kilkenny, who realised that they could take advantage of Ireland's artists' tax exemption to base themselves at home and keep a lot of their earnings. And in doing so, they laid down the template for others to do the same. In his 2023 autobiography *Crazy Dreams*, Paul Brady who found international success penning hits for Tina Turner and others, revealed that he'd believed that the tax exemption was only for foreign acts and classical music until U2's accountant passed on the good news.

As U2 marked the beginning of something new, in a way they marked the end of rock music's classic age. They were the last in a line of stellar acts who believed it was their mission to change the world, a line that started with Dylan and The Beatles and continued on a line that included The Stones, The Kinks and other agents of the counterculture. Counter-intuitively, it was from Led Zeppelin – an outfit with no discernible social conscience – that U2 borrowed their entire hard-nosed business model. Looking down from the top of the world, manager Paul McGuinness remarked, "I only had to get lucky once", but he'd arrived on his lofty perch by leaving little to luck. U2 became the last of the giants from a heroic age when rock music appeared to have the power to change the world, and before it became just another consumer choice from an ever-expanding menu of console gaming, internet porn, online betting addiction and mobile phone trolling. For U2, Live Aid was the launchpad to world domination with their next album, *The Joshua Tree*. For the young people of Ireland, Live Aid felt empowering, a coming of age on the international stage. This was presumably how their parents and teachers had felt when Dana had won Eurovision with 'All Kinds Of Everything', but to the power of a billion.

In the immediate afterglow of Live Aid there was an unmistakable feelgood factor in the air. U2 were the name on everybody's lips, Ireland had out-donated every other country and

Bob Geldof was being fast-tracked for sainthood. The downside would come a year later in the summer of '86 and its name would be Self Aid.

The wild success of Geldof's Band Aid and Live Aid all-star productions sparked a musical mid-80s Aids epidemic featuring such projects as Sports Aid, Farm Aid in the States, and Hear'n'Aid (spandex and poodle perms against want). Staged at Dublin's RDS 10 months after Live Aid, Self Aid was a misbegotten attempt to translate the dynamics of famine fund-raising into resuscitating a national economy. I wrote half of the official concert programme entitled 'Self Aid – Make It Work'.

The Wall Street banker JP Morgan is credited with the maxim that there are generally two reasons for doing something – a very good reason and the *real* reason. This was the firm view of old-school leftie Eamonn McCann writing for *In Dublin*. "The concert came first," he asserted. "The cause was attached later." The idea of an Irish Live Aid had been floating around the Montrose home of the national broadcaster since Geldof's global megabash the previous summer. All the vital elements were in place. By the middle of 1986 a dizzying proportion of young Irish people – now increasingly referred to in business and political circles as "our greatest national asset" – seemed to be signed to major international record labels as the industry frenetically searched for "the next U2". Despite the continuing drain of emigration, half of Ireland's population was under 25, so they could make up the audience. Best of all, the rotating Live Aid Wembley stage was available.

Nobody questioned the organisers' good intentions. It was just that their plan seemed largely based on the fable of the Pied Piper and his magic flute. McCann spelled out the obvious. This scatty attempt to attract 'pledges' of jobs and investment capital by bashing out a few tunes was doomed.

The jobs simply weren't there, he observed, and no amount of well-meaning diminished chords from Christy Moore would subvert the basic rules of capitalism. State agencies were spending £450 million each year trying and failing to create jobs. At tops, Self Aid might generate an extra seven million. It just didn't add up.

Worse, charged McCann, some of the bodies involved in Self Aid were actively engaged in swelling the dole queues. RTÉ itself, the hub of the hubba-bubba, was targeting 320 redundancies. At best Self Aid was a smokescreen, at worst an instrument for diverting blame away from the forces responsible – government and business – and onto the jobless themselves for being jobless. "Major rock stars have become as lightning conductors," argued McCann, "attracting the energy of the urban young and running it safely to Earth." These pampered stars flattered themselves that they were part of the solution when in fact they were part of the problem.

It was in this context that *In Dublin* launched a swingeing attack on headliners U2 for endorsing a sham. The magazine's cover headline laid out the charge: 'The Great Self Aid Farce – Rock Against The People'. As the big day neared, newspapers reported that several companies had held back job announcements in order to reap free publicity on Self Aid day.

At the end of the day, the Self Aid totaliser had limped up to £500,000 in cash donations, a small fraction of Ireland's contribution to Live Aid for Ethiopia. The register of new jobs pledged by business read 1,332, but this figure didn't bear up to close scrutiny. One hundred McDonald's jobs, 150 at Irish Life and 20 at the ESB had to be removed because they would have existed irrespective of Self Aid. One caller to the studio switchboard had phoned in with an idea for creating 100 jobs. They were mistakenly added to the total pledged. One switchboard operator confided to the *Irish Independent* that a large part of her day was spent fending off cranks, drunks and callers with a conscription fixation for giving lazy youth a harsh dose of square-bashing.

"The figures are not a measure of success," stated one of the organisers as the last stragglers left the RDS. U2 manager Paul McGuinness agreed. "Fuck it," he said. "This is National Mood Day."

The hard-nosed music mogul was being glib, of course, but his words captured something very real. A mood had settled on the land, and it was the best mood ever. It was there in the unrealistic expectations of what pop might deliver overnight. Far from being put off by the abject failure of Self Aid to raise a single boat in Ireland's sunken economy, the country's politicians, bankrupt of any other ideas, seized upon pop music as a possible source of salvation. After generations of trying to suppress youth culture in general and pop music in particular, both were to be encouraged and rewarded, and within a couple of years of *The Joshua Tree*'s global conquest, local councillors, mayors and civic officials were falling over themselves to award the freedom of their city, town or village to the local spotty youths who were about to venture out into the world as "great ambassadors for Ireland".

Many at the very top level of government felt they had a special relationship with, and understanding of, pop music. This was because many had come either directly from the showband scene, or had made money from it via a range of business relationships. In the words of Robert Ballagh, a '60s showband star turned state-sponsored artist, "The showband crowd are mostly running the country now. Albert Reynolds ran a chain of ballrooms. He's paid me on occasions, but I'm sure he doesn't remember me. The name of the game was everyone was trying to maximise their profits. I don't think it was an honest profession."

At the time of Ballagh's comments in 1989, Albert Reynolds was Minister for Finance on the fast track to becoming Ireland's first music biz Prime Minister. Other managers and promoters who'd been forced to move on by the collapse of the ballroom scene were now colonising the media, the hospitality sector, property investment and all levels of politics. These ex-showband hustlers were foot-in-the-door salesmen who'd been drawn to the ballroom scene solely on the grounds that it was a big earner. Most were still young-ish, energetic, and on the lookout for the next money-spinning opportunity.

Together with his brother, Reynolds built a chain of ballrooms that encircled half the country by the late 1960s. He had a reputation for being hard but fair. Paddy Cole attested, "Up to that time you would normally be given a slice of ham so thin you could read the *Evening Press* through it. But the Reynolds family would bring you to a hotel or a house for a hot meal before you started."

The biggest draw on early '70s circuit, Joe Dolan, confirmed that Reynolds was respected by the performers as a square dealer, with the caveat, "He wasn't in the business to do anyone a favour. He was in it to make bread." Reynolds made a huge amount of bread during the '60s in an unregulated, cash-in-hand business that went out of its way to stay one step ahead of the taxman. As a government minister and ultimately Taoiseach, he prided himself on being a no-nonsense "one-page man" with little patience for long meetings and bureaucratic red tape.

As *The Joshua Tree* sat at the top of the global charts Reynolds was about to become Ireland's Minister for Finance. I buttonholed the minister-in-waiting at a Fianna Fáil think-tank at Dublin's Westbury Hotel on how best to capitalise on U2's world conquest and make showbiz work for the country. With a general election weeks away, the party was making a pitch at the youth vote by talking up its new interest in pop music and the job opportunities it might generate. There had been plenty of gilded words but no specifics, so I was there to see what – if anything – the party had in mind. It took about five minutes to find out that the answer was nothing much. Walking around the conference room at the Westbury it became clear that while the political party had the scent of money to be made on the back of U2's massive success, there was no understanding of what exactly U2 did or how it could be tapped. There were no representatives there from U2's generation. Instead, the place was wall-to-wall with middle-aged showband veterans and management heads who'd migrated into the mainstream business world, all catching up and trading tales of good times past.

Midway through my chat with Reynolds we were interrupted by The Wolfe Tones' silver fox Derek Warfield. Reynolds, a lifelong teetotaller, chuckled, "The Wolfe Tones played together for the first time ever, for me, for a bottle of whiskey – between them!" Warfield clasped Albert's shoulders from behind and vouched, "It was distilled by Lockes of Kilbeggan."

The interview ended when we were joined by a very merry Jim Hand. Hand was one of the brashest and most successful showband moguls in the room. Having cut his teeth as a door-to-door salesman of anything and everything from washing machines to bibles, he'd become the owner and trainer of a stable of big ballroom draws including The Dubliners and The Freshmen. At the time of Albert's think-in, Hand was enjoying huge album sales in Britain with The Fureys. He was fond of boasting that he turned down the Boomtown Rats because they were "brutal". He brought over big international stars to tour Ireland and famously took the likes of Tom Jones and Billy

Connolly to the family home to meet his parents. He persuaded a young singer called Sean Sherrard to change his name to Johnny Logan and then apparently lost interest until Logan won the Eurovision Song Contest in 1980 when Hand asserted his management credentials in court against Louis Walsh's then employer Tommy Hayden.

Like virtually all showband figures, Jim Hand was a vocal supporter of, and contributor to, Fianna Fáil, who since 1932 had identified as 'the natural party of government'. Despite his close proximity to the levers of power he'd never been drawn towards entering politics. He explained, "Politics is a vocation. I don't think there's any money in it. If there was money in it I'd go, but I don't see any readies." He added, "I insult people when I'm drunk. Basically I don't give a fuck about anyone anyway, but when I'm drunk I *really* don't give a fuck. So I insult people. Especially Fine Gael people."

He hated Radio 2 because they insisted on playing Prince and Rod Stewart instead of his mawkish balladeers, dubbing the station 'Radio Downtown Fucking Burbank'. He hated the pirates for the same reason and the biggest of the superpirates, Radio Nova, run by Chris Cary, for the additional reason that "it's English-owned, which I resent very much".

So despite great gales of lip service from the country's politicians, Irish pop and rock was mostly left to find its own way in the brave new world of global music. The lip service, though, did become a done deed when it came to showing up for any opening or launch that would guarantee a photo opportunity.

I accompanied my *Hot Press* colleague Bill Graham to the Dublin suburb of Ballyfermot for the ribbon-cutting of Ireland's first Rock School. As we were setting out from the office Paul Woodfull of the art department had acted out a scenario where a grizzled musician from Dublin's pub circuit would draw on a blackboard his chord sequence for writing a sure-fire No 1 smash hit single. It's fair to say that the idea anyone could learn to be a rock star in a classroom was met with a big dollop of cynicism by those in the know. So Bill and myself went along to have a look. An unloved orphan less than a decade earlier, rock music was now Official Ireland's mollycoddled Golden Child, and hopefully its Golden Goose. Proof positive was the heavyweight government turnout to launch this starter course for wide-eyed young job trainees.

There was the leader of the nation himself, Taoiseach Charles Haughey. He was flanked by the country's deputy leader, Brian Lenihan and the government's deeply dodgy Mr Fixit Liam Lawlor.

One after the other the speech-makers trotted out the latest line in fad platitudes about how U2 were "great ambassadors for Ireland abroad", how the future prosperity of our country lay with "our greatest national asset", our young people, and about how half the population was now "under the age of twenty-five" which was fantastic news. This last statistic was indeed worth a mention, given that the nation's young people had been fleeing in a forced emigration not seen since the darkest days of the '50s.

Every off-the-peg speech that day was built around the lazy assumption that rock music is a trade that can be learned by taking some classes and serving an apprenticeship, like plumbing or plastering. "So wrong," said Bill.

Happily, U2 by now had moved far beyond caring about the puny priorities of Ireland's parish pump politics and within a couple more years would unveil the much broader scope of their political aspirations.

In August 1992, the Dubliners were guests on the Rockline phone-in radio show which had listeners across the USA. A

"Bill from Little Rock" came on the phone and engaged them in a round of friendly banter. The lame exchanges didn't rise much above…

Bono: "Do I call you governor?"

Clinton: "No, you can call me Bill."

Bono: "And you can call me Betty."

That was the level of it, but U2 and Bill Clinton had clicked.

U2 were touring their Zoo TV live experience. Bill Clinton was on the road in the latter stages of his campaign to become the next President of the United States. Two weeks later the paths of their rolling revues crossed in Chicago. As the sun rose over the Ritz-Carlton Hotel, Bono, Edge and Larry held an hour-long summit with the first time Democratic candidate. Adam wandered in from his breakfast in time to hear the self-assured Clinton invite the Fab Four to play at his inauguration.

The new best friends renewed their acquaintance that same evening where they carpooled their motorcades for a Chicago Bears game, sharing a single police escort.

The band's endorsement of the confident young challenger drew a quick response from the incumbent, President George H Bush. Bush did not appreciate the fact that the band had added the White House to the phone numbers Bono rang as a nightly stage gimmick on the tour.

In a televised speech to a campaign rally, Bush jeered, "You may have seen this in the news. He (Clinton) was in Hollywood seeking foreign policy advice from the rock group U2! I have nothing against U2. You may not know this but they try to call me every night during the concert. The next time we face a foreign policy crisis I will work with John Major and Boris Yeltsin, and Bill Clinton can consult Boy George!"

Labouring his point, the President went on to assert that if Clinton was elected, "you too" would suffer higher inflation, "you too" would pay higher taxes, and "you too" would soon regret it.

Installed in the Oval Office, President Clinton began giving thought to reversing the long tradition of US non-intervention in Britain's running of Northern Ireland. In the face of stern opposition from the British government, some in the Irish government and a segment of American politics, Clinton opened new channels of communication with Sinn Féin with a view to bringing the turmoil in the North to an end.

There were no visible traces of regret three years after the U2/Bill from Little Rock dawn summit when President Clinton and his wife Hillary accepted the acclaim of 80,000 happy campers in Dublin's College Green, telling the crowd that the shadow of the gunman had been banished for good from the island of Ireland.

Chapter 14

THE ENGLISH PIRATE WHO RULED DUBLIN'S 'BAY AREA'

"This is the birthday of George Orwell who predicted the end of the world in 1984. Was Orwell right? Let's stick around another year and find out!"

– Pirate radio DJ Lawrence John, 1983

IN THE opening days of the 1980s, Ireland's newly installed leader Charles Haughey derisively declared that Northern Ireland was "a failed political entity". This sounded rich to many observers at home and abroad who charged that the South had become "ungovernable".

If proof were needed, Haughey would furnish it himself next time around with his second administration – notoriously known as the 'GUBU' government – that did not even last out the calendar year of 1982 before crashing in flames. GUBU stands for grotesque, unbelievable, bizarre and unprecedented, and Haughey's administration delivered all that and much more.

The sorry saga is best told in *The Boss*, a book by Joe Joyce and Peter Murtagh which remains the perfect expression of history on the hoof. Rushed out in 1983 when the smoking guns were still warm, *The Boss* is as chillingly jaw-dropping four decades on as it was the day it hit the bookshelves.

After the initial shock of the revelations made public by Joyce and Murtagh, business as usual quickly resumed amongst a disreputable political class, a compromised judiciary and a police force that was clearly unfit for purpose. In fact, there were effectively two police forces, the plain clothes Special Branch and the uniformed Garda on the beat. They didn't like each other and they didn't mind who knew.

Known to all and sundry as the Heavy Gang, the detective branch had been handed an ever longer free rein to tackle the threat of subversives since the outbreak of The Troubles, to the point where civil liberties campaigners, opposition politicians and concerned citizens complained they had gone rogue. The public perception of the Special Branch was brilliantly captured in the 1986 illustrated book *Irish Wildlife* by John Little and Noel Kelly. The satirical profile of *Specialus Branchus* included the following:

> **What It Wears:** Leather bomber jacket, beard or moustache, jeans and a Walter pistol in a shoulder holster.
>
> **What It Watches:** Football matches on pub TVs, the Russian embassy, Sinn Féin HQ. Likes programmes about the North where it can practise its habit of spotting faces
>
> **What It Hates:** High risk escorts for cash deliveries which preclude the chance of 'refreshments' i.e. a quick drink.
>
> **What It Likes:** Pints of Guinness and shorts. Overtime. Talking to Provos with their arm up their back. Looking down its nose at uniformed members of the force.

That was what you'd expect from a satirical caricature, but everyone knew the rot was real and that the armed detectives were running roughshod over the laws of the land, and their political masters were either unwilling or unable to put a halt to their gallop.

There are many disturbing stories from the time that illustrate the point, but here's one on a lighter note.

One afternoon in the mid-80s, a record plugger pal of mine arrived into the office with a fresh batch of discs for review and a bizarre tale of a couple of nights before. He'd been driving home southbound around three in the morning, very, very drunk after a night in the Pink Elephant. As he passed the old Jurys Hotel he hit a bollard, swerved across the road and ended up on the footpath outside the hotel railings. Mercifully there was no-one about. As he sat at the wheel, dazed but unharmed, a car screeched onto the path inches from his bonnet. It was a blue Ford Avenger, standard issue of the Special Branch. Two burly men in bomber jackets hopped out, yanked him out and patted him down spread-eagled against his car.

They flipped him around and began shouting in his face.

His response silenced his captors. Laughing madly and pointing at their black docker's beanies, he delivered a quick snatch of 'Geno' and told them that they looked like Dexys Midnight Runners.

This completely threw the armed detectives.

Handing him his keys they told him to lock his car, get a taxi, and if they ever saw him again he would be sorry. And with that they hopped back into the blue Avenger, did a U-turn they'd copied from 'The Sweeney' and headed at breakneck speed back towards the Leeson Street strip.

The plugger was sufficiently legless to believe that despite the fact he could barely stand, he'd be okay to drive the rest of his journey. The only trouble wasn't that he was very likely to crash again, but that he'd burst a tyre when he hit the kerb outside the hotel. Incredibly, he decided to change the tyre. He opened the boot to get out the spare, which was buried under a heavy pile of vinyl albums. He set about pushing the pile to the back of the boot to uncover the spare and the next thing…

He lifted his head out of the boot and blinked in the glare of bright summer daylight. He had spent hours bent over, his upper half slumped in the boot while his feet stayed planted firmly on the ground. He turned groggily to get his bearings and found he was yards from a bus-stop with a line of commuters on their way to work who were giving him some very strange looks that ranged from deep scowls to wide smiles.

The antics of the Heavy Gang caused such disapproval that one politician attempted to harness public disquiet for electoral gain. The Fianna Fáil leadership was angered and dismayed when one of the party's election candidates, James Gallagher, appeared to officially endorse the public image of the rogue cop. Gallagher placed an advert in the *Sligo Champion* which asserted, "Our Garda force are preservers of peace and order and should be seen as such, and *not as thugs* who execute repressive legislation."

This acknowledgement of the force's thuggish element earned Gallagher a rebuke from a Fianna Fáil hierarchy that was striving to make law and order a main plank of the party's election platform. A spokesman for Gallagher then came out and sheepishly apologised for "mistakes" in the ad copy. The line referring to the guardians of law and order as thugs was "a typing error".

By the start of the 1980s the old chestnut of who polices the police had become a hot topic. One episode which lent weight to suspicions that the police were not only policing themselves, but that the police tail was even wagging the government dog, came as early as 1973 when a tantalising story appeared on the front of the *Sunday Independent*. The short report centred on the nocturnal habits of one unnamed government minister. Members of cabinet were under a perceived threat from both Republicans and Loyalists so they were shadowed by Garda minders. However, some of these plain clothes bodyguards felt they were being overworked beyond the compensation of their lavish overtime pay. The newspaper reported that at least one detective had submitted a complaint directly to Taoiseach Jack Lynch, "about the conduct of one over-amorous member of the Cabinet in his extra-curricular activities". Lynch denied ordering a hush-hush inquiry into the matter while politics watchers wondered who the Casanova could be, given that the usual suspect, Charles Haughey, had been fired over a plot to funnel arms to Republicans.

And while the Special Branch were throwing their weight about as a law unto themselves, their uniformed colleagues were caught in a perpetual no-man's-land between trying to please their capricious political masters and trying to enforce the law without stepping on too many toes in tight-knit communities.

One result was that the enforcement of the licensing laws could vary from station to station in the cities and village to village in the countryside. The vast majority of the country's elected and aspiring politicians held constituency clinics and meetings in local pubs, with the result that publicans had a lot of clout when it came to the strict application of the law. For the uniformed Guard, the matter of enforcement was muddied by the bad example set by the country's lawmakers. The spirit of alcoholic indulgence and the sense that Ireland had an untouchable establishment was captured by Brian Lenihan Snr when he famously admitted on *The Late Late Show* that he was caught after-hours drinking with fellow ministers Charles Haughey and Donogh O'Malley. The Guard who attempted to break up the illegal session was given the option, "Will you have a pint or a transfer?" Legend has it that on another occasion O'Malley was stopped by Gardaí while driving drunk the wrong way up a one-way street. When asked if he hadn't seen the arrows, he allegedly replied, "I didn't even see the effin' Indians." A former Minister for Justice, Brian Lenihan was happy to put on the record, "The surest way to ensure that nothing gets done is to do everything correctly, by the file … Everything will be clean and transparent and open and nothing will be done." Reflecting on his calling as a politician, Lenihan's cabinet colleague Padraig Flynn said, "All that pseudo-intellectual stuff about ideals, and why you do it, that's all clap-trap."

With the licensing laws a confusing mess, and their interpretation seeming entirely at the discretion of a random guard or judge, several enterprising go-getters applied their own best guess. And so in the 1980s there was a bar on a canal barge that served long after landlubber closing time, claiming that the law didn't apply on water. Operating on the same principle was a boat that took tipplers on a late night booze cruise around Dublin Bay. The most infamous and celebrated of these water-borne enterprises was the MV Arran AKA 'The Ship That Doesn't Sail'. Owned by the host of BBC TV's *This Is Your Life*, Eamonn Andrews, this floating late night disco moored on the capital's quays. It even had its own helipad to whisk aboard VIPs direct from Dublin Airport. It may have been two fingers to the licensing laws, but that didn't deter a host of senior politicians from attending the gala opening in July 1983.

Throughout the 1980s, one-day booze cruises on the ferries to Liverpool and Holyhead proved hugely popular, but it was a day trip to the Isle of Man that made it onto the national news. One morning a caller told radio host Gay Byrne of his Isle of Man adventure a couple of days earlier. After several hours of serious drinking in Douglas, the blast of the ship's siren signalled it was time to cast off for Dublin. One group of drinkers spied that a young man they knew from their own local was completely passed out, so they carried him to the boat. Docking in Dublin, the man was still very groggy, so as good neighbours they stuck him in their taxi and managed to get his address out of him. They pulled up outside his terraced house in the docklands and knocked on the door, and knocked, and knocked. Eventually a woman leaned out of her bedroom window next door.

"He's not in, luv," she told the Good Samaritans. "He's away for the week on his honeymoon in the Isle of Man."

If the licensing laws were in a state of deep disrepute throughout the 1980s, they were just one of many spheres where a combination of political paralysis, gaping loopholes and arbitrary enforcement rendered the law an ass.

One glaring case in point was pirate radio. In the late 1970s, outlaw radio stations mushroomed in Ireland's towns and cities. The pirates provided pop music that was rationed to tiny portions on the lone State broadcaster, RTÉ Radio 1. Initially, the political class feared the pirates, not because they were spreading foreign pop culture but because they might provide a source of news that wasn't approved by a State obsessed with quelling subversive Republican propaganda. Those fears evaporated when it became plain that the pirates had no interest in current affairs broadcasting. If there was any news output at all, it consisted of reading the headlines from the newspapers or – in the case of a couple of stations – lifting RTÉ's news bulletins and rebroadcasting them.

In the run up to the 1981 general election, as the governing party responsible for upholding the State's supposed broadcasting monopoly, Fianna Fáil officially took a dim view of the pirates. However, some Fianna Fáil candidates just couldn't resist the big localised audiences and low, low advertising rates offered by the law-breakers. One deputy's jingle on Big D Radio chimed, "Jim Tunney here asking you to support Charlie Haughey and Fianna Fáil." Minister of State Tunney went on to tell young voters about his party's policies on education, unemployment and sport. Meanwhile Gerard Brady TD, Senator Michael Donnelly and Junior Minister Sean Moore pooled their funds for a joint advert on Big D which urged voters, "Let's have three for Charlie!"

The RTÉ country 'n' western personality Paschal Mooney, who was working at Fianna Fáil HQ, flatly denied that any of this was taking place. He insisted,"Fianna Fáil has no official contact with the pirate stations – they're all outside the law. Any inquiries from local constituencies have been told not to have any contact with them and, as far as we know, they are going along with this." As a reward for his toils for the party, Mooney was later nominated to the Senate, where he memorably quoted *Hamlet* something rotten to the House, lamenting, "Like they said long ago in a story, something is wrong in the state of Holland."

Meanwhile, back in 1981 and over in Fine Gael HQ another RTÉ man, Bill O'Herlihy, said that the main opposition party had no qualms about broadcasting on the pirates. He stated, "We're using them in relation to our youth policy and Dublin plan." Fine Gael candidates could be heard on Radio Dublin, Big D and Southside Radio. Labour were not using the pirates, but not out of any particular sense of disapproval. "We don't have the money," said a spokesman.

As the more robust of the pirates picked up young listeners in their thousands, then in their tens of thousands, turf wars flared between the rival operators. When there was very little advertising money to fight over, it had been mostly about bragging rights. As the advertising revenue grew to modest levels, the turf wars intensified.

If a station only had a single phoneline for requests, competitions and chat, a rival could easily take it out of commission by ringing up and then leaving their phone off the hook. Chopping down the opposition's mast was another popular method of ensuring dead air. Throughout the early years of the pirate boom, arson was both a weapon against enemy stations and a last resort if the station wasn't performing.

One pirate DJ who went on to become a famous broadcaster told me of the time their boss told them to take the next night off as work needed to be done on the premises, so the DJ went to a gig the following night. Their drive home took them past their workplace, but the way was blocked by two fire brigades fighting a blaze which had clearly been foreseen by the station owner. In another case, one of the most popular stations underwent an unexpected change of ownership when the proprietor died suddenly. Within weeks of the new owners taking over, the station mysteriously burned to the ground. In 1979 *Hibernia* magazine reported that, "ARD (Alternative Radio Dublin) was nearly blown up by a young employee who decided to do chemical experiments on the front steps."

Disgruntled employees were a recurring feature of the pirate scene and the employer who set an uncatchable record for disgruntled employees was Chris Cary, the man who took pirate radio in Ireland to new heights and new lows. The entire outlaw sector fell victim to Cary's success when the domination of his Radio Nova forced the Irish government to finally draw up plans to scuttle the pirates.

Cary arrived in Ireland in 1980, determined to ratchet up the war between the pirates and the State, but mostly to make ill-gotten gains. He set up Sunshine Radio with his old Radio Caroline shipmate Robbie Dale who'd been nicknamed 'The Admiral' by Dave Lee Travis and had taken to wearing an admiral's uniform in response. Sunshine quickly ran into rough seas, first when a rival chopped down their radio mast and even more so when Dale insisted on having some minimum talk content. Cary walked and created Ireland's first true Super Pirate, Radio Nova, in his own image – loud, brash and in-your-face.

He boasted that Nova would be "the McDonald's of radio", elaborating "you always know exactly what you are going to get, no surprises, everything within your expected taste and comfort zone". For Nova's listeners, their city now became "the Bay Area", and in less than a year Nova had blown its pirate rivals out of the water. It had also dethroned the national broadcaster's mild-mannered alternative, Radio 2, as the undisputed champ for listeners and ad revenue. Radio 2 had the poke under its transmitting bonnet to drown out Nova in terms of reach and loudness, but yet another loophole in the State's Swiss cheese broadcasting laws forbade the legal station to pump up the volume.

The man who chopped down Sunshine's mast in what proved a futile act of resistance was 'Captain' Eamonn Cooke, the grizzled godfather of the Dublin underground scene. Jailed in the 1950s for shooting at police officers and ultimately imprisoned for indecent assault, Cooke was undoubtedly the nastiest individual ever to man a pirate deck. At one point when he still considered himself a rival to Cary, Cooke thundered, "Chris Cary treats the Irish like I'd treat the blacks!"

Happily, Cooke's days as a bandit employer were numbered. Cary, on the other hand, ruled Ireland's first Super Pirate with an iron fist, a sharp tongue and a brass neck. Cary had spent two decades buffing that brass neck. After his stint buccaneering onboard Caroline in the Swinging '60s, his next port of call was the infant home-entertainment sector where he made a bundle for his part in marketing the first TV console game (a blipping dot and two dashes that vaguely resembled tennis). After a spell at Radio Luxembourg he moved into pocket calculators and proto home computers. Inventor Clive Sinclair branded Cary an ideas thief and the two sued each other. Sinclair won, except for the lucrative US jurisdiction.

The Bossa Nova played up his reputation as a cruel tyrant. When asked what he did for amusement he replied, "I have a row." One staffer grumbled, "He treats people like toys in a game." Employees worked in daily fear of being fired on a whim. This was known as 'Van Halening', a reference to the sacking of one DJ because the jock's spoken intro to Van Halen's 'Jump' was "too long" for Cary's liking. Having said that, some jocks should have never been allowed in front of a mic in the first place. In June 1983, Nova's Lawrence John (not his real name) told listeners, "This is the birthday of George Orwell who predicted the end of the world in 1984. Was Orwell right? Let's stick around another year and find out!"

A self-proclaimed union-bashing Thatcherite, Cary espoused the conspicuous consumption of the age. Freely admitting that his workers regarded him as "a cunt", he countered that he'd improved their lives beyond measure, boasting, "There are guys working in this building that have nice cars, white shoes, the windjammers, the hair all fixed (stiffened with hairspray). When they first came here they arrived on bikes, the hair all unfixed."

At the height of its success, Nova had around 40% listenership in Dublin and Sunshine had 20%. Radio 2, RTÉ's 'youth' station which had been set up to run the pirates out of business, languished with a mere 11% audience share in the capital.

In 1986 Cary made a hasty exit from Nova and Ireland to

be with his piles of cash awaiting him beyond the reach of a Revenue service that had never been able to lay more than a fingertip on his illicit earnings. Cary blamed the hated unions for the station's closure, but the real reason was that his business partner, smelling a rat, had called in the exterminator. The partner had paid a hefty £60,000 for a quarter of Nova. Or so they'd thought.

In fact the company they'd bought into owned just a few office fittings and 80,000 bumper stickers. Any equipment of value was being leased by Nova from a British company. The extraordinary lease arrangement stipulated that the more Nova earned, the more it was compelled to pay in leasing fees. And the owner of the leasing company was – surprise, surprise – Chris Cary. Leaving his wife behind in Dublin, Cary retreated to Surrey's green and pleasant land with his long-time girlfriend and his sacks of loot.

Shortly before leaving his Irish creditors high and dry, Cary mulled his options if Nova went under. "I'll go and learn about TV," he said. And that's what he did. He learned how to mass produce pirate Sky TV decoder cards and flog them for £450 a go. BSkyB called in the law and in 1998 he pleaded guilty to defrauding Rupert Murdoch's broadcast giant of £30 million. Five months into his four-year jail term his appeal failed. Days later he told the warders at Ford open prison that he was off to fetch compost from the prison farm. On the roadway outside the farm a white Peugeot pulled up and he made good his escape. British police surmised he was living it up with fellow expat crooks on Spain's Costa del Crime and that there was little prospect of his recapture. Murdoch was having none of that. The planet's most powerful media mogul would pursue to the ends of the earth the fraudster who'd had the effrontery to take him for £30 million, when £30 million was still more than petty cash to the Australian. And it was close to the ends of the earth that private detectives caught up with the fugitive who was holed up in New Zealand. He was bundled back to Britain to serve out the remainder of his sentence in a high-security prison.

The government Minister charged with putting order on Ireland's post-pirates broadcasting landscape was Ray Burke, who had first come to national prominence as one of the local politicians that ran Sid Rawle out of Skerries and onto Beatles Island back in 1969. A decade after Radio 2 was set up by the State to crush the pirates, Burke's big idea was to set up the independent national station Century Radio, to crush Radio 2. Despite having Terry Wogan and Chris de Burgh onboard as part-owners, Century crashed after a disastrous two years on the air. Much worse was to come for Burke when he was jailed in 2005 for failing to pay tax on some very large political donations he received from some of Century Radio's backers.

Burke's stint as Communications Minister did, however, bring him a moment of Eurovision immortality. As the closing credits rolled on the 1988 song contest in Dublin, the merry Minister commandeered the microphone and attempted to lead the audience in an ad-lib rendition of 'Molly Malone'. Taken aback, most of the dignitaries surrounding Burke shied from joining his singalong while the winner of the 1988 Eurovision Song Contest who'd surrendered the microphone, Celine Dion, just gaped in utter bemusement at the ways of the Irish.

Chapter 15

JACK CHARLTON'S TEAM OF INTERNATIONAL MISFITS

"When I first joined you had spells when you never knew if you were in the squad. You never got a letter saying you were in the squad until after you got back from an international."

– Republic of Ireland defender Mark Lawrenson

IN APRIL 1990 Ireland's most unlikely television star, Arnold O'Byrne, ushered me into his office with his trademark toothy smile. At the end of 1985 the Dubliner had come home from more than half a lifetime in England with a mashed-up accent that was neither here nor there and a brief to rationalise and re-charge General Motors' loss-making Irish operation. He quickly set himself a far more daunting parallel challenge – to revive the tattered fortunes of the Republic of Ireland football team.

The Managing Director of General Motors explained, "We were the biggest employer in the Irish motor industry yet Ford had the highest profile, so I decided to raise our profile through sponsorship. Ford had the GAA so I couldn't get the national games. No-one wanted the bloody soccer – yet. And I had the advantage of ignorance. As a season ticket holder at Luton I knew that for all the supporters of Luton Town the players' names meant something. I knew nothing of the previous history of Eoin Hand (the recently departed Ireland Manager), the alleged incompetence of the FAI, the mess they were supposed to have made of picking a new manager – I knew nothing of all that, which worked to my advantage. I told my guys nothing of what I was up to. I wrapped up the deal and then told them 'Hey, we're sponsoring the Irish soccer team!' and they went 'Oh shit!'."

While the reaction from his colleagues surprised O'Byrne with his "advantage of ignorance", it would have caused little wonder amongst fans. The Football Association of Ireland (FAI) had provided a long-running object lesson in how *not* to run a sporting body, or any sort of body, since its split in 1921 from the Belfast-based Irish Football Association (IFA) with the foundation of the Irish Free State. If there was some slight excuse the FAI could offer for decades of astonishing ineptitude, it was that the rulers of independent Ireland took every opportunity to wipe soccer from the face of the land.

When the first squad to represent an independent Ireland in a major tournament set off for the finals of football's World Championships in Paris in 1924, there was no big send-off. While a smattering of friends and family waved off the team as they sailed away on their great adventure, the Free State government cold-shouldered the new nation's sporting ambassadors with open contempt.

The young FAI was strapped for cash, and since the Paris tournament was an Olympic event the body had expected some funding from the Irish Olympic Committee (IOC). However, the chief of the IOC, JJ Keane, was a dyed-in-the-wool GAA hardliner who strongly believed that for Ireland to allow itself to be represented in a soccer tournament was to bring shame and dishonour on the newly liberated Gaelic nation.

The FAI managed to scrape together the funding, to not just send 16 players and a trainer to Paris, but to also pay for six officials to chaperone the athletes, shuffle the paper clips and ensure the sights were seen. They fell down on the chaperone part at the first time of asking. One of the players, Ernie Crawford, was also captain of the Irish rugby team. When Crawford's kit bag was searched by French customs officials they found a pistol concealed in his gear. He was eventually cleared to go on his way.

Fears that Fianna Fáil's ascent to power would subject soccer to even greater hostility from Official Ireland proved correct. Newly installed in 1932, the party of self-sufficiency announced plans for an 'entertainment tax' on un-Irish activities like dance hops and foreign games. Only one sports body would be exempt: the GAA. One government TD told the Dáil this was only fair because, "Association football is tainted with professionalism, while rugby suffers from a superiority complex."

John Giles, the Leeds United and Ireland midfield maestro told me how, like generations of potential soccer stars, he was forbidden to play the 'foreign game' by the Catholic Church's educational stormtroopers, the Christian Brothers, who ruled most of the country's boys secondary schools with an iron fist. While soccer was frowned upon but tolerated at Giles' primary school, that all changed when he started secondary. He recalled, "They knew that I was a good soccer player and soccer clashed with Gaelic on a Saturday afternoon so I had to sign a letter saying that I wouldn't play for the soccer team. I didn't mind that – I enjoyed playing Gaelic but not as much as soccer. I didn't like the idea of *having* to play Gaelic. I had no real interest in it."

Despite Official Ireland's endless attempts to suppress soccer over the decades, the game became a rallying point for the plain people to show their disaffection with a broken down, deeply repressive state. Despite the repeated failure of the national team to qualify for major finals, or show any level of consistency, large crowds continued to turn up during the worst years of Ireland's isolation. In 1955, 22,000 people converged on Dublin's Dalymount Park to watch Ireland play godless communist Yugoslavia in loud defiance of a declaration by Archbishop John Charles McQuaid that all Catholics must boycott the fixture. The attendances at League of Ireland games went into decline in the 1960s, with the drop partly due to the arrival of the BBC's *Match Of The Day* and ITV's *Big Match* which were available as overspill signals to viewers along the east coast, home to most of the football strongholds. In the early '70s the domestic league enjoyed a brief revival when icons from the English top flight were lured by clubs on a lucrative pay-to-play scheme. Thousands flocked to see legends like Bobby Charlton, George Best and Gordon Banks strut their stuff. However the league's mini-revival was short-lived. The teams hosting these stars at away fixtures were delighted at the big boost to gate money, but refused to split the profits with the visiting teams who paid the stars.

Finding the money to pay John Giles' good friend and ex-Leeds teammate Jack Charlton was where Arnold O'Byrne played a key role in lifting Irish football from its knees. O'Byrne's sponsorship deal came just weeks after Charlton accepted the Irish job following a farcical sequence of events. Under manager Eoin Hand, Ireland's disastrous qualifying campaign for the 1986 World Cup had ended with a humiliating 1-4 home defeat to Denmark. As the credits rolled at the end of the debacle, the RTÉ continuity announcer remarked dryly, "And there will be more comedy after the break in *Cheers*."

The shambolic merry-go-round that left Jack Charlton as manager of the Irish football team has been well documented. Suffice to say that months after interviewing Charlton in a motorway cafe the FAI couldn't track him down to tell him he'd got the job. So they put the word around in the hope it would reach him somewhere along the grapevine. His friend and former manager at Leeds, Jimmy Armfield, rang him:

"Congratulations on getting the job Jack."

"What job?"

"Manager of Ireland."

"Oh, I'd forgotten about that."

The FAI had their man, or *a* man at least, but now the association had to grapple with a challenge that had never come up before – paying a manager something approaching a going rate for an international post.

John Giles was the departed Eoin Hand's predecessor in the manager's seat. Giles was appointed on a part-time basis and his reward for improving results and bringing a greater professionalism to the set-up was – to be retained on a part-time basis. He told me, "I was a player at Leeds and I was asked to take the Irish job as a player-manager on a part-time basis. I always did it on that basis and, later on, when people's expectations were a bit higher and we were doing reasonably well, I was criticised for only doing it on a part-time basis. It was a no-win situation."

Paying the manager was even less of a consideration when Giles first turned out in an Irish shirt in 1959, in an era when Ireland barely outranked Cyprus and Malta as a footballing power. He explained, "There was a selection committee, the Big Five, who picked the team. The Big Five didn't have a clue, and they changed every year. Not one of them was qualified to pick the team. They were members of the FAI executive, butchers, bakers and candlestick makers or whatever. You never got consistency. You pick him and I'll pick him..." Indeed, a story still persists that following John Giles' departure the ex-Portsmouth player Eoin Hand won the selector's vote for Irish manager over ex-Chelsea defender Paddy Mulligan because one of the selecting panel believed that Mulligan had flung a sticky bun at him on a train journey in Poland.

The blazers of the FAI could generally find consolation after yet another desperately disappointing away result through fine wining and dining on the Association's expenses tab. For some of these butchers and bakers these exotic junkets offered a rare chance to experience new cultures. As a group of FAI execs sat down to breakfast in a European capital, one was asked by the waiter what type of omelette he'd like?

"An egg omelette," he replied, as the assembled hacks at the table scrambled to take note.

With Ireland's international stock on the floor the FAI finally grasped the painful nettle of paying for a proven manager, and World Cup winner Jack Charlton had always known his worth. Once Charlton confirmed with his people that he had actually landed the job, it was Arnold O'Byrne's sponsorship money that sealed the deal. The General Motors boss told me, "In the initial stages the FAI had no money. No doubt about that. In my opinion our sponsorship helped the FAI pay Jack's wages. Early on it did."

The benefits of O'Byrne's deal to General Motors came early too, giving the country perhaps its most implausible and certainly one of its most well-liked TV personalities of the decade. For two years the avuncular Arnold O'Byrne fronted a series of TV ads for Opel cars (Vauxhall in Britain) and as Irish football prospered on and off the pitch, Opel cars took over the roads. Much like Jack's back-to-basics approach on the pitch, Arnold's masterplan was simplicity itself. He explained, "At the time what you were seeing were cars being dropped out of airplanes, cars doing all sorts of stupid things. My idea was that the guy out there on the street didn't want to see a car being dropped out of an airplane. He wanted to hear about a car and see who he was buying it off. The original idea was to put the marketing director on TV but the marketing director was not Irish."

When the first Opel ads ran, all the money spent was there to see up on the screen – almost nothing. As Arnold put it, "I would be lying to you if I said those ads were masterpieces. There was a whole amateurish approach." The crowning glory and the hook of the whole clunky affair was the closing punchline of his comically wooden sales pitch. Written down it read "Put the boot in", referring to the spacious trunk, but in his fused Irish/English accent this came out as "Pud de bute in". Virtually overnight the unknown MD of GM Ireland was the most impersonated person in the land. "Pud de bute in" became the "Drink! Feck! Arse! Girls!" of its day, an off-the-peg interjection for every occasion.

Attempting to make sense of his overnight celebrity, O'Byrne said, "Two guys would go into work and say 'Jeez, did you see yer man on the telly last night? Christ, he's got a neck!' So instead of turning it off when it came on, they'd sit there and say 'What a brass neck!', and so it became a talking point and it caught on."

By the summer of Euro '88, when the Irish squad and tens of thousands of fans set off for the country's first ever tournament, Arnold, Jack and Jack's wife Pat had formed a tight snacking circle based on a shared love of an English institution. He explained, "I'm very partial to Marks & Spencer's Eccles Cakes, but you can't get them in Ireland, so every time Pat comes over she visits M&S first and brings me a bag of Eccles Cakes."

Charlton and his backroom team brought in a fresh draft of players and a new regime with Jack as Supreme Ruler and found instant success. When the Republic qualified for the Euro

'88 Finals in West Germany a vibrant new cottage industry in mugs, scarves, caps, t-shirts and anything else that would take an imprint of the cheesy Charlton grin flew off the shelves and the back of lorries. By Euro '88 Big Jack had well overtaken Arnold O'Byrne as Ireland's new merchandising king, his grinning mug endorsing an endless range of products, while the ceramic mugs bearing his likeness had pride of place alongside the precious China in living rooms across the land.

When the draw for Euro '88 took place, to every deflated Irish supporter it seemed like the party had been pooped before it had even started. Our first ever game in our first ever tournament was to be against one of the hot favourites, England. Coach Bobby Robson had an embarrassment of riches all over the park, from Peter Shilton in goals through Tony Adams, Brian Robson, Barnes and Beardsley, Hoddle and Waddle, all the way to the top scorer at the 1986 World Cup, Gary Lineker.

The game took place on a hot June Sunday afternoon, which happened to be a *Hot Press* production Sunday, which meant every staffer was on deck to finish the magazine. But that particular afternoon, the office resembled the Marie Celeste. The workplace was abandoned and everyone but me went to the International Bar next door. Foreseeing a scoreline of Lineker 4, Ireland 0, I slowly walked up Grafton Street and around Stephen's Green and circled a deserted city centre until it was all over. And when it was all over, Ray Houghton's far-too-early sixth-minute goal had worked a miracle and started a party that would last the next six years.

A few months into the Charlton regime, ace defender Mark Lawrenson pronounced himself well pleased with the improvements Jack had brought to the Irish set-up, remarking, "It's now being run like a football team should be run." For one thing, he said, "When I first joined, you had spells when you never knew if you were in the squad. You never got a letter saying you were in the squad until *after* you got back from an international."

Possibly the greatest of Jack's improvements to was to fully embrace and exploit the "Granny Rule" which allowed foreign-born players to turn out for the Republic if just one grandparent was born in Ireland. John Giles had used it to cap Lawrenson, while Eoin Hand had brought on board Chris Houghton, Mick McCarthy and Liverpool's Michael Robinson. But, alerted to the scheme, Charlton told his people to go at it full tilt.

He had cards placed on the notice boards of top English clubs inviting English-born players with even the skimpiest Irish roots to declare for Ireland. Some in England saw this as an act of brazen treachery from an England World Cup winner, while some in Ireland suspected something deeply anti-Irish afoot. Jack's gruff response was, "You want me to compete with the best in the world, I've got to have the fucking best in the world. And if it's not here in Ireland that I can find it, I've got to go to England to find it, or Scotland. Now if you don't want me to do that, tell me and I'll fucking concentrate on the League of Ireland and we'll win nothing."

His policy was an instant success, with Ray Houghton and John Aldridge making their debuts in his very first game in charge. Stalwarts like Tony Cascarino, Jason McAteer and future captain Andy Townsend followed.

At a point in time when Britain's Prime Minister Margaret Thatcher was the number one global hate figure for most of the Irish supporters, the Iron Lady was greatly admired by many of the Republic's players for tax reasons. Playing in the era just before the advent of the Premier League instant millions payout, Mark Lawrenson revealed, "I have bought old houses, lived in them and sold them. The profit is tax free."

Even though Lawrenson and his fellow high-earning professionals were still paying 60 pence in the pound in 1986 under the Tories, this was still a cut below what they had been levied under the last Labour government seven years earlier. He observed, "All the footballers who pay the top rate of tax are in favour of Mrs Thatcher."

In leading his multinational band to the country's first ever World Cup Finals in 1990, Charlton achieved sainthood (he and his players were granted an audience with the Pope) and he received a degree of verbal infallibility. As the Republic's footballing stock shot through the roof, Big Jack became the living embodiment of Victor Hugo's dictum that everything bows to success, even grammar. Or, as put by Humpty Dumpty in *Through The Looking Glass*, "When I use a word it means just what I choose it to mean – neither more nor less."

And so in that spirit of carefree invincibility, several household names were recast in Jack's image. Paul McGrath became 'John'. Denis Irwin became 'David' and Liam Brady became 'Liam O'Brady'. When Jack was in full swash, the English language buckled. He once contended, for instance, that, "If, in winning the game we only finish with a draw, that would be fine". On another occasion he confounded geographers everywhere by observing that the English people "fought two wars against the Germans. We probably got on better with the Dutch, the Belgians, the Norwegians and the Swedes, some of whom are not even in Europe."

As Lawrenson pointed out, under Jack's management players now got a letter in the post informing them they'd made the squad *before* the game in question. But by Charlton's own admission, the same courtesy didn't apply to those whose use to the manager had come to an end. He unapologetically admitted, "It is true that I don't write letters to people or call them on the phone to tell them they are finished. That, for me, has an air of finality about it."

Having missed out on Euro '88 through a combination of injury and suspension, the man dubbed Liam O'Brady by the Ireland manager had his dreams of Italia '90 whipped away with just months to go. In his prime, Brady had masterminded the midfields of Arsenal and Italian giants Juventus, but with Ireland's World Cup debut tantalisingly within reach he was told he was surplus to requirements in a cruel and unusual public humiliation.

By the time Ireland took on West Germany in a home friendly in 1989, Brady had lost a yard of pace and puff, besides which the gifted midfielder didn't fit in with Big Jack's basic and highly effective game plan which was to bypass the midfield and use the prodigiously long-kicking goalkeeper Packie Bonner as his playmaker.

On a marathon car trek from Dublin to Sligo and back again in 1994, Charlton revealed to journalist Paul Rowan the thinking behind Brady's humiliating substitution after just 35 minutes in what was billed as the midfielder's testimonial game. The Irish fans who worshipped Brady, complained Charlton, "would expect me to call him up for every international match in spite of the fact that he's not quick and not playing. So I put him on display."

And so Brady was paraded, and swiftly and, many thought, callously, withdrawn to drive home the point that Jack picked the team, not the supporters. "The Irish don't give up their heroes easily," he remarked, "so you've really got to show 'em." It was earmarked as Brady's big feast day, but it turned out Jack had him earmarked as the sacrificial offering. "I'm not going to give up a result for Liam or anybody," stated the manager.

The glee that accompanied Euro '88 was just the warm-up for

the mass hysteria that followed when the team qualified for the Italia '90 World Cup Finals. Having fought heroically but failed to get out of the so-called Group Of Death at Euro '88, the Irish at Italia '90 found themselves once again cast into the pit with England and the Netherlands, two formidable outfits. For some in the Gaelic Games community this was a good thing which would put a quick end to the nonsense distracting the people from Ireland's traditional summer sporting fare.

As the big kick-off neared, the *Evening Herald*'s GAA writer Eugene McGee warned the straying masses, "There is a concerted effort to convince millions of people... that they will be outcasts of Irish society if they do not become soccer fanatics next June. It is largely a commercial marketing ploy."

Jack Charlton's withering rebuff to the hostile GAA camp was, "I'm always suspicious of games where you're the only ones that play it."

In the summer of 1990 Italy blissfully surrendered when it was love-bombed by a mass movement called Jack's Army whose very existence was resented and ridiculed by a hardcore of 'real' supporters who'd paid their dues freezing on dank terraces stoically swallowing swigs from a hip flask and cruel doses of grinding disappointment. The accusation that the blow-ins couldn't tell one end of a ball from the other bounced off the tens of thousands who sold their grannies to go to Italy for the three group games, and stayed aboard as the magical mystery tour kept going.

The 'real' supporters weren't the only ones to cast jaundiced eyes upon this new model good-time army. One ITV commentator branded the team "Jack Charlton's team of international misfits". No-one got too upset, in part perhaps because there was a morsel of substance to the charge.

Looking back, Niall Quinn told of events in the dressing room minutes after Ireland made their exit against Italy in a close-fought quarter-final. Taoiseach Charles Haughey entered and Londoner Tony Cascarino wondered aloud, “Who the fuck is that?”

Quinn hushed him, “Shut-up, it’s the Taoiseach.”

Next, another Anglo, Andy Townsend, asked Cascarino who was the guy in the suit, getting the reply, “Dunno, but he owns a tea-shop.”

The impact of Italia ’90 on Ireland’s self-image and on the image of Ireland abroad was immeasurable. The feelgood factor was more widespread and intense than anything U2 had ever brought to the party because the whole nation was loved-up, including that large part of the population that didn’t ‘get’ pop music or youth culture. Of course, U2 had to be in there somewhere and drummer Larry Mullen produced and co-wrote the Irish squad’s official song ‘Put ‘Em Under Pressure’ with its ‘*Olé Olé Olé*’ hook which remains an anthem for all things joyfully Irish.

In the summer of 1994, Jack’s Army exported the country’s charm offensive to North America, but that proved to be the manager’s last hurrah. A series of poor results and lamentable performances brought the damning comment from former admirer Mark Lawrenson, “If Plan A fails, try Plan A.”

Charlton was shown the red card by his employers just weeks before the tenth anniversary of his appointment. In a show of genuine love, admiration and gratitude he and his wife were showered with civic honours. “I’m as happy as a pig in muck,” he said, accepting honorary Irish citizenship.

His contribution to the health and happiness of the nation was beyond words.

As the Temple Bar campaigner Frank McDonald put it to me, “1990 was a pivotal year on several fronts. The public mood in Ireland was changing. Through Italia '90 we managed to reclaim our flag after years of seeing it draped over the coffins of IRA men. Now it could be waved with enthusiasm for a heroic soccer team coached by an Englishman, Jack Charlton."

Chapter 16

THE CATHOLIC CHURCH ATTEMPTS TO COLLAR YOUTH CULTURE

"My mother was so religious she wouldn't talk to me for six months because I was playing Judas in Jesus Christ Superstar. Anyone but Judas, she'd say."

– Broadway star Colm CT Wilkinson

IN THE dying days of the 1970s, Pope John Paul II arrived in Ireland on the third leg of his world tour to reignite the holy spirit of Catholicism across the globe. Ireland's faithful felt honoured to be placed so high on his to-do list which would eventually run to 146 different lands. He underscored the purpose of his pastoral visit in a specially dedicated youth mass in Galway where he declared, "Young people of Ireland, I love you." The fact that this was instantly lampooned from the smallest school child to the drunkest pub goer as "yong peopol ov Ireland I loof you", was an early indication that reclaiming the country's straying flock would not be easy.

Ireland facing into the '80s was a marketplace for new religious ideas as the young deserted the Vatican in droves, but rather than turning straight to hardline atheism they splintered into as many religious tribes as musical ones. This slip sliding away had been apparent to church authorities since the 1960s, as seen in two public information films made by the church's own media unit. One, from the '60s, entitled *Good Manners In Church*, sought to curb bad practices such as loitering down the back during Mass, sneaking off home during Communion and stepping out for a sly smoke during the ceremony (the film omitted mentioning that having a sly smoke *inside* the church was not unknown amongst post-pub attendees of midnight mass).

Another instruction film from the '70s borrowed its trendy title from a Rory Gallagher album entitled *Messin' With The Kid*. The title would take on unfortunate undertones in later times, but the intent behind the film was to reassure concerned parents that just because their youngsters liked rock music it didn't necessarily make them card-carrying Satan worshippers.

Like the dreaded folk mass imported from the States at the start of the '70s, *Messing With The Kids* merely underlined that the Catholic Church had not the faintest clue of how to deal with, or appeal to, young people. And so the ideas market-place expanded to fill the vacuum. When one of our friends announced he'd signed up for the Hare Krishnas, who hosted free vegan lunches in Dublin's city centre, we felt so sorry for him. We threw him a party in a Drumcondra flat to mark his final night of freedom, plying him with joints and strong liquor in the hope he might relapse into lapsed Catholicism and leave it at that. He crawled away into the night and I, for one, never saw him again.

Another good friend, who was part of the U2/Virgin Prunes Lypton Village collective, urged anyone who'd listen to join the reborn Christian movement which listed Bono, the Edge, Larry,

Guggi and other local celebs as proud members of the congregation. It seemed like indecent haste to join another branch of Christianity so soon after quitting Catholicism on the grounds that it was rubbish, so myself and my friend Bart said no.

We also had grounds to suspect that some bright young things were signing on to be reborn not from any spiritual epiphany, but because it brought them directly into U2's circle. Our friend's enthusiasm for being reborn ebbed after he began sharing a house that was purpose rented for reborn Christians. He told us that his daily purchase of the liberal *Irish Times* caused tiffs with housemates who didn't want any non-scriptural material crossing the threshold. Ditto, his preferred viewing choices – in a city with only five channels – were a constant source of friction. So he left the house, though not his newfound faith.

The real rival to reborn Christianity as an alternative to Catholicism in the Finglas/Ballymun area was to become a disciple of Guru Maharaj Ji, an eastern mystic who self-identified as the "perfect living master". For many of his local acolytes known to me, "living perfect" translated into a well-structured criminal work-life balance. Aged between their late teens and mid-twenties, the male members of the Maharaj Ji cult would sign on at the local dole office, take the cattle boat midweek and sign on with the DHSS in the English midlands. They would then carry out a series of burglaries on one of the countless routes off Spaghetti Junction and celebrate all night long on the ferry back in time to start up the whole process again. On the face of it, the Maharaj Ji cult seemed the most appealing of the alternative religions – they had the best girlfriends, the best cars, the loudest bling, and you were always guaranteed an uplifting platitude of how to live well courtesy of the Guru himself – but you just knew that most of them were going to end up in Mountjoy and that's exactly what happened.

At the end of September 1979, John Paul II arrived in what had forever been a safe constituency but was now at a tipping point. The Catholic Church in Ireland had never been in this position before. The bond between Church and State had been at its most adamantine in the 1950s, when the population sunk to its lowest in recorded history on the back of mass exodus of the county's youth as economic migrants.

Midway through that most dismal decade, a couple of mild-mannered Jehovah's Witnesses spent a placid Sunday afternoon knocking on doors in the Clare village of Clonlara, asking if people had heard about the One True God. After a series of friendly chats they were packing up to leave when a truck pulled up in front of their motorbike, blocking their exit. They found themselves surrounded by an angry mob led by the parish priest, Fr Patrick Ryan. "Are you the men going around distributing and selling heretic books and articles?" he asked, not particularly looking for an answer. The men – Stephen Miller and Henry Bond – were given a good beating and, after watching their books given a ceremonial burning, were told to get out and never set foot in Clonlara again.

Men of their convictions, Miller and Bond took the priest and 10 accomplices to court where the local Bishop turned up to support the mob who cheerfully admitted to assaulting the two men. Before delivering his verdict the judge stressed that the courts were obliged to be non-sectarian, *but*, while "we have a fairly average reputation for religious tolerance in this country" he was going to make an exception for the "blasphemous" Jehovah's Witnesses. Even though the charge of assault was proven, he would dismiss it under the Probation Act. And as for all the other charges, he would dismiss them too. He fined the victims £200 each, a massive sum in 1956, and threatened them with three months jail if they talked themselves into getting beaten up again. Their outraged solicitor told the judge, "Your worship's decision is contrary to the law of the country." The judge didn't care. There was no public outcry over this glaring piece of rough justice. The only paper to comment was the liberal Protestant *Irish Times*, which took pains to express disdain for the men's religion. A simple truth prevailed – God was a Catholic. And as long as that remained the case, the Witnesses and their ilk would be unwelcome interlopers at large in a hostile state with no invisible means of support.

By the early 1970s a casual head count at any Sunday mass would have confirmed a distinct imbalance between the elderly, the very young, and the missing middle where the teens and twenty-somethings used to be. The Catholic Church was slowly but surely losing the battle to put bums on seats but it still wasn't going to put up with any rival attempting to poach its flock. This time the unwelcome interlopers in the dock were five Hare Krishnas hauled before Dublin District Court in 1973. A Garda detective accused the men of "walking down Grafton Street playing music and making a lot of noise. I had cautioned them on previous occasions not to play music to the annoyance of the inhabitants of the street... They were walking in single file but people had to walk in the roadway to avoid them."

The judge asked if any of the accused spoke English, learning to his displeasure that three of them were Irish born and bred. Visibly angered by the disrespect shown in particular by one of the men who had a small drum hanging from his shoulder, the judge berated the tangerine-clad defendants, "Why are you dressed in those ridiculous garments? I could sentence you for contempt for wearing a scarf like that. I can warn you, you were lucky not to have been assaulted by the crowd. Any decent Irishman would object to this carry on. My only regret is that I can't have you locked up." The judge then came up with another regret which was that he didn't have the power to confiscate their "nonsensical" bells and leaflets. He fined them seven pounds each. As they left the court, a uniformed Guard scolded, "You should pray in the church."

Six years later, towards the close of 1979, the Church made its big play to consolidate its position as the most powerful cultural source in Irish society and to staunch the snowballing defection of young people to the Dark Side of Satanic heresies or none of the above. The plan was that John Paul II would reaffirm the special place of the Catholic Church in Irish life before 1.5 million people at Dublin's Phoenix Park, before winning back the dithering multiple choice generation with a special youth mass the following day in Galway.

And so for one momentous day, I was a teenage Papal Punk in the Phoenix Park. That is, a Papal Punk Steward charged with the smooth running of the event. I made no apologies for it back in 1979 and still see nothing odd about swapping my regulation leather jacket and snot green drainpipes, mail ordered from the *NME*, for a yellow-and-white Papal sash draped over my brown flared ex-Sunday Best suit. In the '70s, suits, carpets, wallpaper and curtains all came in two colours: brown and orangey-brown. And besides, it was just for one day.

Being a lapsed Catholic didn't mean you stopped being a cultural Catholic and everyone in 1979 was a cultural Catholic by upbringing and often by inclination, except for Protestants and pesky foreign sects bent on rocking the boat. Besides, there was the star factor. John Paul II was the first rock star Pope and there was no other show in town. Literally. Since the Miami Showband massacre three years earlier, Ireland had been effectively a no-go area for stellar visitors apart, inexplicably, from Eric Clapton, who appeared to have a monthly residency at the run-down National Stadium.

So, draped Miss World fashion with a Papal sash, and armed with a Papal flag to wave, a flask of stewed tea and corned beef sandwiches, myself, Bart and our fellow orderlies led the faithful of Ballymun's Lady Of Victories parish in procession to the Phoenix Park in the dank pre-dawn. Subversively, Bart and I wore zig-zag Day-Glo punky neckties to signify an ironic detachment from our duties. In Cabra, our column of pilgrims passed a hardware store which had opened its doors at 5am with hundreds of fold-up wooden chairs racked up on the footpath outside, bathed in light from the shop window. With more than a million people expected to start arriving at the Phoenix Park from 5am opening, the faithful had been giving advance warning that "only invalids and the aged" would be provided with benches. At £3.57 each these chairs cost a pretty extortionate penny, but it was going to be a long day standing in that big field and they were already flying out of the shop.

Armed with a site-map for giving directions, at around breakfast-time we began to marshal our flock (women, children, grumpy men) into Corral No.18 which resembled a large sheep pen and may indeed have been a large sheep pen, where they settled into the long wait for the Pope's helicopter. Besides pointing out the nearest loos, we were to keep the swarms of circling hawkers from infiltrating the Mass area, much as Jesus had expelled the traders from the temple. That didn't happen. Coke cans, Mars Bars and ice-creams flew across the fences into the compounds at unholy prices. Cries of "See the Pope for one pound!" filled the air and when John Paul II finally appeared on the vast stage, a serried sea of cardboard periscopes went up to have their pricey £1 view blocked by the sea of periscopes in front.

Any smug satisfaction I felt at living a day of virtuous self-sacrifice was punctured by the thousands upon thousands of fellow teens blaring out Bob Marley and The Clash from the park's tree-canopied margins which were shrouded in a pungent Lebanese haze and littered with spent flagons of cider. There had never been a greater concentration of Gardaí in one place but, stretched beyond their limits, they gave the punky reggae party crashers a free pass. There was not a mention in the national newspapers or broadcast media of this very large, very loud, very in-your-face, alternative festival going on within the grounds of the Phoenix Park. The sole focus of the media was to spread the good news gospel.

The lawbreaking Alternative Mass Ireland jamboree piggy-backing the main event was not the only episode left out of the edited highlights of a media that pronounced the visit a seamless triumph. Twenty years after the event I met up with Polish-born Dublin travel agent Jan Kaminski who'd been selected to welcome the Polish Pope to Ireland, watched by more than a million mass-goers, with a brief greeting in Polish. In 2008, the Polish Embassy in Dublin estimated that some 200,000 Poles were living in Ireland. In 1979 when the Papal visit was announced, newspapers numbered Ireland's Polish community at "almost 100". With the visit confirmed, Kaminski quickly founded the Irish-Polish Society and the number claiming Polish roots jumped to 400.

Waiting in the wings of the vast Phoenix Park stage, Kaminski's moment finally arrived. On cue, he strode with purpose towards the Pope on the altar. Too purposefully for the twitchy security spooks. "As I approached the Pope, they jumped on me," he told me. "They thought I was an assassin. I have press photos showing me in their grasp, gasping with shock." If Frederick Forsyth had been in charge of security for the Mass, as he'd offered, the embarrassing incident would almost certainly have been avoided.

Dublin's city centre was a ghost-town, with no shops open, no public transport running, no litter collected from the filthy streets. Empty. The biggest gathering spotted in central Dublin during the mass was a group of five people at a Grafton Street burger stall.

The next day the deserted streets of Galway City told the same story. Even as the Pope was telling his people to go in peace at the Phoenix Park, a cavalcade of cars and coaches carrying many of the young people of Ireland slipped out of Dublin, carrying their tents, sleeping bags and slabs of beer. Taking advantage of the empty roads, the motorcade, which stretched 12 miles in length, set off in the direction of Galway where the Pope would hold a special youth mass the following day, supported by Bishop Eamon Casey and Fr Michael Cleary.

There, John Paul greeted a cross-section of Irish society who presented themselves two-by-two in the style of Noah's Ark. Even half-a-century ago, these figures represented an idealised, pastoral Ireland that seemed bizarre and alien and ancient history to the Pope's target audience, a vanished world that even a Papal miracle could never bring back. They included "a national school teacher with cap and gown", "a lame person with stick or crutches", "a carpenter's apprentice in dungarees", "an itinerant", "a deaf person" and "a farmer and a dog".

If the oddball parade was a source of merriment to the estimated 300,000, the scene stealing efforts of the Pontiff's two star sidekicks met with less good humour. The young people of Ireland were already only too well aware of the cleric leading the mass sing-songs. For years Fr Michael Cleary had toured his All Priests' Show around Ireland, with himself out front throwing shapes as 'The Mod Priest'. It was as good as it sounds. A man with few filters, Fr Cleary openly admitted he made the most unpriestly priest. He said, "By a process of elimination I came to the horrifying conclusion of the priesthood. I didn't want it because it meant giving up football and girls, and I was very interested in both." In time the country would learn that he'd given up nothing. Typically, he didn't blame himself, but laid all fault at the Church's screening process. "I went in hoping that I'd be found out and thrown out, but I wasn't."

A decade after Michael Cleary and his colleague Bishop Eamon Casey – who organised the event – attempted to pass themselves off as trendy young things singing on the Youth Mass stage, both were to play a huge part in turning those same still young people away from the church forever as their betrayals of their creed and those who trusted them went viral.

Cleary had always been regarded as an unstable element, which worked in his favour when he landed a gig as a clerical shock jock on a Dublin radio station, and a newspaper column which granted licence to rant. He marked one National No Smoking Day with a piece headlined: Why I'm Definitely Not Giving Up Cigarettes This Lent. Challenging centuries of Church teaching bigging up the penance of self-denial, he asserted that, "Lenten exercises should be aimed at making us easier to live with, rather than more difficult." He backed this up with a parable drawing on a recent flight from Bristol, for which Aer Lingus had imposed an experimental no-smoking ban. He raged, "Locked in a small plane unable to smoke, I experienced real panic. The kind hostess offered me a glass of brandy, which I declined. Apparently I could get plastered drunk and become a nuisance and a danger, or I could pop pills or shoot heroin, but I could not smoke."

Bishop Eamon Casey's fall from grace was perhaps the more surprising, given his reputation for good deeds which he'd put up front and centre as the caring face of the Church in Ken Loach's groundbreaking and transformative BBC documentary *Cathy Come Home*, while working with Irish rough-sleepers in Britain. In 1986, Casey again projected himself as the compassionate face of the Church, appearing close to tears in an interview where he said his heart told him he should vote Yes to divorce in the upcoming referendum, but he was bound to vote No by way of just following orders. Mirroring the confessions of Michael Cleary, the Bishop was happy to admit, "I'm as sexual as anyone else and there are a thousand ways in which I express my sexuality." But remembering his duties as a role model he added, "We're in an era of time when self-control seems to have been put aside as a value."

In the near future a shocking lack of self-control would lead to the downfall of the Bishop and the Mod Priest, and would start the tremors that would bring their Church crashing to earth.

With the credibility and integrity of the Catholic Church on the line in the '90s, the two frontmen set the task of reconciling Ireland's youth to the faith of their fathers, were both confronted with the sins of fatherhood. Casey had syphoned large amounts of diocesan funds to his secret son in the USA, while Cleary had started a family with his young housekeeper.

Looking back upon the euphoria of the Galway Youth Mass of 1979 from the viewpoint of the transformed Ireland of the '90s, it could be argued that the most enduring impression the Papal visit left on the young people of Ireland was a generation of teenage boys named John Paul. The records show that in the year following the visit, 10% of all male newborns were named after the rock star Pope.

Between 1983 and 1986 Ireland was torn asunder by a vicious tug of war for the nation's immortal soul. In 1983, even though abortion had always been illegal, the two major parties decided to hold a referendum to make it even more illegal as the plain people edged ever closer to the normalisation of artificial contraception. Opposed by the Left but supported by most politicians backed up from the pulpit, the referendum predictably passed with a big majority. Three years later, the liberal thinkers making up the biggest part of the Fine Gael/Labour government pushed through the wording for a referendum on divorce. Some reforming politicians believed they'd been double-crossed when the Catholic bishops threw their full heft behind the 'No' campaign, having seemingly indicated that they would let civic society sort out the divisive issue. One senior government minister let his displeasure with a particular bishop be known when he said that he'd like to "get dug out of that bastard". This was a sign that the battle of the traditionalists and modernisers had entered the unknown. Bishops had never been spoken of in that manner before, at least not in public. A bitter civil war had ignited in earnest. In general terms – but not in every case – the warring sides broke down into 'rural vs urban' and 'older vs younger'.

The decisive victories of the traditional, rural, older side in the 1983 abortion and 1986 divorce referenda seemed set to keep the country on the same safe course for a generation or more to come. No-one in 1983 or 1986 could in their wildest imaginings foresee that in the space of a dozen years the young, progressive city types would be claiming total victory as the Divorce Ban was cast aside and the trusted pillars of Catholic truth crumbled. In the summer of 1985 the world's media descended on the tiny Cork village of Ballinspittle for a feelgood silly season story marked by a truce in the civil war. A statue of the Virgin Mary had begun a nightly dance in her roadside grotto. Many witnesses swore they'd seen her lips move and her shoulders shrug. One even claimed that her face had contorted into that of Jesus with a long nose and a beard. The official message from the Catholic hierarchy was "nothing to see here". Top theologians were rolled out to assure the public that the movements of the statue were an optical illusion caused by the mind of the viewer playing tricks. There was even a name for this illusion, the auto-kinetic effect, which meant that when viewing an object from a distance in a dim setting the viewer's eyes will do all the moving.

The crowds came day and night but the Virgin seemed at her most jiggy after dark when she was surrounded with distorting lights and the crowd was at its most boisterous. Skeptics pointed to the fact that the village pubs had never had it so good, while those who'd assumed the duty of crowd control kept the public at a distance of 20m from the Virgin so that scientific tests were out of bounds.

The Church hierarchy said there was nothing to see, but they were disobeyed by excited gaggles of priests and nuns, who in turn were far outnumbered by throngs of young party people who declared a cease-fire with their estranged brethren for as long as the party lasted. And it lasted. Ballinspittle briefly became Ireland's most happening tourist magnet, to the point that the gridlock on the narrow roads into the village made them impassable and farmers had to turn their fields into lucrative makeshift pay-per-day car parks. B&B signs popped up all over the townland although a quick check of the tourist board register showed that there was not a single B&B in Ballinspittle. A fleet of fast food vans dropped anchor with one cleverly finding the perfect pitch between young and old with 'Madonna Burgers' as Madonna's 'Into The Groove' lorded it at the top of the pop charts.

The village of Garryowen in Limerick then went one better than Ballinspittle with a plaster Virgin who was shedding tears of blood and the floodgates opened all across the country as just about every Marian grotto turned out to harbour some miraculous property once the locals looked hard enough. At the height of the delirium, one Bishop went on TV in an effort to call a halt, saying he believed "religion itself will be brought into disrepute". He elaborated, "I've met a number of ordinary sensible people who are taking a second look at statues, and I've caught myself doing it. In this kind of climate we're very open to suggestion." One sociologist suggested that the population at large was experiencing an episode of psychological displacement, with the old time religion responding to being suppressed in one sphere by popping up in another form, in the style of the whack-a-mole game.

It seemed clear that Catholic Ireland was having a psychotic episode manifesting as a bout of mass hysteria. Clear, that is, to the authorities, the visiting media and the footloose youth happy to treat the whole thing as a green light from God to party in the streets. However, it was far from clear to the sober masses reciting decades of the Rosary at roadside grottos from Kerry to Donegal in what one Bishop sorrowfully called "a contagion". As the summer silly season drew to a close and the statues became still again, the forces of Catholic conservatism resumed their war against what one of their leading lights, Míne Bean Uí Chribín, branded "the curse of the Libbies", or liberals.

Just 10 years later, in the late summer of 1995, another bout of holy hysteria, this time in Co Waterford, would effectively bring the religious war to a jarring end with the world's media again on hand to bear witness.

Between the '85 moving statues craze and the '95 'Yes' to divorce turnabout, the inter-referenda hostilities would throw up some bizarre episodes which captured a society in the throes of an existential struggle. In September 1987, the Hare Krishnas found themselves the vegan filling in the civil war sandwich as

Catholic Ireland mounted an opportunistic counter-offensive to get itself off the backfoot.

A shocking torrent of spite and even hatred was unleashed when Dubliner Tony Murphy went on RTÉ's *Liveline* radio show with a mind-boggling tale of abduction, island captivity, and indoctrination at the hands of the Krishnas. What really caught the public's imagination, though, was the drugged ice cream.

The 25-year-old had been on the missing persons list for a week when he turned up at his local Rathfarnham Garda station to report his abduction. His story began at the Hare Krishna restaurant on Dublin's Crow Street. A fine free veggie meal was finished off with ice cream. Drugged ice cream, he later learned to his cost. He blacked out and came to in a different room where he was offered more food. Surprisingly, given how his last snack disagreed with him, he ate it.

Next thing he knew he was on an island on Lough Erne, County Fermanagh. When he begged to leave, he was told "Krishna said no". A chance to escape arrived when he was taken to Enniskillen Hospital with a minor neck tweak. But he didn't breathe a word of his captivity because he thought the doctors and nurses were "in cahoots" with his captors. When he made good his escape it was in a manner worthy of 007. He climbed out a window, shinned down a pillar, navigated a leaky boat, stole a car and fled back over the border.

His distraught parents called in their parish priest, who arranged for Murphy to recount his terrifying ordeal on the national broadcaster's flagship talk-in show. In the face of a barrage of abusive calls from concerned Catholics, a Krishna spokesman denounced the whole thing as a pack of lies, insisting Murphy had gone to the island voluntarily. The saga occupied a second show, then a third. The terms 'cult' and 'brainwashing' were much bandied about as the Krishnas took a mauling from listeners.

It was 14 years since a judge had lamented that he couldn't put the Hare Krishnas off the streets and in the heightened religious hostilities of the mid-1980s, tolerance of difference was in short supply. On the second *Liveline*, Murphy's parish priest took to the air. He said he knew nothing about the ways of the Hare Krishnas, but it seemed obvious that Murphy should be taken at his word.

What happened next recalled the Monty Python sketch where a man claiming to have written the plays of Shakespeare is reminded that the works in question were penned 300 years before his birth. He concedes, "*That* is where my claim falls down. I was hoping you wouldn't bring that up."

Tony Murphy's whereabouts on the day he claimed he'd been kidnapped were no longer a mystery. He'd been on national television. RTÉ had filmed him demonstrating outside the Soviet embassy in support of imprisoned Russian Krishnas. In fact, he was holding up the main protest banner. This bombshell provoked a third *Liveline* where, instead of accepting that Murphy had led everyone a merry dance, diehard callers argued that his amnesia actually *proved* the ice cream had been drugged.

Bowing to Hare Krishna demands, the Gardaí launched an investigation. Murphy was in a deep hole, but planning to lodge kidnapping charges. The police told him to stop digging. He wouldn't. When it came to court, the judge dismissed his "smear" as "outrageous" and imposed a three-year suspended sentence for wasting Garda time.

As the judge delivered his verdict, a Hare Krishna spokesman gave his. He stated grimly, "The involvement of the Catholic clergy in this case merits further investigation."

It was an in-between time. Ireland was on the brink of entering a brave new world of mobile phones, satellite TV, personal computers, international celebrity culture and transformative cheap flights, all of which would be life-changing. But at the close of that September week in 1987, it was abundantly clear that although they'd lost this particular battle, those who wanted to drag Ireland back to their comfort zone of the 1950s were still very much alive and dangerous in the war.

Two years after the latest go at the Hare Krishnas, the spirit that moved the multitudes to Marian shrines in the summer of 1985 was back on the front pages, although this time localised to just one modest terraced house in the north Dublin suburb of Coolock.

It was in response to an irresistibly large print headline that myself and my colleague Liam Fay arrived at a modest semi-d where a line of perhaps 20 people snaked around the small front garden. The lead story on the *Evening Press* claimed that an image of Jesus was currently appearing in a bedroom door there and that long queues were forming at the door to have a peek. We turned up on spec and were greeted by three middle-aged women and a priest. They brought us upstairs and showed us the door. There was indeed a pattern in the grain, but it could just as well have been Kurt Cobain as the man upstairs.

We behaved with impeccable politeness and said our goodbyes, but as we made to leave they took us aside to show us their latest discovery which they hadn't yet made public. In an airing cupboard they'd found an image of the Virgin Mary. Again we manfully resisted the temptation to collapse in a heap. We did wonder, however, why we had been specially favoured with a preview of the Virgin in the airing cupboard. As we finally got back to the front door, we discovered why. We weren't asked if we were trainee priests from the seminary, we were *told* that we were because we had that priestly look about us. We didn't disagree. We just said goodbye and thanks.

Our experience in Coolock provided the inspiration for the episode of *Father Ted* entitled 'Kicking Bishop Brennan Up The Arse'. The writers, Arthur and Graham, borrowed the idea and had Ted and Dougal paint an image of Brennan low down on a skirting board in order to get the Bishop to bend over for his kicking.

The moving statue summer of 1985 had seen a good-humoured time-out in the religious wars between the defenders of the faith and the swelling legions of unbelievers. The conflict would quickly resume into a fight to the bitter end.

Ten years after the world's media descended on Ballinspittle to watch the Irish throw a hooley for a plaster cast Madonna, they were back in force to the little Waterford harbour town of Dungarvan, and this time it was serious. The normally sedate hamlet had been visited by mass hysteria – Sunday Mass hysteria – when Father Michael Kennedy unleashed a homily that no-one present would ever forget. He told his startled congregation that a young woman, recently returned from London, was deliberately infecting the young men of the area with AIDS. The unidentified hussy, he claimed, was offering sex to all comers with just one condition – no condoms. The priest said that already some 80 young men in the district were infected.

By lunchtime that Sunday the town was in a panic. By Tuesday, Dungarvan's faceless 'AIDS Avenger' AKA 'The Angel Of Death' was splashed across all the front pages. By Wednesday, camera crews and print hacks from across the globe were in a bidding war for B&B billets. Fr Michael Kennedy was a distant relation of the White House Camelot Kennedys so the story went viral in no time. In fact, he'd recently officiated at the glitzy wedding of the murdered Robert Kennedy's daughter Courtney to the Guildford Four fit-up victim Paul Hill. When it was put to the priest that every shred of scientific evidence gave the lie to his claims, the cleric countered, "Ask the medical men to sleep with a girl who has full-blown AIDS and they can come up with an answer themselves." Hardly scientific, or rational even, but it made good copy. By Thursday, the fed-up people of Dungarvan just wanted to be left in peace, and on Friday a health official called for the priest to be prosecuted if he didn't pass on potentially life-saving details. At this point, Fr Kennedy said that the AIDS Avenger had gone back to England to die. End of story. Dungarvan's notoriety as the world's deadliest seaside resort had lasted just a week, but what a week that was.

Fr Michael Kennedy's personal meltdown came at a time when the once almighty Catholic Church in Ireland was dazed, confused and in shocking freefall. The sudden and absolute manner of that fall from grace was rammed home two months after the priest's panic attack when the Irish people reversed their Church-ordered referendum ban of just nine years and Ireland legalised divorce.

Chapter 17

STEPFORD WIFE-SWAP AND THE RE-DISNEYFICATION OF IRELAND

"Dublin is a world-class city. I'm completely in the woodwork when I go around Dublin. Even if people recognise me they're very cool. The Irish don't stand on ceremony about that sort of thing. When Bono Himself walks amongst them he is very quickly reminded – lest he ever should forget – that he is a mere mortal."

– Carole King

IN JUNE 1995, I numbered amongst some 800 souls shoehorned into Dublin's modest Tivoli Theatre for a show by pretty, crop-haired, singularly-voiced Sinéad O'Connor. Meanwhile, across town at The Point a crowd 10 times the size was filling the capital's largest venue for The Cranberries, fronted by pretty, crop-haired, singularly-voiced Dolores O'Riordan. Some sort of Stepford Wives-swap had taken place, but how and why?

The why is easy. Sinéad was trouble. There's a popular misconception that the Dubliner blew her career when she tore up a photo of the Pope on NBC's ratings-grabbing *Saturday Night*

Live in 1992. That protest stunt brought a memorable disclaimer from the show's producer, Lorne Michaels, who said, "We were sort of shocked, the way you would be at a houseguest pissing on a flower arrangement in the dining room." But if Michaels had done two minutes of homework he'd have known that Sinéad was never cut out to be the model houseguest. She was too prone to tugging at carpet corners, looking for anything swept underneath. In fact her controversial reputation in the world's biggest and richest entertainment market began two years earlier when she refused to allow the American national anthem to play before a show in New Jersey, an act which earned her radio bans and a flea in the ear from Frank Sinatra who said he'd like "to kick her ass". Her curt response was, "I'm not the first woman he's threatened to hit", adding that she was delighted that Frank Sinatra knew who she was.

So that's the *why*. The *how* of this Stepford Wife-swap was standard showbiz procedure.

Responding to Sinéad's second transgression of polite performer norms, the industry in all its manifestations decided enough is enough. In his study, *The Global Jukebox*, author Robert Burnett set out how the industry groupthink works. He explained, "As soon as capital pays its lip service to risk (for which profit is its just reward) it gets busy trying to minimise it. The marketplace, the intended recipient of the product, is an abstraction and an imperfect guide. It cannot tell the anxious executive what to do. Therefore the music industry constantly tries to develop new ways to control both supply and demand." And so, the plan was and is that if you control the demand end – like music outlets, TV and radio etc – you can ensure that the consumer is set up to want what the suppliers are set up to supply.

There's no suggestion that anyone actively conspired to usurp the angry and unpredictable Sinéad and replace her with a near lookalike angst-free singer fronting an outfit with a line in pleasant, dreamy, radio melodies and whose biggest selling album was entitled *No Need To Argue*. It's just how the system is set up to work.

In the same month, June 1995, that the story of the doppelgangers was being played out across Dublin, the Irish dance sensation *Riverdance* vacated The Point to decamp for a lengthy run in London, where separate royal command performances would be staged for both Prince Charles and Queen Elizabeth. As it made its triumphant progress to every corner of the globe, *Riverdance* joined Enya as the ultimate expression of the re-Disneyfication of Ireland for global consumption. The two became three with the arrival of the gentle multi-platinum shifting Corrs toting their tin whistles, fiddles and bodhráns.

The commercial pendulum had swung all the way back to the '50s when John Wayne and Maureen O'Hara defined Hollywood Irishness in *The Quiet Man* and Walt Disney himself turned up in Dublin for the premiere of his pet project *Darby O'Gill And The Little People* starring Sean Connery as a loveable leprechaun catcher.

In 1988, as Enya's gauzy, chocolate box confection 'Watermark' was covering the planet in a Celtic mist, a very different version of Ireland went on limited cinema release. With music by Elvis Costello and a notable cast led by Gabriel Byrne, Patrick Bergin, Cait O'Riordan and Ian Bannen, *The Courier* was a grim tale of heroin turf wars in tumbledown modern Dublin. Unimpressed, the *In Dublin* film critic Gerry McCarthy, dismissed it as "brutal". Completely misunderstanding that "brutal" meant "one to avoid", the English producers splashed the Dublinese put-down across the movie's posters thinking it signified "very violent".

In truth it probably didn't matter if *The Courier* had been another *Godfather* – the odds of finding acceptance abroad would have been vanishing. The world didn't want to see an ugly, gritty Ireland. If they wanted grit at all they wanted pretty gritty, which is what they soon got with *The Commitments*, filmed through an affectionate English lens by director Alan Parker and scripted in the main by Britain's kings of situation comedy Dick Clement and Ian La Frenais.

One man who saw which way the wind was blowing and warned where it would lead was Bill Graham, the music writer who had played matchmaker to U2 and Paul McGuinness. In September 1990, the great and the good of the music industry, from home and abroad, gathered in Dublin for a seminar on how to make the most of Ireland's new pop prowess. The speeches and workshops covered all aspects of the business, from how to get to grips with the new-fangled rave culture to setting up a stadium-sized sound system. It was all business as usual until Bill got up and delivered a withering *J'accuse* which none of those present could unhear, much as they might want to. The writer had already deplored "the triumph of hip capitalism" that had directly followed Live Aid. The music industry, he charged, had a vested interest in slowing the spread of new musical forms, in stabilising trends and in freezing anything that looked like runaway free-thinking.

Now he took aim specifically at the rot in Irish rock. The huge increase in Ireland's musical output had been matched by a flatline in quality. He characterised "the identikit hopeful Irish rock star" as male, middle-class and "probably from a south Dublin suburb" mindlessly churning out "songs of generalised emotional assertions" which he derisively branded "Irish emotionalism". In other words, "Irish rock is the corporate ventriloquist's dummy, mouthing the second-hand language of others."

This identikit wannabe inhabited rock's comfort zone, never straying close to any dangerous edge. "Instead he operates off an all-purpose, non-specific, indiscriminate and meaningless mysticism that dissolves all differences in vacuous goodwill. Deep, green and meaningless, his potential record company hopes naïve American audiences will fill the gaps between the dots." He reserved his special ire for "the '70s generation who've succeeded the showband mafia as the commercial powers of Irish music and had a clear agenda to modernise Irish popular culture" but had sold out on that mission.

In a final swipe at his music biz audience he charged that, "Irish rock is increasingly becoming a middle-class leisure pursuit with little content. Increasingly, its only justification is in its commercial success which must be counterfeited when it's not happening."

That was 1990 when U2 and Sinéad O'Connor – no corporate puppets – sat astride the world of pop. Two or three years later, Bill Graham's damning depiction of Irish rock had become painfully plain to see as the second generation of 'Next U2s', expensively packaged for international consumption, were binned one after the other before they'd even had the luxury of suffering 'Difficult Second Album Syndrome'. The glaring exception that disproved the rule were The Cranberries AKA The Next Sinéad.

As I mentioned, a portion of that music convention in 1990 was given over to rave culture and specifically how to deal with the threat of ecstasy fuelled dance music which was both baffling and disruptive to an industry based on bog-standard rock with guitars, vocals and lyrics. Around the same time, I ran into the most unlikely individual to have given rave music the warmest embrace.

Three years earlier in 1987, I had first met Liam Ryan in

a greasy spoon café around the corner from the Olympic Ballroom, which he owned. In his capacity as Secretary of the Irish Ballroom Proprietors Association, the former priest wanted to put the case that ballrooms were being ill-treated under the licensing laws. "We're being strapped by unfair competition," he complained, pointing out that while pubs, clubs and hotels could serve drink seven nights a week, the ballrooms were restricted to six drink licences per year. Jobs in the industry had plummeted from 5,500 in 1975 to under 200 when we spoke. After our chat, he put down 20 quid to cover the fish, chips and house speciality, mushy peas. He stood up and as we shook hands across the table, he passed a roll of notes into my palm.

Flabbergasted, I told him, "I can't take this. Honestly, you have a really good point. You don't need to pay to get it printed."

But he was out the door. I counted it. Two hundred quid, more than two weeks wages. Liam Ryan was showband old school. Greasing palms was how you oiled the wheels of industry. Inevitably, my publisher told me to return the payola, which I did feeling the genuine pain of loss. Three years later, around the time of the music seminar, I ran into Ryan on the street and asked how life was treating him.

"Wonderfully," he beamed, explaining that the acid house phenomenon meant he was packing in 3,000 ravers every Friday and Saturday and not one of them wanted alcohol. I was genuinely happy for a nice man.

By the mid-90s it was becoming abundantly clear that the Irish music industry had backed the wrong rockin' horse in its bid for world domination. The business did adjust however and once again the chief driver was an old showband hand.

A young Louis Walsh first stepped onto the bottom rung of the showband ladder in the mid-70s, learning his trade as a general factotum in venues established by future Prime Minister Albert Reynolds. In 1993, noting the teen hysteria building around Take That, Walsh reasoned that the current fad for all things Irish – in rock music and in movies – could readily cross over into an exploding boy band market. That November he auditioned 300 hopefuls in Dublin's city centre, each required to take a stab at George Michael's 'Careless Whisper'. Future Hollywood star Colin Farrell didn't make the cut. Six UK Number Ones later, Boyzone had fully vindicated their manager's instincts about the marketability of Irishness. In 2002, one British newspaper described Louis Walsh as "the man who owns the UK Number One slot". It was now official, Walsh had succeeded Reynolds as the most powerful figure ever to emerge from showband management. The ultimate revenge of the showbands can be gauged in the huge success of manufactured boy and girl bands including Boyzone, Westlife and B*Witched, which in turn fed into the global saturation of 'synergy', karaoke TV and 'reality' entertainment. While U2 pursued and attained Andy Warhol's 'mythic fame', Walsh would become a giant in the not remotely brave new world of Warhol's 'peanut-sized fame'.

By the early 1990s, Ireland had suddenly, and surprisingly, taken its place amongst the hip nations of the Earth. In 1992, the narrow cobbled streets of a resurgent Temple Bar were given a coating of fake snow on the orders of top director Ron Howard for a scene featuring Hollywood's power couple Tom Cruise and Nicole Kidman. *Far And Away* turned out to be a stinker, and Cruise's *Oirish* accent continues to be nominated in the 'Worst Ever' category, but that was hardly the point. The point was that they were here. Ditto when Mel Gibson arrived in 1994 to shoot *Braveheart*, lured by the imaginative tax breaks devised by then culture minister and future President of Ireland, Michael D Higgins. And with Ireland now firmly on the map as a hip and happening place, the planet's pop royalty kept coming both for tax reasons and simply because it was the place to go.

The derelict downtrodden Dublin of Def Leppard, Spandau Ballet and the Frankies at the start of '86 had all but vanished by the close of '94. In a November issue of *In Dublin* that year, Djinn Gallagher noted how Temple Bar had been transformed from a deserted, dangerous place after dark, into the city's new funzone.

She wrote of how the district had become "a veritable monument to youthful bohemianism, brightly coloured paintwork and avant-garde haircuts. Fuelled by hormones, hash and designer beer, the young people of Dublin congregate at night in the pubs and clubs of the area, and small bistros flicker in and out of existence like fireflies. Although the civic plans for Temple Bar originally proposed razing the beautiful, crumbling buildings to the ground and building a delightful bus station in their stead, the influx of bright young businesses cashing in on the low rents and short leases has transformed the area into a vibrant business community. Temple Bar is a heartening example of the way enthusiasm and energy and youthful vigour can bypass the plodding suburban vision of the men in suits."

The week that appraisal appeared, I found myself sitting early one morning in a granite Victorian factory building, recently retooled as a plush hotel to accommodate Temple Bar's heavy new tourist footfall at its most well-heeled. The guests coming down for breakfast that morning didn't come any more well-heeled, well-respected or indeed legendary than Ray Davies of The Kinks, the songsmith behind some of the greatest classics in pop music history, including 'You Really Got Me', 'Sunny Afternoon' and 'Waterloo Sunset'.

Paradise, to the warbling narrator of 'Waterloo Sunset' is a "dirty old river" that keeps on rolling as he looks at the world from his window, feeling dizzy at the "people so busy" in the "chilly chilly" outside.

It was chilly, chilly along the Liffey on the dark winter morning we met to discuss, amongst other things, how and why six years earlier Davies had fetched up as the most fabled of all Ireland's '80s rock refugees. It was a pleasant if slightly dislocated meeting. Although just turned 50 there was an unmistakable frailty to him – in his faltering voice, in the niggling cough that punctuated his talk and in the way topics of conversation would slip in and out of focus – and for one moment into what seemed pure 'Waterloo Sunset' *deja-vu*.

"Sorry," he said, craning to look out the window at the early morning bustle along the quays below. "I've just realised how much I love this place. That's the Ha'penny Bridge. I wrote a song about the Ha'penny Bridge. I never put it out."

Unlike Sting and the MTV millionaires that followed, Davies hadn't come to Ireland seeking tax reliefs. And unlike most of the others, he shunned the bright lights and creature comforts that were rapidly turning Dublin into the big ticket venue for Europe's 24-hour party people. Just a couple of doors down from where we sat that morning, the cleaners were at work scrubbing the capital's newest hotspot, The Kitchen, based in U2's Clarence Hotel, for the evening's intake of beautiful people.

The boss Kink, who was married to a Cork woman at the time, moved to her hometown in 1988 after collapsing on a European tour that was about to land in Ireland. He didn't realise the gravity of his situation when he was checked into a London hospital and he asked to be discharged so he could play out the rest of the dates.

"I told the doctor in London that I've got to go to Ireland, and he asked if I wanted to die in London or in Ireland, adding that I might die on the airplane. I'm glad that I did come to Ireland.

There are some things that happen in life that you pull yourself through. I could have checked into a posh London clinic and I probably would have died."

Because the illness threw him back into the throes of the manic depression that had plagued him all his life?

"Yeah, but I fought back. I particularly disliked England at this time. I remember saying, 'This country, England, is not going to hurt me'. So I went to Cork, to this little hospital. The doctor saw my readings and he said, 'I'm a big fan Mr Davies, and I'm terribly sorry but you're seriously ill'."

The singer's chuckles dissolved quickly into pensive tones.

"I loved that city very much. I've lived there and got close to it. The hospital was poor, it didn't have enough sheets, but I was glad I was there instead of London."

His healing time in Cork "was like the shedding of a skin".

"I told myself I must change my whole environment, so I adopted that place as the place I would be. I would begin or end there. I just realised there how lucky I am to be alive. You don't think about all the things you're gonna do, you just look out the window and say 'It's incredible out there'. You go down to the Old Head of Kinsale and you look out to sea and you think, 'Shit! It's a long way to America, or wherever'."

A long way from America, or wherever, was where he needed to be just then.

"I just relaxed, and waited for the day I could walk up the 200 steps of Patrick's Hill. That was my target. That was the only target I had, to walk up that hill."

Rolling Stones' guitarist Ronnie Wood arrived in Ireland around the same time as Davies. Like Joe Elliott, Lisa Stansfield and others he came for the tax year and stayed for the sheer love of the place.

"The Irish community took me to heart," Wood told me six

years into his Irish residence, "and to this day remains hospitable and welcoming to me and my family. Ireland has become a tranquil haven for me. More than once it has allowed me to escape the madness of life as a Stone and quietly recharge my batteries without being disturbed." On many occasions over the years, however, recharging his batteries meant late nights as Kingpin of the Pink Elephant's pool tables.

At other times Wood imported his wild life as a Stone to his home in the little village of Clane, County Kildare, inviting a host of famous friends to visit and record in his home studio and to party hard. He's told of how U2's Edge taught him "a thing or two about guitar effects", and how house-guest Bob Dylan would break off their recording sessions "throw on his big coat, flip up the collar and go for long walks. He looked like he was walking down Fifth Avenue, avoiding stares, when in fact he was in a muddy field in Co Kildare." Playing guitar in the late '60s to mid-70s with The Jeff Beck Group and The Faces, Wood was a bona-fide rock star, but joining The Stones was like landing on "another planet". He had to learn 200 Stones songs in just weeks, *but*, he confessed, "The music was the easiest part of becoming a Rolling Stone. The steep learning curve was *living* like a Rolling Stone. We had groupies with The Faces, but The Stones had so many. They had male groupies too, who nearly all seemed to be doctors." At a time when even rustic Kildare couldn't keep the occupational hazards of life as a rock megastar at bay, new Irish resident David Bowie presented him with a book called 'Living Sober' which he put behind the bar of his custom-built pub.

Two-time world champion Alex Higgins would arrive regularly to play snooker with Wood and they would go to the races together. However, Wood lamented in his autobiography, "It was always difficult being there with him because he had to avoid so many people, especially bookies. He couldn't go near them because he owed this one four grand and that one two grand." According to Wood, Higgins climbed into bed with him one morning dressed in the guitarist's wife's tights and armed with a pencil and tip sheets for that day's races. As a racehorse owner, the Rolling Stone was named Ireland's Small Breeder Of The Year for 1998.

When he settled in Clane, there was one Kildare native Ronnie Wood did not want to run into. Born nearby beside the Curragh racecourse, Billy Gaff had found huge success in the world of music, working with a portfolio of acts including Cream, the Bee Gees, Status Quo, Peter Frampton and The Clash. One of the first bands on his books were The Faces, fronted by Rod Stewart and starring Wood on guitar. On an early '70s US tour with The Faces, Gaff pulled a stunt which earned him a thumping. Rod Stewart had begun having solo hits, and Gaff decided to capitalise. In his autobiography, 'Ronnie', Wood recalled, "None of us knew it at the time, but as that tour progressed, we were starting to get billed as 'Rod Stewart and The Faces'. We were never meant to find out, so someone would arrive in a town and take down all the signs that we might see along the road from the airport or the hotel to the gig. But one night in Detroit, a few were missed. We arrived at the gig and there was Rod's name in big bold letters." Gaff was made to regret his actions that day by the other Faces, but Rod was happy with the situation to the point that when Gaff set up his own record label, Riva, the singer signed just as his career went multi-multi-multi platinum. Years later, Billy Gaff would arrive in Dublin with the express purpose of signing a hot band called U2. By his own admission, he got dead drunk, missed U2's gig that was supposed to seal the deal and instead signed a dead-end outfit called The Lookalikes.

Dramatist Peter Sheridan and his brother Jim also had a

young U2 on their roster at their Project Arts Centre, but Peter thought there were better acts playing there regularly. In 1996, Peter pulled off what was undoubtedly the greatest coup of his illustrious career when he persuaded the great singer-songwriter Carole King to take an acting role in Dublin's tiny Tivoli Theatre a stone's throw from Temple Bar.

One sunny afternoon that June, over soup and sandwiches backstage, the pop legend told me why she had been drawn back to Ireland time and again after first living here four years earlier. She loved the new improved Dublin. She'd lived a while in the countryside but the stillness of rural life didn't sit well with her busy New York state of mind. She said, "Dublin is a world-class city. I'm completely in the woodwork when I go around Dublin. Even if people recognise me they're very cool. The Irish don't stand on ceremony about that sort of thing. When Bono Himself walks amongst them he is very quickly reminded – lest he ever should forget – that he is a mere mortal."

Recalling that summer when he enticed the music giant into a small space in the Liberties, Sheridan said, "Carole had always loved acting. She'd done it as a youngster and then much later she'd done *Blood Brothers* on Broadway. I don't think it was a happy experience for her. I don't think it worked out. But she was looking to do something again, though not on the scale of Broadway. She wanted to get a break from New York so she came to Dublin. She was coming for a stay of a couple of months to work with Bill Whelan (*Riverdance* composer) and catch up with people she'd met along the way. *Riverdance* had taken over the world about a year earlier and it was huge in America where she'd met Bill. She knew music so she could tell that Bill was the real deal and not just a chancer. So she came over with her boyfriend, Johnny, and I met them at a reception in the US ambassador's residence in Phoenix Park. Johnny came up to me and said, 'You're a writer. I'm researching a story on the 1916 Rising. Would you be interested in coming in on that?' Oh yeah, I said, so we got together. He was a great guy. A real New Yorker and the loveliest man you could ever meet."

Johnny had secured funding to make a short film in Ireland and Sheridan came on board to recruit the local cast and crew. To his amazement, Carole King decided to become part of the crew.

He recalled, "She was lovely. Immediately we were friends and we hit it off straight away. She was coming from a background when she was 16, 17 in a New York where you just got up and did things. So we shared that energy where if you had the idea to do something you just got up and did it. Like myself and Johnny deciding 'Let's make a movie.'

"So I said to her she should really come to Ireland to do something. She said yeah, but she didn't want to do music. At the time she was doing a lot of community based music work with kids. She was always working with young people, young musicians, young singers who were just coming through. She loved the idea of giving something back. Shortly after, the theatre producer Pat Moylett was looking for a show to do in Andrews Lane Theatre and *Brighton Beach Memoirs* came up. I knew the play and as soon as I re-read it I said, 'The mother is Carole King. The Jewish mother! Carole is very Jewish so she'll totally get it'. So I said to Pat, 'Will I ring her?' And she said you'll never get her. I said there's nothing to lose and I rang her. I said, 'Carole, I've a mad idea for you. Come to Dublin for a few weeks to play the mother in *Brighton Beach Memoirs*. Have a read of it. The part is made for you.'

"Two days later she got back and said, 'I love this play. I want to come to Dublin to do it.' So she came to Ireland completely under the radar. There was no big publicity push. In the posters and adverts there was no 'STARRING CAROLE KING'. She got equal billing with everyone else because that's what she wanted. She just wanted to be part of an ensemble and she had the best time of her life! We made Noel Pearson (the producer of '*My Left Foot*') Carole's PA. One day she came running into the rehearsal room shouting, 'There's been a shooting, there's been a shooting on the Naas dual carriageway! Veronica Guerin!' Carole was so upset. She'd met Veronica at some do. I'll always remember the look of sheer horror on her face. But that aside, we did the show, it was a big success."

Radically different though they are, New York and Dublin have a shared attraction in that they're both walking cities and the day we hooked up for lunch backstage, she explained that what she loved most about Ireland's capital is that she could walk everywhere. She could walk to rehearsals, she could walk home. It's not a sprawl city like London or LA where you need a car to exist. She loved the size of Dublin and the sense that it was a community. She was particularly impressed with the transformation of Temple Bar in the space of just a few years.

She later wrote in her autobiography, *A Natural Woman*, "The truce (in the North) and the economic expansion have brought positive changes. In 1992, while walking at night in Temple Bar I had seen a disproportionate number of men in various stages of intoxication sprawled on the streets. In 1995, the neighbourhood was a lot cleaner. Customers still got intoxicated but most did so indoors. Dubliners' optimism was reflected in the new office buildings and elegant residences either under construction or already completed. In contrast to 1992, Ireland in 1995 seemed a place of peace, growth and opportunity."

As Ireland's celebrity headcount continued to soar, Bob Dylan was joined on stage by Carole King, Van Morrison and Elvis

Costello who – while they hadn't exactly been plucked out of the audience – happened to be living close by.

After endless encores King rejoined the other three to take a final bow. The backing band exited stage left, Bob, Van and Elvis by an exit at the back of centre stage, and Carole found herself left behind. She decided, "The stage right black curtain seemed the logical exit for me. I thought it would lead to a stairway. But when I stepped through the curtain there was nothing under my feet." Next thing she knew she was in the Mater Hospital with a head wound and a broken wrist. Dylan eventually rang to apologise for going to the after-show party and not even realising she wasn't there. He passed the phone to Van who characteristically had little to say and quickly passed to Elvis who wouldn't shut up. She was told she'd be kept in overnight so she used the time to ring family and friends in the States, one of whom told her they'd already heard, and the story going around was that Bob had pushed her off the stage.

Chapter 18

THE IRISH COMEDY EXPLOSION – MADE IN BRITAIN

"Ted was made by British companies. Ted would never have been made in Ireland."

– Arthur Mathews, co-writer of Father Ted

IN THE late 1980s stand-up comedy was on the way to making a remarkable transition from being as terminally unhip as your grandad's pipe and cardigan to fulfilling the fresh minted prophecy that "comedy is the new rock 'n' roll". In fact, that now famous line was never meant as a prophecy.

Legend has it that it was uttered in frustration by Englishman Dave Cohen as he set up his mic for a 1988 London gig before an audience of six men and a dog. He was drawing what consolation he could from the fact that he was about to perform on a stage where many of his punk heroes had strutted their stuff a decade earlier.

As it happened, one of the six men looking on was a hack from the *City Limits* listings magazine, who opened his review with Cohen's throwaway line that comedy was the new rock 'n' roll. A couple of weeks later Cohen saw his quote go viral when Janet Street-Porter used it on TV. They say that timing is everything in comedy, and the analogy proved perfect for the alchemy that was bubbling under just then.

British stand-up in the '70s and '80s was a grim affair dominated by Brylcreemed men of a ripe vintage with pot-bellies tucked under their cummerbunds, huge bushy sideburns and a line in gags that began with "My mother-in-law is so fat". Irish stand-up comedy was usually more gentle but veered little from that formula. Dermot Morgan was a rare honourable exception. Morgan had been around the block too often to be the new anything as he scratched a hand-to-mouth existence trying to do something different in the guise of his pre-Ted Father Trendy. He got the odd TV slot before finally landing his own radio show with *Scrap Saturday* in 1989. Co-written with Gerry Stembridge and co-starring Pauline McLynn, *Scrap Saturday* lampooned the great and the good and became a sensation, with weekly tilts at the Taoiseach, Papa Doc Haughey, his 'let them eat cake' lover and his conniving henchman Mara. In fact it became so much of a sensation that RTÉ dropped its biggest ratings winner when it was the closest thing the broadcaster had to required listening. RTÉ insisted that the show had not been axed, but had simply run its natural course – a line that found very few buyers.

A year after yanking *Scrap Saturday* from the airwaves, possibly realising they'd killed their ratings golden goose, RTÉ greenlit Morgan and Stembridge to make a TV version entitled *Newshounds*. Station execs were still nervous about the banished *Scrap Saturday* to the point that when Morgan suggested resurrecting it as the best title for audience recognition "there were no takers". In the end it didn't matter because the broadcaster then axed *Newshounds* at extremely short notice before it hit the screens. Executives gave off-the-record briefings that it was scrapped because it was simply not funny, while Montrose insiders said it had come down with a severe bout of cold feet. Two days after *Newshounds* was binned I sat down to breakfast with Dermot Morgan. He was down in the dumps, not that you'd notice as he peppered his chat with his usual manic laughter and demonic voices. Besides, he'd been jilted many times before.

He groaned, "I hate having to expend so much time and energy *not* doing my job, but *trying* to do my job. There's so much hassle it wears you out. Your head gets done in by that shite and I don't need it. I appreciate that you have to hustle, but I'd like to think I could get to the stage where someone would say, 'You've paid your dues. Go and do what you do well.'"

He'd paid his dues the hard way. "The comedy bug bit" when he was a student at University College Dublin in the '70s and he set out to make a living doing what he loved, but "Ireland didn't have a comedy circuit in those days so I ended up dying in places I shouldn't have appeared in at all. They were unsuitable and I shouldn't have been there but I didn't know my business. Once I did a Sunday morning stag thing and they didn't even look up from their newspapers. How I managed to string a career together at all is a wonder, the gigs were so few and far in between."

He was rescued from stag morning purgatory by broadcaster Mike Murphy who gave him a regular slot on 'The Live Mike' TV show. It was there that he introduced the Irish public to Fr Trendy. Looking back, the satire was almost reverential, but in '70s Ireland it had audiences tittering guiltily.

"I ran a mile from Trendy very quickly," he told me, explaining, "I was terrified of *becoming* that priest rather than Dermot Morgan who does characters." Ironically, it was his time served as the mild-mannered Trendy that would put him in pole position when the auditions came around for Father Ted Crilly a year after the frustration of seeing *Newshounds* pulled from under him.

Morgan reported that just the previous day, he had been cold shouldered by one of his *Scrap Saturday* targets who would have popped up on *Newshounds* had it been aired. Ireland, he accepted, is a tight-knit village, which makes satirical comedy very difficult. He said, "We're not as open a society as we should be. I believe that broadcasting has an important role to play in opening up society, but there's an inertia [in RTÉ] wrought of their own o'erweening monopoly. There's this showbiz ethos in Ireland that you never really stick the boot in, but if you're going to be sincere about your satire you have to kick all around, and those who can take it can take it. If people can't understand that's me doing my job, tough."

While Ireland's state broadcaster was maintaining its deep-seated mistrust of comedy, Channel 4 in Britain was giving a young Irish comedian his big break. With his pin-up good looks, 26-year-old Sean Hughes looked every inch the picture of comedy as the new rock 'n' roll. Two years earlier he'd become the youngest winner of the prestigious Perrier Comedy Award at the Edinburgh Festival, following in the footsteps of Stephen Fry, Hugh Laurie and Emma Thompson. Now, in the spring of 1992, he had become a TV star playing a surreal version of himself in *Sean's Show* which was nominated for Best Comedy at that year's British Comedy Awards.

With the show's second series ready to roll, London-born Hughes explained that when his family moved back to Ireland his accent brought him some grief, though not where he might have expected it. He said, "At school, in a sense, the toughies did like me because I was a smartarse and I was trouble to the teachers. The problem was around the local area where they'd just give me a kicking anyway." Buffing his rock 'n' roll outlaw cachet, the spin-off book from the TV series, *Sean's Book*, contained instructions on how to shoplift the volume with the use of a football bag. "Easons was the shop I was thinking about," he said. "I did that one Christmas. I filled up the bag. It was very exciting. I was very good at thieving. I was the second best in my neighbourhood. Then I got caught twice and I lost my bottle. I just love the idea of someone stealing books because they're not like sweets or microwave ovens, they are knowledge."

Following his Edinburgh Perrier win, and because he was one of our own, Hughes could always be sure of a full house whenever he came back to Ireland. No other Irish stand-up came close as a series of comedy venues opened and quickly closed at the start of the '90s. But while stand-up was wilting on its feet, two comedy acts with a strong musical element were packing them in a mile apart from each other in Dublin city centre. No-one knew it, but contained within The Joshua Trio and The Baldy Fella were the two estranged futures of Irish comedy which would leave Sean Hughes trailing in their tracks as he moved sideways to become a team captain on the BBC's comedy quiz *Never Mind The Buzzcocks*, while *Father Ted* and *Mrs Brown* went stratospheric. Many years later I got to work closely with Sean on two radio comedy series a year apart. Three months after recording the second series Sean died at the terribly young age of 51. He was a good-natured, gentle soul and the aura of melancholy he carried with him was real. During our first encounter he said, "I have a wonderful life. I just don't particularly enjoy it." It was a good line, the more so because it rang true.

Just as U2 reached the point where it seemed they couldn't get any more overbearing, they did just that with the release in late '88 of the *Rattle And Hum* epic double album, movie and tour. Even the lovesick *Rolling Stone* lamented their efforts to hoist themselves into the pantheon of rock's greatest legends as "misguided and bombastic".

The antidote to this swollen head disorder arrived in the form of an outfit calling themselves The Joshua Trio, a spoof U2 tribute act. Made up of Paul Woodfull (stage name Wonderful), his bassist brother Kieran and drummer Arthur Mathews, the jazzy combo had tasked themselves with a quest even more ambitious than U2's bid for parity of esteem with The Beatles and The Stones.

The Trio's first major interview was with the newest addition to the *Hot Press* stable of young guns, Graham Linehan. Frontman Wonderful told him, "Our mission is to bring the music of U2 to a wider audience."

The drummer elaborated, "We want to wean people *on* to U2. We want to bring U2 to the old, the sick, the infirm."

A year earlier I'd been teaching journalism at Coláiste Dhúlaigh in the Dublin suburb of Coolock. As the students exited one session, a lanky teenager sidled in the door and introduced himself as Graham from the communications course. He said he'd written some reviews and asked if I would look at them. The following week he tendered three typed reviews. Two appeared in the next issue. As his scribblings began to appear regularly, something happened that had never happened before. Fan mail in praise of Graham began to pile up on my desk as Letters Editor. Naturally, we all assumed that he was writing the love notes to himself, but we eventually had to face the fact that at least most of them were genuine. No sooner was Graham installed as the mag's film critic than he started taking movie reviews down surreal new paths, angering some readers and delighting others. Some reviews were three words long, while others completely ignored the film at hand. It was in this surreal spirit that Graham's words made the comical Joshua Trio even funnier.

Like their hero Bono, they understood that every band on a mission needs a creation myth which supersedes the mundane facts of what may or may not have actually happened. They pointed out to Linehan that the world had been set alight by an album called *Rattle And Hum*, not *Rattle And Humdrum*. In this light, Arthur explained, "Paul used to heal people at the U2 wall outside Windmill Lane, and soon he and Kieran were holding daily workshops for guitarists who wanted to be invited up on stage by U2 to play some songs. I thought this was important work and asked if we could get together and jam."

Paul interjected, "I was practising a few, um, whatjacallem... *chords* a few weeks ago when Kieran walked in and said, 'Hey, that really sounds like The Edge!' I just... I just couldn't... I threw down the guitar, went to my car and drove deep into the country. I honestly thought that would be the end of the band."

Graham described how an awkward silence descended, followed by a white dove that circled three times above Paul's head before shooting off.

"That's been happening a lot lately," muttered the singer. "I wish they'd just fuck off altogether."

The interview with Graham lit the touch paper on the next phase of The Joshua Trio's career. The beginning of 1989 saw their residency move from upstairs at The Baggot to the much bigger space downstairs which U2 themselves had made their own midweek stomping ground 10 years earlier, ably supported by The Blades.

For the first show of the Baggot residency, Paul arrived on

the back of a donkey, wearing a white blood-splattered toga, a crown of thorns and a medallion bearing the likeness of Bono. In addition to U2 covers, their set included rewrites of old standards into glowing tributes such as 'The Edge Has Got His Hat On, Hip, Hip, Hip Hooray!' and 'All Kinds Of Everything Remind Me Of U2'. One early review applauded, "On this showing The Joshua Trio are simply and categorically, far and away the second best band in the world." Their first superstar fan was Joe Elliott, whose Def Leppard had been knocked off their perch as the World's Biggest Band by U2. The singer hired The Trio to play at his Dublin wedding.

When U2 caught wind of all the fun being poked their way, Bono astutely turned the tables to disarm the clamouring naysayers accusing his band of getting too big for their stack-heeled boots. Asked by *Rolling Stone* to name his favourite band, the singer nominated The Joshua Trio. This in turn prompted a feature on the satirists in America's self-styled rock 'n' roll bible, and this whetted the appetite of my pay-masters at MTV Europe for the continuing adventures of the threesome.

For months on end the music station's priority list for stories from Ireland ran: U2, then rising star Sinéad O'Connor, then The Joshua Trio, and then the latest video fodder put in the shop window by the major record companies, generally more in hope than expectation.

Over a Christmas lunch at the close of 2023, Paul and Arthur recalled to me the beginnings of The Trio and the band's chaplain who would go on to even greater things, Father Ted Crilly. Both creations came into being in the offices of *Hot Press* on the long and late production weekends that happened every fortnight, when the magazine was put together in an intense three-day blitz. Arthur Mathews, then Art Director, had already featured several times in Britain's million-selling *Viz* comic with illustrated stories such as 'How To Improve Your Golf Handicap After The Holocaust'. His creations for *Hot Press* included 'The Footballers' Guide To The JFK Assassination' and the provincial newspaper *The Border Fascist.* One 'Locals Abroad' column began, "Congratulations to Cootehill man Jimmy Clinton who recently seized power in the central African state of Bogawonga after a bloody coup." A large-print advert for a hearing-aid store was headlined 'ARE YOU FUCKING DEAF?'

With the arrival of Paul Woodfull as Arthur's design assistant, the humorous banter of production weekends took a turn for the crazy as the office turned into an open mic session minus the mics. The characters that emerged and evolved included The Trio's version of Bono, Father Ted Crilly and Father Dougal McGuire. Ted the chaplain emerged as the most regular of a host of interval guest impressions which included cyclist Stephen Roche, celebrity chef Darina Allen, and Arthur as Arnold Schwarzenegger doing readings from John McGahern's Booker-nominated *Amongst Women*. Recalling another of his spoof acts, sleazy crooner Tony St James, Paul added, "We'd regularly do a set as both the Trio and Tony, and Ted would give his sermons in the interval. I remember one show in the Olympia where some yobs in the audience thought he was a real priest and they were shouting abuse. Get off the fucking stage!"

When I put it to Graham Linehan in January 2024, nearly three decades after its first broadcast on Channel 4, that *Father Ted* was the ultimate expression of comedy as rock 'n' roll, he demurred, "That's not for me to say. It would be very arrogant for me to say that, but I do remember someone once saying that 'Ted' was Ireland's punk and I was so flattered and delighted by that. It gave me an insight into how much the show meant to people and what it did to the Irish consciousness. In the same way as the Sex Pistols were attacking the foundations of their society, we were too. The Catholic Church were still a force and you weren't really allowed to make fun of them. Things were relaxing but it was still quite bracing, I think, for Irish people to see the Church not being treated with kid gloves. So it was quite anarchic – and Arthur was a punk so that was in the mix."

While the new wave of politically correct stand-up comedy was struggling to get a foothold in Dublin, the long queues outside the Baggot Inn for The Joshua Trio were being matched by the lines outside The Rathmines Inn to see Brendan O'Carroll giving Cilla Black's ITV smash *Blind Date* a car crash of an Irish makeover.

And so it was there on the Rathmines Road one spring evening that the two future superhighways of Irish comedy crossed paths. A contingent that included Arthur Mathews, Paul and Kieran Woodfull, Graham Linehan and myself had to elbow our way from the front door to the bar where t-shirts hung for sale bearing the legend 'I Saw The Baldy Fella At The Rathmines Inn'. The Baldy Fella was the stage name adopted by the chirpy motormouth from Finglas, Brendan O'Carroll. The double part of the entendre was that it might refer to his thin covering up top or to a thickness of girth below the belt.

After his band ambled through a hodgepodge of pop covers, The Baldy Fella came on as his own warm-up before the main event. "My mother was a prostitute," he began, giving a foretaste of what was to follow over the next two hours. Our jaws pinned to the floor, myself and my *Hot Press* colleague Liam Fay could still scribble notes. It was meant to be a night off, but this demanded a write-up. And so it was that Brendan

O'Carroll's first print review would pass judgement that, "The Baldy Fella wasn't funny in any conventional sense. He wasn't funny in any unconventional sense either. He was just racist, sexist, homophobic and very, very dumb."

Five years later, riding high on the success of two blockbuster live videos, a bestselling Mrs Browne novel, *The Mammy*, and a hit play *The Course*, the demolition job myself and Liam Fay did on the Baldy Fella following that night still rankled with O'Carroll. As for being "slagged to fuck" over a wisecrack about the Miami Showband, he said, "I regretted that. Another thing that guy Damian Corless said in *Hot Press* that gutted me was the suggestion that I was a real cunt because I was sexist. I gave the article to (his then wife) Doreen to read and she said, 'You're not sexist Brendan, this guy doesn't know what it means'. But I wrote to Corless pointing out where I fucked up and I was only starting out."

Two years later in the summer of 1992, the Brendan O'Carroll of *Blind Date* was no longer 'only starting out'. He had moved a short way down the Grand Canal to The Barge where, serving up a similar bill of fare, he had Sunday lunchtime tipplers eating out of his hand. I had now moved on to the editor's seat at *In Dublin* and at my suggestion a female colleague, Djinn Gallagher, went along. After the show, Djinn put it to Brendan that on the evidence of his routine he was a "racist, sexist, homophobic misogynist".

He opened his defence with, "It's usually girls who tell me I'm sexist. You never have a fella telling me I'm sexist." Having rebuffed Gallagher's other charges ("That show you were at was the only racist joke I've ever told." "I love queers. I do, big time.") he got to the nub of the matter, "The audience manufactures me. I don't manufacture the audience."

Looking back on the *Blind Date* show more than 30 years

on, Paul Woodfull said, "I saw Brendan O'Carroll a few times around then because I knew someone who promoted his gigs. And he would storm those audiences. Two hours doing jokes basically from the schoolyard, but he had a real talent. He had the funny thing. He could win over an audience with his force of personality. He was very clever. But it wasn't for us."

"He was much cleverer than his audience," Mathews added.

"There's a comedian I know and he told me that your audience decides what you are," Woodfull said, "and if you're playing the clubs in Dublin, Ireland or anywhere you'll end up doing material that works for your audience. It might not be material that you'd prefer to be doing. You might like to do something more challenging but if you don't do what works you don't have an audience."

According to Arthur Mathews, when Brendan O'Carroll auditioned for *Father Ted* for the part of milkman Pat Mustard, "His audition was great. I can't remember what happened. I think he might have turned it down, or he might not have been available when it was time to shoot it. But he was very good."

Arthur Mathews, Graham Linehan, Paul Woodfull on the legacy of Father Ted:

I put it to Mathews that when *Father Ted* first screened on Channel 4, British audiences were surprised to discover that on this remote Craggy Island (which didn't feature on any maps) off this remote island of Ireland, the natives would be arguing the merits of Blur versus Oasis or fretting about drive-by shootings like in *Boyz n the Hood*. I proposed that *Ted* expertly exposed the two-way-mirror relationship between a fully modern Ireland and an unseeing Britain. We knew everything about them while they knew virtually nothing about us.

Mathews: "Yes, absolutely! They knew nothing about Ireland and still don't. Yesterday I heard some TV presenter try and fail to pronounce Taoiseach, and Drogheda is always pronounced *Drogg-heeee-dah*. The examples are countless. When I moved to England nothing I encountered came as any surprise because I knew everything. The only thing that struck me as being different was the milk cartons. The first thing I did in England was go to watch games in all the football grounds that I'd seen on *Match Of The Day*. Every week I'd go to a different ground. It was totally unsurprising, except it was much more multicultural than Ireland."

Linehan: "We were coming from an interesting position where the Irish were always getting blanked by the British on one side and America on the other. We were sat in the middle of these two countries seeing all of their culture and them seeing none of ours, so you could almost say that *Ted* was a bit of revenge. Us throwing back all these cultural references that we'd been picking up for years. We were in an ideal position to do that."

So was part of the initial appeal of *Father Ted* to British audiences that they were presented with an Ireland that flew in the face of the one they thought they knew? (Obviously leaving out that half the population were priests and nuns.)

Mathews: "I think it was in one way. Then there was the basic ruralness of it. It was set in the middle of nowhere. The big stand-alone parochial house. The weather. And the locals. So there was all that, but I also think it's like Reginald Perrin with all the catchphrases and the surreal bits interrupting mundane reality. I think it was a mix of *Hall's Pictorial Weekly*, *The Simpsons*, and *Seinfeld*. Graham was a huge fan of *The Simpsons* so a lot of the little cutaway scenes were like that show. But part of the attraction was the classic scenario of people with nothing in common stuck together somewhere they didn't want to be, and one of them, Ted, having a mission way beyond his capabilities.

"Another feature of *Ted* that's brilliant for a sitcom is that every priest in the world knows every other priest in the world. That was a seeming reality that I grew up with, that every priest knew every other priest. And that's great for a sitcom because you don't have to explain new characters or spend time giving them a back story, they just appear and Ted knows them."

Woodfull: "I think one thing the English would have seen that Ted captured perfectly was that Irish Catholicism is not very spiritual. It's like, it's the most natural thing in the world to be a Catholic and you don't have to give it much thought. The pilgrimage to Lourdes was huge, but most people who went did so for the craic. 'Ah, I went. Not for a cure though. There was nothing wrong with me but the sing-songs were great!' So if you're a priest, that's just your job like any other job."

Mathews: "That's very much how I felt about my uncles who were priests – that it was just a job."

Woodfull: "I remember you telling me Arthur that one of your uncles was talking about another priest who was having apparitions and holy visions, and your priest uncle thought he was mad. My uncle priests would never discuss anything too spiritual. They'd be embarrassed to talk about apparitions. I also remember the religious programme 'Radharc' where they used to have priestly discussions on the issues of the day, and they'd always refer to 'the laity' as if the world was divided 50-50 between clergy and non-clergy.

Mathews: "Yes, like they were equal partners in humanity."

When *Father Ted* aired for the first time, elements of the Irish media fabricated an 'anti-Irish' backlash in the hope of stirring opposition and generating column inches. The most ludicrous objection came from Ireland's top broadcaster Gay Byrne who chastised Dermot Morgan to his face for having anything to do with a show that was "just not funny" and which, if it had been made by RTÉ, would have been "laughed off our screens".

Mathews: "*Ted* was made by British companies. *Ted* would never have been made in Ireland. I remember that one of the Irish newspapers got a priest to review it. And he did that classic thing of saying 'I didn't find it offensive at all. I just thought it wasn't very funny.'"

Woodfull: "My reaction to *Father Ted* was that even though it was so surreal and silly, it came the closest of any film or drama to capturing my real experiences of the Catholic Church. That's what it was like growing up. I'd been to a seminary because a friend of mine was thinking of becoming a priest, and that was that world. I had friends who'd be in a bedsit listening to Pink Floyd and Led Zeppelin but they were going to become priests."

Father Ted showcased an entire generation of upcoming Irish comedic talent. In addition to giving Dermot Morgan his deserved reward after decades of fighting blandness, it brought stardom in Britain and further afield to Ardal O'Hanlon, Pauline McLynn, Tommy Tiernan and Graham Norton. Almost three decades after it first aired, *Father Ted* is as fresh as ever, enjoying perpetual heavy rotation on the box. It is woven into the cultural fabric of these islands. The *Father Ted* Defence – "the money was just resting in my account" – has entered the legal and business lexicon. Placards urging "Down With That Sort Of Thing" show up at every manner of protest. The show's legacy is profound.

Linehan: "When we wrote it, we wrote it thinking this is the best thing ever. We just thought it was the bees knees, but we never thought it would ingrain itself into Irish society so much. We were actually worried that Irish people wouldn't like it and we crafted it in such a way that it would reassure people that it was an Irish comedy show rather than a comedy show about the Irish."

In doing so they crafted a truly divine comedy.

Epilogue

A LAND TURNED ON ITS HEAD AND SPUN ON ITS AXIS

"Ludicrous. Ridiculous."

– The 1989 edition of the Collins Concise Dictionary defines the word 'Irish'

IN CHRISTMAS 1995, US President Bill Clinton and First Lady Hillary addressed a delirious crowd of 80,000 on Dublin's College Green. Clinton had been instrumental in brokering the arms decommissioning process that he pledged would pave the way for a permanent peace and assured prosperity on the island of Ireland. The crowd that cheered him were a changed people, changed utterly in self-belief and outlook from just a few years before.

I've picked 1995 as the closing chapter in a cultural civil war that had reached its most belligerent in the middle years of the 1980s. In 1983 a bitter referendum on the so-called Pro-Life Amendment to the Constitution drove a wedge between traditionalists and modernisers in Irish society. Abortion was already illegal. The decisive and divisive vote to make it even more illegal paved the way for another poll that would again set old Catholic Ireland against young liberal Ireland. With the full weight of the Church once again deployed, the bid to legalise divorce was soundly defeated in 1986.

The cultural war against the forces of reaction continues with a renewed intensity in the present day of toxic social media. Within a decade of that second setback for liberal values there was no longer the remotest prospect of Irish society being dragged back to the dark days of suffocating Church and State repression. The first Taoiseach with a clear liberal agenda was Garret FitzGerald, who brought his so-called constitutional crusade to government in 1982, in the face of fierce opposition from a hardline Catholic rump within his own Fine Gael party. For instance, Louth TD Brendan McGahon came out against his own leader's support for divorce, saying, "There's much that's made of women's rights, in inverted commas, but what about the rights of the children? What about [women's] duties? I mean, you can't wean a calf from a cow overnight."

With Charles Haughey's Fianna Fáil committed to opposition for the sake of opposition regardless of the issues at stake, FitzGerald knew that his only hope of achieving his aims was to get young voters onside. U2 answered his call early on, inviting him into a Windmill recording session for a photo opportunity and a joint appeal for a new Ireland.

It is a measure of the profound transformation this country underwent, that a mere nine years after rejecting divorce, the people spurned the instructions of the bishops and gave it their blessing. For Ireland's youth, this was a huge symbolic victory which, for many, signalled that the civil war between the forces of enlightenment and entrenchment had been won. But not all the young people were delighted. A small but noisy group calling themselves Youth Defence had entered the world kicking and screaming in 1992. Making their presence felt with street protests and shrill taunts, they claimed 3,000 members, although the wrinkle count at their rallies suggested they operated a very permissive young at heart admission policy. Stridently militant in their language and posturing, the group represented the youth wing of the Society for the Protection of Unborn Children (SPUC). Praising the hardline tactics of these Young Turks, SPUC founder Phyllis Bowman claimed, "Our first mistake was to sound reasonable." That would never be a problem for Youth Defence, who fought rowdily for the rejection of the 1995 divorce referendum. Their defeat effectively put a halt to their march, although the firebrands of SPUC vowed to continue the fight to return Ireland to the 1950s. Scores of journalists were on hand at the RDS count centre to witness the reaction of SPUC's Úna Bean Mhic Mhathúna to her enemies' victory.

"You're only a shower of wife-swapping sodomites," she snarled.

"And you're only an old Bible-basher," retorted a young man wearing a 'Yes To Divorce' badge.

"I don't give a shite about the Bible," snapped the Catholic mother of nine.

"You *do* give a shite about the Bible," the man informed her.

"Shuddup you," she countered.

"You're a lunatic," he concluded.

Watching all this, one of Youth Defence's leaders was stoical. She'd lost. "But we really can't lose," she argued, "since everything we said would happen will happen now. We won't take any pleasure in that, but we did warn people."

Like every other previous religious prediction that the world was about to end, this one would let down its oracle. In fact, next up on the schedule was the Celtic Tiger goodtime boom and, at the end of 1995, Ireland was ready for anything. In the world of stocks and shares, market sentiment can mean more than hard facts or any other factor. Market sentiment was now with Ireland and the country's stock was going through the roof not just in economic terms but as a cultural influencer. The term is Soft Power.

The constitutional amendment legalising divorce was signed into law by the first female President of Ireland, Mary Robinson. Dermot Morgan had notched up another black mark with the powers that be when he mercilessly pilloried government minister Pádraig Flynn on *Scrap Saturday* after Flynn attacked Mary Robinson's bid for the Presidency, claiming that her "newfound interest in her family" was an electoral gimmick. Morgan told me, "I was outraged by the Flynn crack at Robinson, not because I'm partisan in politics, but because I thought it was disgraceful." Flynn's intervention backfired spectacularly, bringing many women voters over to the Robinson camp.

In the '70s the notion that a woman could occupy any of the State's highest offices was so far-fetched that *The Irish Times* drew up a fantasy female cabinet for a laugh. The newspaper's judging panel selected the young Senator Mary Robinson as leader of this neverland government. The paper accepted that many readers would find the exercise either redundant, far-fetched, or both. It editorialised, "An all-women Cabinet? What sort of silly election joke is this? What we're offering is a very unlikely coalition that will never take place."

Just as *The Irish Times* was giving its readers a good chuckle with its fantasy female government, Fianna Fáil's Joe Lenehan argued that it was self-evident that some women weren't equal to some types of work. The Mayo deputy reasoned, "How could I employ a local secretary? If I got a local lady, the first dance she would go to, out would come your business. You wouldn't want that." As to why Fianna Fáil should be returned in the next election, he told a crowd, "What you got, stick to it. These buckos would tax the farmers."

As the '80s began, a woman's place was always in the wrong. The Victorian law of Criminal Conversation remained on the statute books, having been invoked in a sensational infidelity trial just a few years later. At the close of that trial, the judge told the jury that the infidelity was proven, so their only task was to put a price on the loss of a wife to a husband. The judge declared, "In this country a wife is regarded as a chattel, just as a thoroughbred mare or cow, and the jury is concerned merely with compensating Mr Braun for the value of the loss of his wife and the damages to his feelings." The jury put that value at £12,000, the price of a four-bedroom house in Dublin.

One of the non-negotiable conditions of granting Ireland membership to Europe's go-ahead club in the '70s was that the inferior status of Irish women must be addressed with urgency. The European Economic Community (EEC) ordered the government to start by putting equal pay on the statute books by the end of 1975. The politicians compiled by drafting the legislation, but then steadfastly refused to enact it. By 1985 there had been little improvement to women's status as second class citizens. The trade unions charged with promoting equality quickly demonstrated that some (men) were more equal than others (women). Meanwhile, the Federated Union of Employers raised furious objections to paying women the same as men, insisting it would banjax the economy.

The Church threw its considerable weight behind the politicians, unions and employers. Reverend Brother Vivien Cassells scolded, "There is still a high percentage of women working for no valid reason, though they realise that by doing so they are depriving many young people from starting their careers in the civil service, banking or teaching. These people are not willing to forego the perks that a second salary can bring, like a trip to the Costa Brava, that second car or that well-stocked cocktail cabinet."

By the close of 1995, Irish women had access to divorce, contraception outside of the '*bona fide*' prescription system restricted to married couples and many other rights denied to them in the '80s. Successive governments continued to foot-drag on issues like equal pay and equal opportunities as they had with legislation to decriminalise homosexuality, which was ordered by the European Court of Human Rights in 1988 but not reluctantly enacted until 1993. Generations of prejudice did not evaporate with the passing of a law, but removing the legal sanction on gay acts led to a gradual change in attitudes and was the first step towards the 2015 referendum in which Ireland became the first country in the world to endorse same-sex marriage by popular acclaim rather than have it imposed from above.

The cultural civil war that sundered Ireland in the '80s didn't just manifest as a tug-of-war for the nation's moral values, it broke down in parallel to a matter of cold, hard cash. In March 1980, the biggest civic protest in Irish history took place when 700,000, mostly urban, PAYE workers took to the streets of towns and cities around the country to protest that the burden of taxation fell massively and unfairly on their shoulders. The anger of those trapped in the Pay As You Earn open prison was magnified when the government caved in to farmers' protests against paying a token 2% levy on incomes that had been massively boosted by EEC subsidies.

At this point, rural Ireland was approaching the peak of a giddy boom. Membership to the EEC had greatly enriched the farm sector with new export markets and a range of generous subsidies. Best of all were the intervention payments which guaranteed top prices to produce the goods to build up the

EEC's Beef and Butter Mountains, Milk Lakes, Gravy Trains and other peculiar additions to the European landscape.

After a spending splurge on brand new combine harvesters, the denizens of rural Ireland embarked on a building spree which would suck the life out of the towns and cities, with the hollowed-out centre of Dublin the most obvious victim. Environmental writer and Temple Bar activist Frank McDonald takes up the story, explaining,"The vast bulk of these homes were not designed by qualified architects, but rather plucked from pattern books such as *Bungalow Bliss* by Fianna Fáil Senator Jack Fitzsimons, that was so popular it ran to 12 editions. Nobody was writing about this phenomenon, so I coined the term 'Bungalow Blitz' for a series of articles in 1987 documenting what was, in effect, the suburbanization of rural Ireland. More and more people were now car-dependent, living as they did at a distance from shops, schools, churches and workplaces. This turned narrow rural roads into the most dangerous in Ireland – unsafe for both walking and cycling and particularly hazardous for anyone pushing a baby-buggy. It also had knock-on effects on towns and villages. As people moved out in greater numbers, the upper floors of once-inhabited shop buildings were left vacant with no sign of light after dusk. Ultimately, these buildings became endangered through lack of use."

For his troubles, McDonald was branded Public Enemy No 1 by rural politicians and the newly enriched farming class who felt that how they spent their newfound riches was nobody's business but theirs. He was attacked from the floor of one planning conference by the founder of the Irish Rural Dwellers Association, who accused him of siding with the Royal Town Planning Institute in London, which wanted to impose its 'foreign' standards on Ireland.

Perhaps the most striking pop culture expression of this rural resurgence was the coronation of JR Ewing as the poster boy and role model for keeping it country. The official records of the Dáil and Seanad are littered with references to the antics of JR, the shower scene featuring his brother Bobby, the 'Who Shot JR?' plotline and the whole *Dallas* phenomenon which spawned a fashion craze for stetsons and Southfork Ranch-style gates. For as long as anyone could remember, one of the unwritten but unbreakable rules of post-independence Irish society was that if you've got it, you *don't* flaunt it. Flying in the face of convention, rural Ireland in the 1980s went big on bling, widening the prickly urban/rural social divide.

By the middle of the '90s, progressive values had largely toppled regressive views and this translated to cosmopolitan urban values ousting provincial rural views. Dublin had reclaimed its standing as a capital city deserving of that title. The term 'Celtic Tiger' was first coined in 1994 and would shortly come to pass. However, although the newly created International Financial Services Centre (IFSC) would breathe vital new life into the city's docklands, before too long perceptive observers were branding it Ireland's lawless "financial wild west" storing up the seeds of future financial ruin with reckless trading facilitated by light touch government regulation.

Ultimately, Dublin was rescued from utter ruination by the young people of Ireland and of Europe, drawn in their droves to spray-paint love notes to their heroes on the U2 wall at Windmill Lane or just party hard in a city suddenly made cheaply and readily accessible by the arrival of Ryanair. After surviving several attempts to smother it at birth by Aer Lingus and British Airways who were determined to protect their stranglehold on the Dublin/Heathrow route, Ryanair revolutionised Irish tourism, the fortunes of Dublin, and Irish society itself. For as long as anyone could remember, the price-fixing Aer Lingus/BA duopoly had put air travel beyond the pocket of all but the wealthiest, forcing travellers to and from Ireland into a tiresome, time-consuming slog by coach and cattle boat.

While many of Ryanair's practices were deeply customer unfriendly, the newcomer opened up a cheap, fast and direct route from Britain and the continent which fitted tight young budgets. In doing this, Ryanair turned Irish tourism radically on its axis, shifting the cash-cow from rich middle-aged Americans landing at Shannon to young Europeans with disposable income landing and staying in the east. While the numbers flying into Shannon Airport increased modestly from 152,000 in 1980 to 277,000 in 1995, visitors from Britain and Europe soared from 551,000 to 1,799,000 in the same period, putting on another spectacular spurt by the end of the 1990s to 3,047,000. For many Dubliners, the natural order of things had been restored and they had their capital back from the brink and back as a vibrant living city after a fierce struggle. The new reality was sealed in 2008 with the final elimination of the Shannon Stopover, which had obliged transatlantic flights to land in Shannon even though the technical need to refuel had long ceased.

Not only did this new ease of access by air give tourism a huge boost, but it changed the nature of emigration and of society itself. In the cattle boat days of the 1980s, Irish migrants to Britain and Europe tended to stay put in their new dorms because it was too much of a long haul and too expensive to come home, apart perhaps for Christmas. Ryanair changed all that so that the back and forth of people and jobs and ideas suddenly became fast and fluid. Young Irish people would continue to emigrate through the Celtic Tiger years of massive inward migration, but now it was rarely out of economic desperation. It was to take a gap year working in a different culture or simply travel the world safe in the knowledge that they'd be back.

The '80s youthquake that shook Ireland from its long slumber cleared the ground for a new open, forward-looking and economically dynamic society. In the decades that followed pop music, politics, comedy and all the rest have been absorbed into the mash-up of new technology that has made the entire world virtually unrecognisable from what it was a generation ago. Ireland emerged from the key period of transition in the '80s and '90s resilient and versatile and fully plugged into the matrix. Today, thanks to it's highly educated English-speaking workforce and its enticing outlier tax laws, Ireland is *the* destination location for the glitterati of the IT world, with Google (Alphabet), Facebook (Meta), Microsoft, Amazon, Airbnb and IBM amongst the tech giants settled in and around Dublin's Silicon Docks. The richest of all the world's companies, Apple, has had its European Headquarters in Cork since 1980.

In June 1994 when Navan man Pierce Brosnan was announced as the next James Bond, the *Times of London* carped sourly, "Was it wise to select the Irish as heroes, when in this tame new world after the demise of SMERSH and SPECTRE they might be needed to play the evil empire?" That remark only served to expose a mindset unable or unwilling to come to terms with a radically new Ireland.

Two years later Brosnan set up his own Hollywood movie production company. He called it Irish DreamTime. Ireland was indeed in dreamland.

SELECTED SOURCES

BOOKS

Albert Reynolds, The Longford Leader. Tim Ryan.(Blackwater Press).

The Beatles and Ireland. Michael Lynch, Damian Smith. (Collins Press).

The Destruction Of Dublin. Frank McDonald. (Gill & Macmillan).

The Global Jukebox. Robert Burnett. (Routledge).

Irish Wildlife. John Little, Noel Kelly. (Phoenix).

John Lennon, The Life. Philip Norman. (Harper Collins).

A Natural Woman. Carole King. (Grand Central).

One Train Later. Andy Summers. (Griffin).

The Outsider - My Life In Intrigue. Frederick Forsyth. (Penguin).

Robert Shaw: Jaws, Deoch & Deora. TV documentary. Brian Reddin.

Ronnie. Ronnie Wood. (Macmillan).

Rotten: No Irish, No Blacks No Dogs. John Lydon. (Picador).

Still A Dream. James M. Moran (Moran Cartur).

Tell Roy Rogers I'm Not In. Tim Ryan. (Blackwater Press).

2RN And The Origins Of Irish Radio. Richard Pine. (Four Courts Press).

U2 At The End Of The World. Bill Flanagan. (Bantam Press)

U2 By U2. U2. (Harper Collins)

You Never Give Me Your Money. Peter Doggett. (Bodley Head)

SELECTED SOURCES

PUBLICATIONS

In Dublin
Irish Independent
Irish Press
Irish Times
Hibernia
Hot Press
Magill
Phoenix
Central Statistics Office.
National Archives.
National Library of Ireland.
RTÉ

ACKNOWLEDGEMENTS

John Kelleher. Frank McDonald. Francis Rossi. Robbie Fox. Peter Sheridan. Faith O'Grady. Arthur Mathews. Paul Woodfull. Graham Linehan. Brian Reddin. Paddy Dunning. And many thanks to Christine Costello for the indispensable help with knocking this book into shape.